Fooling Ourselves

Recent Titles in
Contributions in Psychology

Counseling Refugees: A Psychosocial Approach to Innovative Multicultural
Interventions
Fred Bemak, Rita Chi-Ying Chung, and Paul B. Pedersen

Health Related Counseling with Families of Diverse Cultures: Family, Health,
and Cultural Competencies
Ruth P. Cox

Acculturation and Psychological Adaptation
Vanessa Smith Castro

Progress in Asian Social Psychology: Conceptual and Empirical Contributions
Kuo-Shu Yang, Kwang-Kuo Hwang, Paul B. Pedersen, Ikuo Daibo, editors

Vygotsky's and Leontiev's Semiotics and Psycholinguistics: Applications for
Education, Second Language Acquisition, and Theories of Language
Dorothy Robbins

The Arts in Contemporary Healing
Irma Dosamantes-Beaudry

The Politics of Stereotype: Psychology and Affirmative Action
Moises F. Salinas

Racial Sensitivity and Multicultural Training
Martin Strous

Counseling American Muslims: Understanding the Faith and Helping the People
Ahmed N. Kobeisy

Thriving in the Wake of Trauma: A Multicultural Guide
Thema Bryant-Davis

Nurturing Nonviolent Children
Elsie-Jones-Smith

Working with Cultural Differences: Dealing Effectively with Diversity in the
Workplace
Richard Brislin

Fooling Ourselves

Self-Deception in Politics, Religion, and Terrorism

HARRY C. TRIANDIS

Contributions in Psychology
Paul B. Pedersen, Series Editor

Westport, Connecticut
London

Library of Congress Cataloging-in-Publication Data

Triandis, Harry Charalambos, 1926–
    Fooling ourselves : self-deception in politics, religion, and terrorism / Harry C. Triandis.
        p. cm. – (Contributions in psychology, ISSN 0736-2714 ; no. 52)
    Includes bibliographical references and index.
    ISBN 978–0–313–36438–9 (alk. paper)
    1. Self-deception. I. Title.
    BF697.5.S426T75   2009
    155.2'4—dc22   2008033679

British Library Cataloguing in Publication Data is available.

Library of Congress Catalog Card Number: 2008033679
ISBN: 978–0–313–36438–9
ISSN: 0736-2714

First published in 2009

Praeger Publishers, 88 Post Road West, Westport, CT 06881
An imprint of Greenwood Publishing Group, Inc.
www.praeger.com

Printed in the United States of America

The paper used in this book complies with the
Permanent Paper Standard issued by the National
Information Standards Organization (Z39.48–1984).

10 9 8 7 6 5 4 3 2 1

Contents

Series Foreword

Psychology is to this millennium what theology was to the previous millennium as an "engine of change." The field of psychology is going through rapid and radical alterations to match the changing society in which psychology is applied. While there is some disagreement about the paradigm shift, there is almost universal agreement that profound changes are taking place in the field of psychology. The books in this series have been selected to help chart the progress of psychology as a discipline going through these changes. To the extent the changes are being mediated by controversy, this series will be controversial. In any case, the emphasis is on applications of psychology to particular social problems. Some of the social problems addressed in the series have included identity issues, moral development, ethical thinking, self-representation, culturally competent therapy, and hostage trauma.

This book, *Fooling Ourselves*, fits very well in this series because it is focused on basic psychological truths that we accept without explanation. These statements of "truth" are seldom challenged, and if you are asked to defend yourself on one of these belief statements you will likely respond, "I don't know why it is true. It just is!" and . . . you will become angry. It is difficult to accept the degree to which our basic assumptions are arbitrary and not subject to empirical verification. We are much more vulnerable to "fooling ourselves" than we would like to believe. Using the "test of reasonable opposites," you will quickly learn that the opposite of what you have always believed is just as reasonable as what you have believed. Of course, our thinking is so fuzzy it is usually hard to identify the opposites, but once you have done so you will quickly see how that opposite is also reasonable...from its different viewpoint. Until and unless you challenge these basic assumptions, you will never learn about that "other world" of reasonable assumptions you have overlooked in the past.

Triandis does an excellent job of showing us how we can avoid fooling ourselves about the information we process. Just as our basic assumptions are typically culturally learned then the multicultural path of analysis provides the most direct access to those belief assumptions...usually without even recognizing our mistake! Triandis then turns to a sample of fields and disciplines to frame the contexts of politics, religion, and terrorism. Conventional thinking has assumed culture to be a subset of context. Triandis shows us how context is rather the subtext of culture! Our framework of understanding is first and foremost culturally learned.

In his last chapter Triandis offers suggestions about what we can do to regain control and diminish the extent to which we are fooling ourselves. Readers will emerge from this book with a clear understanding of the basic belief assumptions in their life, and as a result the reader will likely "think differently" in the future. It is not just the content of our thinking that must be examined but the very process of thinking itself. This book is sometimes not comfortable to read and often challenges the reader at sensitive points, but it provides a valuable service and perspective for the future.

                                        Paul B. Pedersen, Series Editor

Preface

Perhaps the sentiments contained in the following pages are not yet sufficiently fashionable to procure them general favor; a long habit...raises at first a formidable outcry in defense of custom. But the tumult soon subsides. Time makes more converts than reason. (Opening paragraph of Thomas Paine's 1776 *Common Sense*)

It is difficult to make a man understand something when his salary depends on not understanding it. (Upton Sinclair, cited in Gore, 2007, p. 211)

The Sinclair quote can be stated more generally: "Motivation can trump cognition." When we fool ourselves, our needs, hopes, and desires trump our cognitions. A technical way to say that we fool ourselves is to say that we use self-deceptions. Self-deception occurs because we often see the world the way we would like it to be rather than the way it is. Psychologists have studied it since the 1930s (Frenkel-Brunswik, 1939).[1]

The essence of self-deception is the selection of positive information and the avoidance of negative information. That does not preclude the possibility that most of the thoughts that humans normally have might be

---

[1] As been studied also seriously by scholars in both philosophy and psychology (e.g., Ames & Dissanayake, 1991; Greenwald, 1988; Hartung, 1988; Hayana, 1988; Janoff-Bulman, 1989; S. Langer, 1960; M. Lewis & Saarni, 1993; Lockard, 1988; Lockard & Mateer, 1988; Lockard & Paulhus, 1988; Monts, Zurcher, & Nydegger, 1977; Moomal & Henzi, 2000; Myslobodsky, 1997; Paulhus 1988; Paulhus, Friedhandler, & Hayes, 1997; Sackheim, 1983, 1988; Sackheim & Gur, 1978; Sarbin, 1988; Snyder, 1985; Solomon, 1993; Welles, 1988; Whittaker-Bleuler, 1988; Wiseman, 1997).

negative. In fact, when most thoughts are negative the positive information is especially welcomed.

This phenomenon has subtle and profound effects on everyday life. It explains how and why humans engage in some aspects of the war on terrorism, politics, religion, and many other aspects of everyday life. Humans have the illusion that they see the world "realistically." Social psychologists call this *naïve realism* (Pronin, Lin, & Ross, 2002). In fact, humans are biased in the way they see the world; they often engage in wishful thinking without realizing that they do this.

The human environment is filled with positive, negative, and ambiguous information. Humans prefer to sample the positive and often ignore the negative information; thus they use self-deceptions that allow them to see the world the way they want it to be rather than the way it is. Humans construct the way they see the world (Taylor, 1998b) and often also use cognitively simple self-deceptions to build it. Self-deceptions are frequently fabricated out of their wishes, hopes, and needs.

Even more specifically, humans are biased in their information processing. Out of the trillions of bits of information in their environment they are especially likely to pick the information that fits their hopes, expectations, needs, and prejudices, and is consistent with their culture and their prior frames of reference. Ideology (e.g., liberal–conservative) also influences the way information is selected and organized (Jost, 2006). At the same time, humans tend to ignore information that is undesirable or anxiety-producing. Of course, that does not mean that they always ignore negative or undesirable information. When a tiger is charging them they pay attention only to undesirable information. Following the 9/11 events some people became paranoid, expecting another terrorist attack. In short, people frequently select the positive and ignore the negative information, and that is what I call *self-deception* because it tends to make people see the world the way they would like it to be rather than the way it is. However, under crisis conditions, self-deceptions are switched off. Depending on the situation and the behavior, people receive much or little feedback from reality. Certainly, in most everyday life situations, one receives a good deal of feedback from reality. However, in the case of situations that cannot be confirmed by empirical observations (e.g., experiments), such as those that occur in the case of religion, politics, and terrorism, as well as when the outcomes of a decision can be observed only many years after the decision has been taken, self-deception is likely to be an important factor. For example, when one has invented something, or when a businessman takes a decision that may turn out to be good or bad several years later, self-deceptions are likely to be important factors. Furthermore, there is also reverse self-deception, where people pay attention only to negative information and ignore positive information (Strachman & Gable, 2006). For example, individuals with avoidance social motivation remember more negative than positive information.

In Africa, some tribes believe that everyone has enemies. They explain illness, crop failure, or an unsuccessful effort, by attributing the event to magic carried out by their enemies (Adams, 2005).

A fantasy can be defined as any concept or idea that is not linked to an objective reality. Many fantasies are inconsistent with common sense (hence the opening quote from Thomas Paine). Self-deception is a special case of a fantasy, in which individuals construct a belief on the basis of needs, wishes, hopes, or desires, rather than because it corresponds to reality. We will understand self-deceptions better if we consider some examples.

Paul Wolfowitz, undersecretary of defense in 2002, claimed that American forces would be received with flowers in Iraq. At the very same time, German intelligence was warning about a possible insurgency. Thus, Wolfowitz used his wishes, and ignored the negative information in constructing his perception of the war. Additionally, he claimed that the war would cost very little, because Iraqi oil would pay for the country's reconstruction after the war. The reality is that the war will cost more than $1 trillion. (This is the estimate of the bipartisan Iraq Study Group.) A recent study that took into account the macroeconomic effects of the war and the obligations for support of the wounded veterans for 50 years estimated the cost at $3 trillion (National Public Radio [NPR] Report, 2008). In any case, there is a major discrepancy between the perception of the war before it started and the reality after it began.

A majority of those surveyed in Indonesia, Egypt, Turkey, and Jordan said Arabs were not responsible for the 9/11 attacks (Pew Research Center, June 23, 2006). That is, they feel good that Arabs did not do it, and ignore reality.

The importance of the phenomenon that motivation trumps cognition is shown in a May 2007 PBS interview by Bill Moyers of Carlo Bonini of the Italian Intelligence Service. According to Bonini, a man by the name of Rocco Martino was interested in making some money. He fabricated a story that Saddam Hussein was getting yellowcake (intermediate step in processing uranium; when concentrated it can be used in weapons of mass destruction) from Niger. In short, Hussein was developing an atom bomb. Martino had a friend in the Embassy of Niger in Rome who supplied official-looking documents with the fabricated story. Then Martino took the documents to the intelligence services of Italy, Britain, and the United States and was well paid. Prime Minister Berlusconi came to see President Bush in October 2001, a month after 9/11. He told him that Iraq was going to get an atomic bomb. Bush "confirmed" the story with British intelligence, but the CIA was skeptical and they asked the French Intelligence Service to check the story. Since Niger was a former French colony the French had the best entrée to Niger. The French reported that there was nothing substantial about the story. But the Bush Administration needed a reason to go to war with Iraq. So, in his State of the Union speech in 2002,

Bush reported that British intelligence had "confirmed" that Iraq was buying yellowcake from Niger. The need that Bush had was converted into the cognition that there were weapons of mass destruction (WMDs) in the works in Iraq. A major mistake of U.S. foreign policy was made because the need for the WMDs was converted into a cognition.

A good example of how a need is converted into a cognition was provided in a report by the British Broadcasting Corporation (BBC, October 7, 2007). In two villages in Bolivia the locals worship and pray to Che Guevara! The fact that Che was a Marxist atheist does not bother them. He helped the poor, so he was a good person, and because they *need* such a person to pray to they converted him to a local saint. His picture is in many homes, and one of the locals who was interviewed assured the BBC reporter that Che answers prayers. He said, "I do not ask for any goods; I ask that my grandchildren make good grades, and they do get good grades in school. Che answers my prayers." If one needs a powerful entity, one creates it.

According to a report on National Public Radio (NPR; December 21, 2006) there is a group of Sunnis who believe that they are the majority of the population of Iraq, although most observers estimate that the Sunnis constitute no more than 20% of the population in that country.

Mohammed Atta, the leader of the group that committed the 9/11 attacks, had a "Manual for a Raid" in his luggage. According to the manual the raid was perceived as "doing God's work." In my opinion, Atta was after glory: the destruction of the superpower. He could not admit even to himself that he was after glory so he dressed his motive in religion, that is, religion was used as a cloak to hide the actual goal. In short, the idea that he was doing God's work was a satisfying fantasy.

In the 10th century, Christians also had such fantasies. Those who died fighting Islam were believed to be "going to Christ." Supposedly, when they died in that situation it guaranteed going to paradise (National Public Television program on Islam in Spain.)

Gunaratna (2002) and particularly Cullison, in "Inside al-Qaeda's Hard Drive," in the September 2004 *Atlantic Monthly,* reproduced correspondence found in al-Qaeda's computers. A future "martyr" dedicated a poem to bin Laden with thanks for asking him to be a "martyr." He wrote to his mother that he is "Going to God...we will meet in heaven." He asks his father to be proud of him. He tells his wife, "This operation, God willing, will turn the tide for Islam and Muslims." He tells her that he will be an exiled tourist in God's land. Note that megalomania and glorious self-perceptions are often aspects of self-deception.

Bin Laden, writing to Mullah Omar (the leader of the Taliban), sees the United Nations (UN) as an alien culture that has "a new religion that is worshipped to the exclusion of God." "The UN imposes all sorts of penalties on all those who contradict its religion. It issues documents and statements that openly contradict Islamic belief, such as the Universal

Declaration for Human Rights, considering that all religions are equal, and that the destruction of the statues constitutes a crime" (Cullison, 2004, p. 64. He referred to the giant statues of the Buddha that the Taliban blew up in Afghanistan). In short, bin Laden used the fantasy that his particular interpretation of Islam is the word of God, and anything that does not agree with it must be rejected.

My examples here frequently come from Islam. But Islam is not unique in the use of self-deceptions. In fact, most religions use self-deceptions. For example, the Mormons believe that their gospel contains the "fullness of the Bible, which is missing in other doctrines" (from their Web site). They think that those who become Mormons become "like God." What could be more pleasant, more positive? In fact, there are some striking similarities between Islam and Mormonism—both depend on revelations received by their founders; both are patriarchic and very conservative about homosexuality, abortion, emphasizing large families; both do not use paid religious practitioners; both require considerable monetary contributions (10% in the case of the Mormons); and both used polygamy (the Mormons dropped that under pressure from the U.S. government, but there are still splinter groups practicing it).

The Bush Administration also advocated a change of the Geneva Convention to give more freedom to interrogators. The implication is that if the interrogators have more freedom they will be more effective. That is also a self-deception. There is psychological research establishing that innocents confess (Kassin, 2007). Interrogations that border on torture are ineffective, produce the information the interrogators want to receive rather than useful, reliable information, and give the country that adopts such methods a bad name, in both the international community and among moderate Muslims. Thus, we have a classic self-deception: sampling positive information (we will get valuable information) and ignoring negative information (we are turning off the rest of the world).

Even intellectual giants such as Nobel Prize winners are susceptible to self-deception. For example, in 1914 the *Manifesto of 93 German Intellectuals* stated, "It is not true that Germany trespassed neutral Belgium....It is not true that the life and property of a single Belgian citizen was injured by our soldiers....It is not true that our troops treated Louvain brutally." In fact, historians report that Germany *did* trespass, some Belgians *were* killed, and the library of the University of Louvain *was* burned, so that there is now a plaque there thanking the Rockefeller Foundation, and several universities for the help received after the war to reconstitute the library. The signers of the declaration were the top intellectuals in the world, at that time. They included Max Planck, who developed quantum theory, which is considered as important as Einstein's theory of relativity, Wilhelm Roentgen, who discovered the x-rays, and Wilhelm Wundt, who established the first psychological laboratory in the world. In retrospect, one can ask, "How could these intellectual giants, sitting in their universities, know what German soldiers did?" Obviously, they had no direct evidence. They just projected their hopes, desires, and needs, the definition of self-deception. They even stated in the manifesto that Germany was the land of Goethe, Beethoven, and Kant and could not possibly have done what it was accused of having done.

The greatest challenge to our civilization comes from global warming. But those who do not wish to have their lifestyle changed have the self-deception that the evidence is insufficient that there is any human-made modification of the environment. Almost 1,000 refereed scientific papers point to the human-made changes of the environment (Gore, 2007). But the mass media, as is required by their professional ethics, have to present both sides of the argument. Thus, they interview some uninformed politician who says that there is nothing to the argument that there is a human-made modification of the environment. The public can then focus on the message that fits its needs. Because the public would rather not change lifestyle, it pays more attention to the uninformed politician than to the scientific evidence. This maybe the greatest self-deception in the world!

There is also some evidence that emotional (our hopes, wishes, fears) and cognitive information are processed in parallel, like two trains running on parallel tracks. At the end of the journey the two systems interact, and often emotions (the way people feel about an issue) take over and reality is ignored. For example, objectively it is much more likely that one will die in a car accident than from terrorism. Yet, most of us do not fear riding in a car nearly as much as we fear terrorism. We overreacted to terrorism, supporting the starting of an unnecessary war to fight it.

The importance of self-deception is underrecognized, perhaps because it is so common. Yet self-deception is extremely important in human affairs. Leonardo da Vinci said, "The greatest deception that men suffer is from their own opinions" (Gore, 2007, p. 112). When we read that Donald Rumsfeld, the former secretary of defense, consulted the generals who did agree with him and retired the ones who did not (Gordon & Trainor, 2006) we did not find it surprising. Yet it reflects a tendency toward self-deception. People who are high in this tendency are likely to make more cognitive mistakes than people who are self-critical. If George W. Bush knew how to recognize the significance of self-deceptions he might have accepted Rumsfeld's resignation much earlier than 2006 when he finally did, and that might have avoided some of the "thousands of mistakes" that Secretary of State Condolezza Rice admitted had occurred in Iraq.

Readers of this book will learn to analyze events by using the self-deception construct. This should help them analyze their own behavior as well as in the behavior of others. *When they identify that one of their beliefs is consistent with their hopes, needs, desires or ideology, they will do well to require of themselves to obtain more information, and to be skeptical of this belief. It would be desirable also if they detect that they sampled mostly positive information and ignored negative information to be especially skeptical of their belief.*

In this book I also discuss individual differences in the tendency toward self-deception, and the differential occurrence of self-deception in different domains, such as in human relationships, politics, religion, economics, philosophy, or aesthetic judgments.

Additionally, humans generally tend to be intellectually efficient or lazy (Zipf, 1949), depending on whether we want to use a complimentary or uncomplimentary label. That is, they pay attention to as little of the information as they can get away with when analyzing complex phenomena. This phenomenon I call *cognitive simplicity*, and it also occurs differentially in different domains. In short, some of us might be very complex when making aesthetic judgments and extremely simple when making political judgments.

For example, when thinking about the war in Iraq, the Bush Administration was both cognitively simple and used much self-deception. The Administration ignored much of the history and culture of the region; and had a superficial understanding of Islam, such as the Shiah–Sunni divisions. They did not prepare by training 15,000 or so military in the Arabic language, as was done during World War II and Vietnam, when 4 to 6 months of language training was provided (Fallows, 2005) before the military arrived in the front. Instead of 1 in 10 speakers of the local language they have only 1 in 150 (Fallows, 2005). They thought that 150,000 military personnel would be sufficient, when experienced generals suggested that 700,000 were needed. They retired the experienced generals who disagreed with them, and kept the ones who agreed with them, thus receiving only information that was consistent with their assumptions and hopes (a classic case of self-deception).

Of course, in this case it is difficult to be sure that these were self-deceptions, because they may have been outright deceptions. But I assume that they are honorable individuals, not liars, so I give them the benefit of the doubt. If we use the two-trains metaphor, one train was loaded with fear and hatred for Saddam Hussein; the other had historical and cultural information. When the decision was made the emotions took over and the cultural-historical information was ignored.

If we are to understand international terrorism we need to understand how humans process information. Both the way our politicians process information and the way the terrorists do are topics of concern in this book. How do people differ across cultures in the way they process information? It is also important to see that we ourselves are biased in our information processing. For example, my hope that I can provide answers to important questions might be my self-deception. This is the way I hope it is, but reality may be quite different. It is desirable to be self-critical, and look for biases, thus avoiding poor judgments.

In short, a major purpose of this book is to help the reader understand how cognitively simple self-deceptions are used by politicians, themselves, and others. It is useful to learn to analyze the statements that people make, and identify cognitive simplicity, such as placing very different entities in the same category (e.g., the axis of evil!), or using their own hopes to make a judgment (e.g., Hamas' statement that they are going to eliminate Israel). Everyday we read in the paper about conflicts occurring in many parts of the world. One common element seems to be that the participants in these conflicts use cognitively simple self-deceptions, which make compromises and the development of win–win solutions unlikely. Self-deception allows a party to stake a position that is unrealistic from the point of view of both its opponents and objective observers. Cognitive simplicity does not allow exploration of multiple paths toward a win–win solution.

Individuals who were convinced that they were doing "God's work" carried out the 9/11 atrocities. This was also a cognitively simple self-deception, and unfortunately humans use both deceptions and self-deceptions when they deal with religion.

There are many kinds of religion. Statistical studies of responses to a large number of questions show four distinct emphases: (a) classic religiosity (importance of God in life, importance of religion in life, frequency of prayer); (b) traditional religiosity (emphasis on religious rituals, religious identity, acceptance of traditional behaviors); (c) emotional religiosity (emotional commitment to religion, and religious values); (d) spirituality (search for meaning, openness to experience, universalism, broadmindedness, concern with social justice, equality, world peace, world of beauty, unity with nature, wisdom, and protection of the environment; Saroglou & Galand, 2004). It is very likely that the terrorists were high on the first three aspects of religion and low on the last aspect.

Spirituality aims at something greater than we are and is necessary for good health (Creagan, 2001). Such spirituality does not require supernaturals. One can feel some spirituality by taking a walk in a beautiful place, by looking at the sky (astronomy), by meditating, by looking at flowers, by listening to great music, such as that of Bach or Beethoven. Nevertheless, religion is also a way to experience spirituality, because religion, like art, is one of the ways to become greater than we are. I see religion in the form of spirituality, as essential for human well-being.

Haidt (2006) experimentally established the importance of spirituality. Certain acts (e.g., incest) elicit disgust, whereas other acts elicit "elevation," which is related to spirituality, and makes salient moral beauty, and the desire to help others. Elevation is a calm emotion that results in new relationships, and a sense of the "sacred." The individual feels wonder, awe, joy, love, and gratitude. Happiness does not come from the outside but from the balance between the inside and the outside. It is a "between" experience. Mystical experiences occur when the self is "turned off." Facing something greater than the self is an essential element of "peak experiences" and well-being.

There are both external and internal religions. The external assume the existence of supernatural entities. The internal, such as original Buddhism, are concerned with internal events, such as reaching enlightenment. The external are classic cases of self-deception. Humans wish to have a God who will protect and guide them, and will control uncertainty, so they invent gods that suit their needs. It is obvious that most humans wish to have an enormous power help them succeed in their hunting, fishing, farming, or wars. Anthropological evidence shows that the gods of each tribe are consistent with the needs of the tribe. When the tribe needs rain, they do a rain dance. If the tribe needs wind, they sacrifice something valuable (e.g., Agamemnon sacrificed his daughter in the *Iliad*). When they need a good crop, they pray and sometimes they get a good one, and that confirms the efficacy of that action. If they do not get one, they explain it by saying that they did not pray correctly, or they failed to pronounce the correct incantations.

J. Campbell (1988) argued, "Geography has done a great deal to shape cultures and religions. The god of the desert is not the god of the plains ... or the god of the rain forest. ... When you are in the desert with one sky and one world, then you might have one deity, but in the jungle where there is no horizon and you never see more than a few yards away from you, you do not have that idea anymore" (p. 101). Thus, it is no coincidence that monotheism was generated in the desert, and polytheism in places where the horizon was cut up.

Although I see external religions as self-deceptions, I realize that most people need some religion. Also, humans need traditions, to guide their behavior. For that reason I favor a religion or a worldview that will incorporate the common ethics of most religions, and will encourage those who wish to use the traditions, rituals, and music (the *Missa Solemnis* by Beethoven is one of my favorite compositions) of their own religion to do so. One can enjoy traditions and music without believing in supernatural entities, angels, devils, heaven, hell, afterlife, which are mere superstitions or self-deceptions.

Internal religions emphasize events inside the person. Spirituality, as described earlier, including the intention to help as many others as possible, including concern for the welfare of others and their physical and mental health, and the protection of the environment can be associated with all religions. Feeling grateful for having food, shelter, and friendship is also part of spirituality. Confessing can improve health, even when people confess to a tape recorder (Pennebaker, 1989)! In this book I advocate internal religions, including the spirituality associated with any religion, and reject external religions, which are superstitious self-deceptions.

I propose the hypothesis that the more religious a sample the more likely it is to use cognitively simple self-deceptions. I am impressed by the extensive use of self-deceptions by some Arabs, who tend to be very religious. For example, during the 1967 (Six-Day) war between Israel and Egypt, the Egyptians had the self-deception that they were winning the war for quite a few days, until their defeat was impossible to ignore. Then they developed the idea that their defeat was due to the help that the Israelis had received from the United States and Britain. But the reality is that there was no help given to the Israelis by other powers. The contrast between the secular Israelis, who viewed the war with realism (religious Israelis did not participate in the war plans), and the Egyptians is so striking that the hypothesis may well receive support if it is researched.

Self-deception is not always undesirable. There are circumstances when it is desirable; for example, when a decision has large benefits and small costs it is desirable for people to believe that they will succeed even if that is unrealistic. Haselton and Nettle (2006) described a variety of situations when "paranoid optimism" provides the best outcome, and can be explained by using the theory of evolution. Self-deception or cognitive simplicity is not always a problem. In some domains it pays to use mild self-deceptions. Patients with cancer who think that they are going to live a long time do in fact live a bit longer than those who give up (Taylor, 1998a). Married people who see only positive traits in their spouse and ignore the negative traits are happier than those who also see the negative (Seligman, 2002, p. 200). In some domains it pays to be cognitively simple. If a problem can be solved by paying attention to only one factor, paying attention to more factors is simply confusing, and reduces the effectiveness of dealing with the problem. Also, when we have personal fantasies (e.g., that we are more intelligent than we really are), that can be helpful when we face criticism. However, when the fantasies pertain to our body politic they can be disastrous. We live in a world where some religious fanatics believe that an atomic war will clean up the earth of "sinners" and only "good" people *like themselves* (!) will survive and thrive. Such mystical beliefs could be lethal for the health of the planet and may result in the end of our species (Harris, 2004).

The definition of self-deception as selective perception of the positive while ignoring the negative aspects of a situation makes a number of phenomena studied by social psychologists special cases of self-deception. Specifically, ethnocentrism (my ethnic group is wonderful and other ethnic groups are "good" to the extent that they are like my group, while ignoring the deficiencies of own culture), impression management (I have wonderful attributes and have never done anything wrong, while

ignoring one's mistakes), the fundamental attribution error (positive behaviors of my in-group and negative behaviors of my out-group are "natural" and "to-be-expected"; negative behaviors of my in-group and positive behaviors of my out-group are unusual, probably forced on that
group by outsiders), and stereotyping (I know with great certainty the attributes of people who belong to particular races, religions, nationalities,
social classes, genders, etc., while ignoring the information that stereotypes have limited validity) are all special cases of cognitively simple self-
deceptions.

In addition to personal self-deceptions there are cultural self-
deceptions. The idea that honor is all important, as found in cultures of
honor (Nisbett & Cohen, 1996), is a cultural self-deception that considers *only* the importance of honor, and ignores the negative information
of what too much emphasis on honor can do. External religions are cultural self-deceptions. Most people accept them without looking for solid
evidence. If told that the world is flat they look around and confirm this
"wisdom" without testing it.

The core of the book is a review of the literature, including experimental
and philosophical studies that point to the validity of the following points:

Some humans developed concepts such as "afterlife" and "paradise"
when they started agriculture, and they saw that plants go through different stages and by analogy thought that humans go through different
stages. They did deny death (Becker, 1973) by inventing such concepts.
A related theme is that the god dies and is resurrected. For example,
this theme was widely held in the Middle East, in the form of the myth
of Aphrodite and Adonis (Frazer, 1960), which appeared in Cyprus and
Syria, in Phrygia (as Cybele and Attis), in Egypt (as Isis and Osiris; Frazer,
1960), and even in Christianity. Humans desired and needed to have eternal life, so they invented concepts that allowed them to think that there is
eternal life. Paradise is a classic self-deception.

Some political leaders used the "if you kill for my cause you will go
to paradise, if you do not do what I tell you will go to hell" argument to
get their followers to sacrifice their lives for a cause. The notion that self-
sacrifice for a cause leads to paradise is very old. For example, Mohammed, the founder of Islam, in addition to being one of the world's
best poets, was an extremely skilled leader. At the battle of Badr, which
marked a crucial point in the development of Islam (in the year 624 CE),
he told his followers that 1,000 angels would come to their aid. Those who
were too scared to fight would go to hell, whereas the brave would go to
paradise. He threw sand in the direction of his enemies, saying that this
would seal their fate. As a result, he was most successful in motivating
his followers. The army of Meccans, who disputed Mohammed's claims
that he was a prophet of God, consisted of 950 men while he had only
324 men (Jannoulatos, 1975/2001). Winning that battle was crucial for the

development of Islam. The thought of having angels fight on your side and going to paradise must have produced an enormous boost in motivation. Incidentally, this may seem miraculous, but we know from studies by industrial engineers that under some circumstances people can triple their productivity. Thus, it is possible for 300 soldiers to defeat an army three times greater.

I am aware that Muslims are easily offended when a non-Muslim mentions Mohammed. Their religion has only five pillars: belief in only one God, prayer (five times per day), charity, fasting (during Ramadan), and pilgrimage to Mecca. That Mohammed is God's prophet is a central belief, and people are trained not to doubt central beliefs. Thus, any expression of even the mildest doubt threatens the *whole* belief system and cannot be tolerated. I have an immense respect for Mohammed as a great poet, leader, human being, but I cannot accept that he has any relationships with supernatural powers.

In other religions or ideologies we also find images of something very positive if the followers do what the leader wishes them to do. For example, nationalists urge their followers to die for the nation, but that is usually much more favorable for the leaders than for the followers. Hitler's image of the 1,000-year Reich (which lasted 12 years!) and the arguments of some Communists (kill for the perfect society), are also examples of self-deceptions provided by leaders to their followers.

This book uses the criteria of (a) good mental and physical health, (b) well-being, (c) longevity, and (d) without degrading the environment, for the evaluation of a society. These criteria are real, measurable. For good mental health, humans need to be linked to each other, and thus this book argues that the purpose of life is to help as many humans as possible reach a good, happy, long life. We review experimental evidence later that shows that doing small helpful acts (e.g., driving a friend to the airport) increases subjective well-being (Larsen & Prizmic, 2008). Whether this realistic perspective can be used widely in Islam, to tell "believers" that they are being manipulated, and suicide does not lead to paradise but to nothingness is empirically testable. Ultimately it is, in my opinion, the best weapon of the war on terrorism. The British Anti-Terrorist Unit estimated on November 9, 2006 that there are in the United Kingdom 30 terrorist plots, consisting of 1,600 individuals. Many of these individuals are planning to be suicide bombers. Clinical interventions to persuade them not to commit suicide, structured as mentioned above, may be worth trying. Many moderate Muslims are trying to re-educate the jihadists. In Yemen (BBC, October 20, 2005), for instance, there is a judge who engages the jihadists who are in prison, in "Qu'ranic confrontations." When they argue in favor of the aims of al-Qaeda he tells them that this is inconsistent with the Qu'ran. Eventually, some of them agree with the judge, and then he lets them out of prison. The government follows these men to make sure that they do not go back to jihad. The judge is moderately successful in converting some of the militants. At the August 2006 meetings of the Asian Psychological Association, in Bali, Indonesia, a psychologist presented a paper that claimed 90% success using the same technique. The psychologist works at the Institute of Defense and Strategic Studies of Nanyang Technical University in Singapore. He claimed that the technique could be used in the rehabilitation of prisoners who have been arrested for collaboration with al-Qaeda. I am not convinced that such high rates of success can be obtained, but it is certainly worth further research.

The four criteria can be used also to evaluate policies and to avoid cultural relativism. Some cultures are more successful than others in meeting these criteria. Evidence is presented later that the most successful cultures are in Scandinavia, especially Norway (de Rivera, Kurrien, & Olsen, 2007; Naroll, 1983), and the least successful (i.e., not meeting the four criteria) are mainly in Africa, south of the Sahara, and in the Islamic world. Furthermore, policies can be evaluated (e.g., democracy is more consistent with the criteria than dictatorships).

The four criteria that I adopted may be too American. After all, they are consistent with the Declaration of Independence ("We hold these truths to be self-evident . . . life, liberty, and the pursuit of happiness"). Life requires physical and mental health, subjective well-being requires liberty. If the environment deteriorates we will have neither life nor happiness. But even if the criteria are American, most cultures would find them acceptable if not highly desirable (Suh & Koo, 2008). Granted, there are cultures where longevity is seen as a problem—too many old people to take care of. But across the world, at least right now, it is seen as desirable.

The first three of these criteria are intercorrelated and are also related to other desirable attributes. Humans who are high in subjective well-being live longer, have stronger immune systems, and thus they are healthier (Larsen & Eid, 2008). Health was related to happiness (Cacciopo, Hawkley, Kaluil, Hughes, & Thisted, 2008) in a major study done in Chicago. Happy people are more sociable, creative, and cognitively complex, make more money, are better leaders, and are better citizens. Nations with high average subjective well-being have more security, more political stability, lower divorce rates, more civil liberty, and more gender equality than nations with low average well-being (Larsen & Eid, 2008; Veenhoven, 2008).

There is the paradox that sometimes cultures that are unsuccessful proselytize other cultures to have them adopt their culture. For example, bin Laden, and according to Darwish (2006) many Muslims living both in the Islamic world and in the United States, believe that the ideal is to make the whole world Islamic. Bin Laden said that if the whole world is Islamic then there will be eternal peace, forgetting that religion is not the only factor in conflict. This kind of proselytizing can be explained by the theory of cognitive dissonance (Festinger, 1957). When a belief system is clearly inconsistent with reality there is cognitive dissonance. Festinger, Riecken, and Schachter (1956) studied a sect that believed that the world would come to an end at a particular date, but the members of the sect would be saved by a flying saucer that would transport them to another world. When the date came and the world did not come to an end they started proselytizing (there is a slight postponement in the date, the flying saucer is on its way). When they are successful in proselytizing they feel less dissonance, since if others adopt their belief system it must be that the belief system is valid. Thus, there are some failed states in the Islamic world, but if others adopt Islam it must be valid.

In summary, the framework I use in this book has four "dependent variables"—good health, longevity, subjective well-being, and protecting the environment. It also has several "independent variables," such as an emphasis on nothing in excess, tolerance for different lifestyles, respect for all humans, facing reality, helping people be happy and healthy so they can live a long time, science not mysticism, and so on. The nothing in excess principle applies also to our tendency to use cognitively simple self-deceptions. It is all right if we fool ourselves a little, as long as we do not do so excessively. If we fool ourselves excessively the consequences can be that the dependent variables do not have a desirable value. Learning about when it is all right to fool ourselves a little can help us live in a better world. Note that this position is cognitively complex. A cognitively simple position would be: "no self-deceptions." Most extremists are cognitively simple.

If we were realists, instead of cognitively simple self-deceivers, we would take the perspective of science. The reality is that we are unimportant creatures of natural processes, such as evolution, in a vast universe. The only thing that makes sense, from my perspective, is to help each other be healthy and happy and to avoid the destruction of our environment. Yet we are foolishly divided in a myriad of ways, violence is common, and we are making a mess of our planet. My hope is that if we learn about self-deception we may start moving toward this realism. But that is probably my self-deception!

CHAPTER CONTENTS

Chapter 1 explores how we can approximate reality and avoid cognitively simple self-deceptions.

Chapter 2 discusses information processing in more detail. Because this is a vast topic, I present only the essentials. My main point is that humans use cognitively simple self-deceptions very widely, and that is often detrimental to their well-being, as measured by objective criteria such as good health and longevity.

In Chapter 3, I discuss cultural similarities and differences and how they are related to different kinds of information processing. Some cultures have self-deceptions of the "I am wonderful" type and others have self-deceptions of the "My in-group is wonderful" type. There is no doubt that the culture of the West and modernity are very different from the culture of al-Qaeda. An analysis of these differences can be helpful. Western culture has problems (e.g., high rates of depression) so we need to be self-critical. As we talk with Muslims we need to admit that they have some points. We are not completely blameless. We need to identify what aspects of modernity and Islam can be made compatible.

Chapter 4 provides examples of poor information processing in politics. This is a domain where deception and self-deception mix in wondrous ways, because politicians have to lie to get elected but when they are caught they may lose an election. If the readers learn to identify self-deceptions in others they might be able to say, as in Hans Christian Andersen's fable, "the emperor has no clothes."

Chapter 5 examines religion. Humans have been extraordinarily inventive in creating gods. In fact, they created an estimated 100,000 religions, dogmas, and heresies (Wallace, 1966). They often create their gods in their own image, and have many self-deceptions, such as that they will have eternal life, they will be protected and helped by supernatural powers and the like. But that is not all bad. Humans need religion because religion provides the illusion that one can control uncertainty. Humans cannot deal with uncertainty. In fact, there is evidence that people would rather receive a strong electric shock that they control, than a weak shock that occurs randomly (Averill, 1973). The illusion that they can control uncertainty is good for their physical and mental health. Prayer reduces stress and blood pressure, and can stimulate serenity. If there is one important finding in psychology, it is that humans need to be connected to one another. Religion provides a community that increases the chances that they will be connected. Humans also need spirituality, that is, a purpose that is greater than them, otherwise their mental health suffers.

Chapter 6 discusses several factors that increase the probability of terrorism, and several kinds of terrorists. Each kind of terrorist has a different kind of self-deception. We can learn how to deal with the different kinds of terrorists better if we understand their self-deceptions.

Finally, Chapter 7 outlines what can be done to increase cognitive complexity and decrease the frequency of large self-deceptions. We need new skills that will allow us to analyze situations with optimal levels of complexity, and avoid major self-deceptions.

Acknowledgments

This book was written after I retired in 1997, after 40 years of teaching at the University of Illinois. The turning point was the events on 9/11/01, which directed me to examine the role of religion in human affairs. The leader of the group that created the 9/11 events had a "Manual for the Raid" in his luggage, which I read in *The New York Times*. How come, I thought, these atrocities were conceived as "doing God's work"? What kind of God requires killing 3,000 innocent people? I knew, because I had studied many cultures, that sacrifice is sometimes involved in religious activities, such as the Aztecs sacrificing prisoners because, according to their beliefs, this was necessary, otherwise the world would come to an end. But the Aztecs killed a few people, not 3,000. So, I read a great deal, and thought a lot, and spoke to a lot of people, and I finally came up with this book.

I hesitated to publish it, because self-deceptions are so satisfying, and people often are better off if they have them than if they are in contact with reality. Yet, much of the conflict in the 21st century is due to various self-deceptions. The war on terrorism includes self-deceptions on both sides of the conflict. Conflict may end our species because we are perfectly capable of blowing ourselves up. Thus, on balance, it seemed better to face our self-deceptions than to nurture them.

Richard Brislin reviewed a draft of the manuscript in some detail and made suggestions that greatly improved it. Michael Bond suggested the title. I am grateful for critical comments and suggestions received from John Adamopoulos, Nicos Ajiovlassitis, Rabi Bhagat, Dharm Bhawuk , Peter Brownfeld, Peter Carnevale, Juris Draguns, Alice Eagly, Gustov Jahoda,

Elaine Hatfield, Yuh-Ting Lee who sent me excellent references to Chinese philosophers and to discussions of shamanism, Paul Pederson, Albert Pepitone, Frank Rosten, Micheal Salzman, and David Trafimow.

My wife Pola read sections of early drafts of the manuscript and made it more readable.

1

How to Avoid Fooling Ourselves

To avoid fooling ourselves we need to become self-critical, become aware of individuals and institutions that "sell hope," and learn how to approximate reality.

BECOMING SELF-CRITICAL

To become self-critical we need to ask if our beliefs might be consistent with our needs, hopes, wishes, and desires. If they are, we should be suspicious! It may be that we have a self-deception. Thus, for instance, if the president of Iran wanted to avoid fooling himself, he would have asked, "Is my belief that Israel will soon be wiped off from the face of the earth consistent with my wishes?" Once he found out that it was he would know that it is a self-deception. Ho Chi Minh, the president of Vietnam, "predicted" in 1950 that by the year 2000 the United States would be a Communist country. Had he used this test he would not have made a fool of himself.

AVOIDING PEOPLE AND INSTITUTIONS THAT SELL HOPE

Astrologers, fortune-tellers, palmists, readers of tarot cards or crystal balls, mediums, prophets of all kinds, faith healers, psychic surgeons, psychics of all kinds, parapsychologists, and other makers of miracles constitute another domain of self-deception. The common thread is that the psychics are supposed to be helpful, or at least provide some entertainment, but, in fact, they acquire power or money. The victims pay for the hope. The "professionals" mentioned earlier tell their victims who they are (the stars made you this way) or what their future is. The victims hope that the information is accurate. A classic maker of miracles might say: "Give me $500 and I will bring your boyfriend back to you." When the boyfriend does not return, the miracle maker might ask for an additional $500 to "try harder." In some cases engaging the services of such individuals may be good for the mental health of the victims, although it drains their finances. The evaluation of the work of such professionals is complex and should consider both the psychic benefits and the financial costs.

A parallel phenomenon is the widespread acceptance of alternative medicines, and "magic" cures. Sampson and Vaughn (2000) reviewed evidence that most alternative medicines are ineffective or harmful. In some cases even placebos have been shown to be harmful. In one study, for instance, 70% of the students who were told that an electric current would pass though their heads reported a headache, even though nothing really happened.

The evidence for acupuncture, chelation, and large doses of vitamin C is generally negative (Green, 2000), and again should be evaluated by considering both the psychic benefits and the costs. Hydrotherapy, aromatherapy, and scores of other techniques tend to increase well-being in the same way that listening to good music does, but there is no solid evidence that they are permanently changing human physiology. Nevertheless, the public is eager to hear the "good news" that the technique works, and avoids information that it does not work. Even physicians often recommend some of these techniques, in the hope that the more "holistic" treatment of the patient will be beneficial. The media are more popular if the carry the "good news" (e.g., they found a cure for cancer!) than if they tell that a technique does nothing.

However, mild self-deceptions do help people. Health maintenance organizations have discovered that people who use some alternative medicines are healthier than run-of-the mill patients (L. Schneiderman, 2000). Even if the therapy is ineffective, the patient's "happiness" is what counts. This is parallel to Taylor's (1998a) finding that patients with cancer or AIDS who believe they will live a normal life do in fact live somewhat longer than those who are more negative.

Hyman (2000) discussed how "ideomotor action" (when expecting that some movement of the hand will occur results in the movement actually occurring), a well-known phenomenon in psychology, can result in "magical" or "supernatural" occurrences, such as in divination, or in spiritualism (e.g., a table moves supposedly because the spirits moved it).

Even in highly developed countries, substantial percentages of the population fall victims to "magic traps." G. Jahoda (1969) asked people in Switzerland to report occult experiences. The study received about 1,200 letters reporting approximately 1,500 experiences, most of which involved self-deception. Approximately 40% of the sample reported seeing ghosts. Fortune-tellers and astrologers were also popular with about 50% of this population. Social class apparently is not strongly related to the tendency to use such professionals. Nancy Reagan had her own. In these self-deceptions, individuals believe that they have some control over events, that is, they can predict the future or they can have good luck. They ignore any evidence that is contrary to their assumptions.

Hope is so valuable that people who have been deceived sometimes do not want to face the reality of the deception. In the 1850s, Margaret Fox exposed her own fraudulent spiritualism, but her devotees refused to believe her and insisted that she continue her work. Thus, she resumed her deceptive career (Welles, 1986).

In many Asian cultures, religious professionals are consulted before any serious decisions are made. Such consultations are sought to determine where and when to build a house, how to orient the house, how to name a child, when to get married, and so on, and the professionals receive a handsome fee. Such traditions travel with the immigrants, so that they persist even in Western countries. Again, although the consultations with these professionals may not bring a tangible outcome, the psychic benefits may be substantial. These consultations also can involve a ceremony, such as when a religious practitioner "blesses" a house. If the event does not cost more than a party it is often accepted as desirable.

The illusion often exists that one causes an event when in fact this is not the case. The self-deception that individuals have special powers is highly enjoyable. The individual who thinks that he or she has influenced the roll of dice, or contributed to the outcome of a sporting event on television ("Did I just jinx them by running off to the fridge?") provides such an example (Wegner, 2002).

Although I am critical of such professionals, I admit that there are places where they must be accepted. In less-developed countries there are few scientifically trained physicians. Thus, the population relies on traditional healers. Vontess (1991) pointed out that the services of such healers are often useful. Some of these healers have studied their craft for 9 years. They have their own "professional societies" that award certificates and make them swear that they will not harm their patients (similar to the Hippocratic Oath). Such healers learn to be exceptionally good observers and are familiar with the medicinal properties of plants. They take extensive medical histories, and know how to select the plants that will be most effective for the particular condition. There may be some placebo effects and some self-deceptions used by both the professionals and their patients, but as long as the patients derive some psychic benefit from interactions with the traditional healers, we must consider these professionals as desirable for the mental health of people who do not have access to scientific medicine. Some modern cultural psychiatrists also advocate this view (e.g., Tseng 2001).

In summary, although some of these practitioners may fool us, we might accept them if they provide sufficient psychic satisfaction relative to the costs. If we make the conscious decision that we want to be fooled, because that is enjoyable, and feel that the costs are "reasonable" then why not accept them?

APPROXIMATING REALITY

There are basically two ways to approximate reality. One is through scientific studies, and the other is through cross-cultural observations, when we establish that multiple observers from diverse cultures believe something.

In science we approximate reality by hypothesizing how the world is, and by collecting data that might support or falsify our hypotheses. We can never be sure that we identified reality because new data can always indicate that a new way of thinking is more correct than our previous belief.

In addition, a belief is likely to be valid when multiple observers across diverse cultures agree.

In the preface I proposed that we test the quality of a culture by examining whether the culture promotes good physical and mental health, longevity, and subjective well-being and does not destroy, or diminish, the quality of the environment.

These beliefs are widely shared. In most cultures people prefer high to low subjective well-being, good health, longevity, and the avoidance of deterioration of the environment. Granted, there are dissenting voices. Not everyone agrees that longevity is desirable, for instance, because demographers tell us that when there are too many old people relative to the working population, society may not be able to support the elderly. One Dutch study argues that ideally people should die at age 65, as soon as they stop contributing to the health system, because the longer they live the more expensive they are to the health system. However, most people believe that such utilitarian, economic arguments should not trump the humane ones.

We must be self-critical when we believe that we know the "truth" about some topic. Truth requires that our beliefs correspond to "reality." However, getting to the truth is very difficult (Russell, 1940) because reality is socially constructed (Berger & Luckmann, 1966). We "see" reality by using constructs (e.g., words) that have been invented by our ancestors. We use ideologies that reflect our culture. We can only approximate reality by checking whether multiple observers worldwide agree about something. It is a reality that humans would like to live in good health for a long time. I think we can construct a morality around the idea of helping others stay healthy, live a long time, be high in subjective well-being, and be kind to the environment.

Because truth is strongly influenced by one's culture, people in different cultures have different truths. Some examples follow:

- An African who does not believe that the spirits of the dead influence an individual's life is likely to be viewed as "crazy" (Boyer, 2001), but an American who does believe this is likely to be thought of as "crazy."
- In 1991, the Iraqis met U.S. Secretary of State James Baker in Geneva. Baker told them very clearly, "If you do not get out of Kuwait we will attack you." The Iraqis interpreted this to mean that the Americans would not attack! They paid attention to *how* Baker said it, not to *what* he said. He was not angry, he did not throw the Geneva telephone book at them, and so they concluded, "He was just talking." In many intercultural encounters people have the self-deception that they "have the truth" (i.e., understand what the other persons are saying and doing), when in fact they are greatly mistaken. Clearly, it is more consistent with one's wishes to think that one understands than that one does not understand. This example indicates that the American truth consists of what was said; the Iraqi truth is revealed by how it was said. In this instance one truth was closer to "reality" than the other truth, because multiple observers, from many cultures, agree that the Americans attacked the Iraqis.

Another way to analyze this episode uses the concept of self-deception. Certainly, the Iraqis wanted to stay in Kuwait. Thus, they may well have sampled the positive elements of the situation, such as "staying is good" and ignored or suppressed the negative elements, such as "we will be attacked."

The following is an example of a time when my truth was inconsistent with reality:

I asked a hotel in Mysore, India, for a room for a number of nights. I received a card that had two options: We are reserving a room for you/we are unable to reserve a room for you. The second option was checked with an X. Thus, my truth was that they did not have a room. I asked my colleague in Mysore to find me another place to sleep, and he arranged for me to stay at the Mysore police vacation pavilion. However, when I got there I noted numerous lizards and insects. He then arranged for me to stay at the palace of the Maharaja, but the room, which was wonderful, required 24 hours to be prepared. Thus, I would have to spend one night at the police pavilion. I decided to go the hotel to see if, by chance, they had a cancellation, and thus I might be able to spend that night there. I told the clerk who I was and he said, "We are expecting you." I said, "You checked that you did not have a room." He answered, looking at me with disdain for not knowing enough about how the world works: "Of course! We cross out the categories that do not apply." In short, my reality was that one indicates the categories that do apply with a check or X and his reality was that one marks the categories that do not apply. When there are only two categories, the two versions of reality are equally satisfactory.

In addition to "universal truths," such as individuals' desire to live in good health for a long time, there are "regional truths," which reflect the particular ecological, historical, and cultural conditions of different regions. Universal truths have greater validity than regional truths. Regional truths have limited validity, and should be accepted with considerable modesty. Unfortunately, the history of the world is full of instances when one group imposed its regional truth on another group, with resulting violence, resentment, and long-term detrimental consequences. For example, the colonial powers view their actions in the 19th century very positively, whereas those who were colonized view them negatively. Most of the countries that were not involved in colonialism agree with the latter. Thus, the validity of the former view is low. People around the world need to learn to be self-critical and understand that often the way they see the world has limited validity.

Another defect we are likely to find in the beliefs held by different people is that they are too simple. Most people see the world too simply and deceive themselves by focusing only on the positive aspects of issues. For example, most Moslems take religion more seriously than people in Europe and East Asia and use cognitively simple self-deceptions more than people in Western cultures, such as "the United States is governed by Jews." Many Arabs, for example, believed that 4,000 Jews were warned not to go to work in the Twin Towers on 9/11 (Friedman, 2002). Ahmadinejad, the president of Iran, and a Turkish newspaper stated that the Holocaust "never took place." It was just Jewish propaganda to justify the formation of Israel (*The Economist*, April 8, 2005). Such pleasant cognitively simple self-deceptions travel well on the Internet and in the irresponsible press.

B. Lewis (2003) stated that not infrequently the Arabic media take one of three positions on the Holocaust: It never happened; it was greatly exaggerated; or the Jews deserved it anyway. People who are psychologically modern have critical tendencies that reduce the acceptance of such simpleminded self-deceptions. Yet most extremists are cognitively simple, saying "my truth is the only truth."

Although external religions are self-deceptions, they are very pleasant and also are related to subjective well-being (Myers, 2008). Religiosity increases longevity, which is one of my criteria for a good society. As seen in more detail later, mild self-deceptions are good for us. Religions provide social support, the illusion that there is a God who loves us, and makes us feel secure, some religions make people more "virtuous" (no drinking, drugs, coffee, etc.) and as a result such people live a little longer. Forgiveness is emphasized by most religions (Myers, 2008), and that is highly desirable because it is associated with increased well-being.

Many of my examples involve Muslims, only because they take religion more seriously than modern cultures. I empathize with Muslims because the colonial powers have created their world without asking for their opinion. That was wrong. But generating fantasies like those just mentioned is also wrong. Muslim resentment of the West is justified because colonization did hurt them. But most of their problems are self-made, and self-inflicted, as the analysis of the Canadian Muslim Manji (2003) has established.

In many parts of the Muslim world there is a mentality that is cognitively simple (Friedman, 2002). When Muslims move from their country to Europe, they are shocked by the complexity of the environment, and withdraw into the isolation of the mosque, the only social environment that is relatively simple and in which they feel comfortable. There they meet the mullahs who have a political agenda, and they learn jihad. European governments that do not train immigrants to become cognitively more complex than they were in their original countries are asking for trouble. There is a literature on how to provide such training (Triandis, 1994).

I propose that governments require anyone who is to be a "preacher" of any religion to pass first a stiff course in comparative religion. We have standards for most professions, but people can call themselves preachers without any qualifications. A person might announce that he or she has been "called by the Lord" to be a preacher and that is sufficient qualification! This is especially important when issuing "religious visas" for people to come from another country to "preach." We need to insist that preachers be cognitively complex, and a course in comparative religion should be helpful. Research does show that cognitive complexity is associated with moderation. However, cognitive simplicity is related to extremism.

What do we have to do to promote the four criteria of a good society? Each of them can be examined in some detail. In the course of doing such work, it will be inevitable that we will criticize some cultural practices. All cultures have faults, some more than others. My inclination is to be realistic, and call a spade a spade.

I expect that some groups will be offended by my criticism of specific aspects of their culture. That is fine. There are two perspectives in anthropology: One is to leave the culture the way one found it. The other is to help the culture get better. I subscribe to the second view. Criticism can help the culture get better. One of my heroes was Alan Holmberg, a professor of anthropology at Cornell when I was a graduate student there. He studied (Holmberg, 1969) the Siriono Indians, a hunting-and-gathering tribe in eastern Bolivia. He found that they were successful in their hunting about once every 3 days. Because they did not have refrigeration, they had to consume what they killed before it spoiled. So they had periods of overeating and periods of going hungry. He introduced rice to them. That, of course, changed their culture, a cardinal sin according to some of his colleagues, but it was an improvement. The Siriono were not as hungry anymore. I approve of such improvements. I know that people all over the world want to be healthy, to avoid pain, and to live a long time. I do not think that it is a case of imposing Western values when we help them reach good physical and mental health. Holmberg also undertook experimental interventions to improve cultures (Dobyns, Doughty, & Lasswell, 1971).

I think there is virtue in calling a spade a spade. Too much discussion about other cultures tries to gloss over defects. Specifically, I believe that violence, especially war, is undesirable because it works against each and every one of the four criteria mentioned above. War cuts short the life of young people; it is unhealthy both physically and psychologically; it reduces subjective well-being; it destroys the environment. I lived through World War II and do not want my grandchildren to see such a war. Furthermore, humans increasingly can hurt each other in more major ways. If they use all their skills they can easily destroy their species. That does not mean that violence must never be used. When an egomaniac such as Hitler or bin Laden threatens the peace and prosperity of the world, violence is necessary.

Thus, I criticize cultures that are more violent than average. Cultures of honor (Nisbett & Cohen, 1996) and cultures that use polygyny tend to be more violent that the average. Cultures of honor are more violent than many other cultures (Vandello, Cohen, & Ransom, 2008). A good predictor of violence is the number of unmarried men in a society (House, Hanges, Javidan, Dorfman, & Gupta, 2004), and polygyny results in too many men remaining unmarried because some men take more wives than their share. The fact that Islam derives from cultures of honor and accepts polygyny explains why there is so much violence in many Muslim countries. In my opinion, most of these cultures need someone like Mustafa Kemal Pasha, later called Atatürk (who reformed the Ottoman Empire) to reform them and make them more peaceful.

I judge a society by the extent it inspires people to help each other, to reach the four criteria mentioned earlier. American culture falls short on these four criteria. On longevity it is 42nd in the world (Andorra is No. 1).

On subjective well-being it is 13th (Tov & Diener, 2007). The average health is not as good as the health in Britain (*Journal of the American Medical Association*, 2006). On protecting the environment it is one of the most polluting cultures. On the other hand, the U.S. Constitution guarantees very important freedoms, including the freedom to write this book. In many cultures, writing this book would put me in jail because it is so subversive. I value also the diversity in this country. In fact, a couple of times when I was in Argentina I found that country "boring," because everybody looked like me (they are of Mediterranean descent). Furthermore, 8 of the top 10 universities in the world are in the United States. Because I chose to be an academic, my choice of living in the United States makes a lot of sense. In short, although America can be improved, I love it anyway.

I strongly believe that cultures can be improved. We need to look at the places where the United States falls short, and develop remedies that will improve the picture. In my opinion, the U.S. health delivery system is in need of fixing. Although Americans spend 2.5 times more than the British, their rates of diabetes, high blood pressure, heart disease, lung disease, and cancer are higher than the British rates (Castilla, 2004). The only statistic that favors the United States is cancer deaths, and that is traceable to early detection of cancer because screening for cancer is higher in the United States than in Britain. The U.S. depression rates of 15% of the population are among the highest in the world. I believe that the country is too unequal (and that depresses most of the above criteria, because the poor in this country have bad health, and a short life span) and too competitive, and in need of more cooperation, and mutual support. American culture in the 21st century is too loose (see chapter 3 for definitions); it was tighter and more to my taste in the 1950s. American culture pollutes the environment and contributes to global warming more than most cultures. The most important point, however, is that all cultures are defective on some of these criteria. To believe that one has a perfect culture is a sure sign of self-deception! We must not expect perfection, but simply work to make things better.

Cultures that result in violence, social disintegration, a short life, and degrade the environment must be criticized, and we need to seek ways to change them. It is important that people develop skills in criticizing and changing cultures that do not meet the criteria discussed earlier, and people need to be trained to critically evaluate their own culture and learn how to get rid of its unhealthy elements (e.g., obesity). Adjusting to another culture, as immigrants have to do when they move from culture to culture, requires an especially critical evaluation of own culture. Part of the skill in changing culture is to make distinctions between the elements of own culture that can be preserved and the elements that must be changed. It is useful to distinguish the public and private aspects of life. In many cases, people can keep their own culture in the private aspect of life (food, family life) but not the public aspects. For example, the traditional pattern of the parents choosing the spouse of their daughters is counterproductive in individualist cultures where women are expected to choose their husband. It results in thousands of suicides by girls who do not want to submit to the choice of their parents (Shweder, Minow, & Markus, 2002).

I strongly believe that cultures can be improved. Note how the violent cultures of Europe have changed with the development of the European Union (EU). What aspects of American culture need to be changed? Among the important attributes are two that are not consistent with ancient wisdom.

Ancient wisdom tells us that we should try to know ourselves and recommends that we use moderation. The ancient Greeks had two inscriptions over the temple of Apollo in Delphi: "Know thyself" and "Nothing in excess." A lot of Indian philosophy includes the "know thyself" point. The Buddha wanted to see the world without self-deceptions and emphasized "the Middle Way." In China Confucius emphasized the "rules of property"; and he objected to both extravagance and parsimony. Lao-Tse as well as Confucius (1909) avoided extremes. Most utopias, such as those written by Plato (1960) and Thomas More (1951) recommended moderation. Post-World War II Japanese childrearing encourages self-reflection and self-criticism (Fiske, Kitayama, Markus, & Nisbett, 1998), which can increase self-knowledge.

Unfortunately, much of modern culture ignores these two pieces of wisdom. To know thyself means to entertain the possibility that you are deceiving yourself. Many of us deceive ourselves and are unaware that we are doing so. Other ancient wisdom also opposes self-deception. For example, the Talmud says, "Thunder exists only to straighten the crookedness of our hearts, to strip away the layers of our self-deception." Under the influence of the advertising industry we are urged to buy more and more luxuries, not realizing that we are overusing the resources of the world.

"Nothing in excess" suggests that we must not do or have too much of any "good thing." Too much food, alcohol, or even jogging, is likely to have bad consequences, such as obesity, auto accidents, or arthritis. Too little water results in dehydration, and too much in hyponatremia (this happens to long-distance runners who drink as they run). Even too much money is not good for us (Kasser, 2002). Muscular men are attractive to women, but the optimal attraction occurs when the man is not excessively muscular (Frederick & Haselton, 2007). In a study done in 1979, the level of happiness of the sample was measured, and in 1994 the participants were asked how much they earned. The top earners were not the ones who were most happy in 1979 but the ones who were next most happy. Thus, even in the case of happiness nothing in excess seems to work! Nothing in excess criticizes the extreme elements of our cultures, such as the extreme materialism of the West but also the extreme nonpossession of anything material as practiced by the Jains in India. It criticizes too much passion and too little passion. It is critical of the fashion industry because it encourages people to spend 1,000 times the daily income of some people in the developing world on the latest style bag or hat. Note that nothing in excess is cognitively more complex than taking any polarized position.

Nothing in excess also applies to self-deceptions. Too little self-deception means excessive realism, and that is often associated with perceiving too many negative elements in our life, and results in depression. Too much self-deception means not being in touch with reality, as found in mental hospitals where some patients think they are God. Too much cognitive simplicity is problematic, but excessive cognitive complexity can leave an individual bathed in thought, unable to make decisions. Knowing ourselves is good advice, but we must become aware of the fact that, in individualistic cultures, such as the United States, people tend to look only inside themselves (attitudes, beliefs, values), when in fact the cause of behavior is often also outside themselves, in the situation, in the actions of others, or in the culture. Thus, in many cases more cognitive complexity is needed.

An interesting example of a good thing that is used excessively, in some cultures, is the concept of "honor." Honor, of course, is a human construction, supported only by "social reality." When used in excess it results in a dysfunctional cultural pattern. Honor is extraordinarily important in some cultures (Nisbett & Cohen, 1996), but is discounted in others. For example, during the 2006 World Cup, Italian Marco Materezzi provoked French team member Zinedne Zidane (probably intentionally), by insulting the Frenchman's mother and sister. Actually, such insults are more common in Italy and Greece than in other cultures, so people are trained to ignore them. But the French football player (with his Moroccan cultural background) could not ignore the insult, and thus France lost the World Cup, resulting in each player of the French team losing $350,000.

For another example, the UN reports that there are 5,000 suicides each year by girls who are told by their family that they must kill themselves because they have "dishonored" the family. The "dishonor" may consist of falling for a boy met in school, or looking at a boy inappropriately. In conservative cultures women are starved, strangled, shot, or buried alive by their family because of their "inappropriate" behavior. These deaths are often called "virgin suicides" because the girls are usually virgins. Whether a behavior is "inappropriate" is of course in the mind of the perceiver, not an objective fact. Even when all members of a culture have the same fantasy that does not mean that the belief is linked to reality. For a belief to be linked to reality it is necessary that multiple observers from diverse cultures see it linked to reality. Modern people (multiple observers in diverse cultures) see the life of the woman as much more important than her supposedly dishonorable behavior. In an example, discussed on the BBC, a Turkish woman was killed by her 14-year-old son, acting on his father's instructions, because she revealed on television that her husband beat her. His honor was lost when his wife agreed to be on television and talk about his behavior. The result of this killing was that five children were orphaned, and the father's remorse led to severe psychological problems. Yet to ignore the loss of honor in that part of the world means that the whole family would be ostracized. Only if the extended family, of perhaps 100 people, moved to another community, where they are unknown, they would be able to live normal lives. Thus, this is a dysfunctional cultural pattern, and too much emphasis on honor supports the wisdom of the nothing in excess principle.

In addition to personal self-deceptions there are cultural self-deceptions. The idea that honor is all important is a cultural cognitively simple self-deception that considers only the importance of honor, and ignores the negative information of what too much emphasis on honor can do.

We can examine what makes a good society in more detail, by reviewing studies that indicate what needs to be done to maximize the four criteria.

THE DETERMINANTS OF SUBJECTIVE WELL-BEING

There is a considerable body of research on subjective well-being (Diener, 1994; Diener, Lucas, Oishi, & Suh, 2002; Diener, Oishi, & Lucas, 2003; Diener & Suh, 1999; Eid & Larsen, 2008; Myers, 1999; Tov & Diener, 2007), which is one index of good health, especially mental health. *Time Magazine* (January 17, 2005) provided a summary that is quite accurate. Low subjective well-being is associated with less physical health, and more depression. Happiness is not just a vague concept; it now has been shown to have definite physiological correlates, and to increase the probability of a long life.

The evidence is that people who are happy have their mind fixed on something other their own happiness (McMahon, 2008). Happiness is derived from many factors, not from seeking it.

Both cultural and personality factors are determinants of subjective well-being. What we do can increase our subjective well-being. For example, "random acts of kindness" can make us happy (Larsen & Prizmic, 2008; Lyubomirsky, Sheldon, & Schkade, 2005). Those who help others perform better on cognitive tasks (Oishi & Koo, 2008), and those who work toward valuable goals are higher in subjective well-being (King, 2008). Feeling grateful (counting our blessings) increases our subjective well-being (Emmons, 2008; Larsen & Prizmic, 2008). Societies sometimes develop rituals that are designed to make people feel grateful (e.g., Thanksgiving). S. Post (2003) advocated eloquently that people should express unlimited love by being altruistic, compassionate and by providing services to others. Humor and laughter are desirable. Cheerful people studied in 1976 earned more money in 1995 than those who were not cheerful in 1976 (Oishi & Koo, 2008). However, in another study, the sample was divided into fifths, and the incomes of those at the top fifth were compared with the incomes of the other four subgroups. Those who were above average in happiness obtained the most income in 1995, not the ones who were in the most happy fifth in 1976 (Oishi & Koo, 2008). A similar pattern was observed for the amount of education of the subgroups. The most education was not obtained by the top fifth in happiness but by those who were in the second, third, and fourth fifths in happiness (Oishi & Koo, 2008). Oishi and Koo (2008) concluded their chapter by stating that happiness is associated with health, longevity, job performance, and close relationships (e.g., successful marriages).

The evidence is that, across countries, a minimum gross national product (GNP) per capita (of the order of $13,000 per person per year in 1995 dollars) is desirable. This level of economic development is typical of the poorer countries of the EU. Countries that have a higher per capita income than that do not show much higher levels of well-being than, for instance, Portugal. Of course, this standard is very high for many of the countries of Africa, the former Communist world, Latin America, and the most densely populated regions of the world. The asymptotic relationship between income and life satisfaction was confirmed by a large study (Deaton, 2007) that sampled more than 1,000 people in each of 130 countries. When income was low, life satisfaction was low, but at moderate levels of income more income did not increase life satisfaction very much.

About 20% of the world lives on less than U.S. $1 per day; another 25% survives on about $2 per day (M. Wagner, 2005). Thus, we humans have not been able to move in the direction of the ideal society advocated earlier. We have a long way to go to increase the income of some regions of the world. Furthermore, we may run into problems of too much environmental destruction and resource exhaustion, if the parts of the world that are now poor were to acquire the standard of living of the rich. China is already suffocating in pollution and is running out of water in significant parts of its northwest. That points to the urgent need for population control and for the development of environmentally friendly technology.

In short, economic development is desirable, but subjective well-being does not increase substantially once most members of a culture have reached an income that guarantees the satisfaction of basic needs (food, shelter, education, medical needs). Maslow's (1954) hierarchy of needs seems supported by this observation. Once low-level needs are satisfied, income is not especially helpful in increasing well-being. One need not be a millionaire in order to be happy. Yet in the modern world we see many individuals who strive to become millionaires, and as a result they are under stress, which is inconsistent with both their physical and mental health. Furthermore, many of these people are characterized by greed and corruption.

That does not mean that a person's situation and income are irrelevant: Biswas-Diener (2008) showed that the average happiness of *Forbes* richest Americans is 5.8 (7-point scale), of traditional Maasai (in Africa) it is 5.4, Pennsylvania Amish it is 5.1, Illinois college students it is 4.7. Calcutta homeless average 3.2, but California homeless average 2.8. Diener (2008) showed that 62% of those with incomes of $300,000 per year say that they are very satisfied but only 45% of those with incomes of $100,000 are very satisfied. About 2% of the respondents in the former group and 5% of the people in the latter were dissatisfied. Thus, income does make a difference. Nevertheless, those who value money above other pursuits, such as social relationships, are less happy (Biswas-Diener, 2008). *Experiential* purchases (e.g., a vacation) are more closely related to well-being than *material* purchases.

Those who emphasize financial success show lower levels of self-actualization and have more behavioral problems (Kasser, 2002). Depression, anxiety, and undesirable physical symptoms were found in societies where people were too concerned with financial success, fame, and physical attractiveness. It is remarkable that immigrants to the United States usually have low levels of depression upon arrival, and the longer they stay here the more their level of depression approaches the 15% typically found in this country. In a society where fame and fortune are overemphasized, it is expected that some segment of the population will fail and become depressed. In short, seeking much material success can be inconsistent with good health. On the other hand, those who emphasize community feelings, self-acceptance (I like myself), and affiliation do not show high levels of depression, anxiety, and undesirable physical symptoms.

Iceland is high in subjective well-being. While spending a few days there I noted that there was much interaction (people often sit in relaxing warm water fed by underground springs talking to each other), little inequality, and a great deal of value homogeneity. Countries like Switzerland and the United States, as well as the Scandinavian countries also have very high levels of subjective well-being. The lowest levels of subjective well-being, around the year 2000, were found in Moldova, Belarus, Ukraine, and Russia. Of course, these countries experienced substantial sociocultural change after 1990, and things had not yet settled down in 2000. Rapid social change is difficult for humans to handle, which is probably another factor accounting for the different rates of depression.

Factors That Have Been Found Associated with Well-Being

Political Freedom. Political freedom is desirable. The average subjective well-being of countries that have freedom of the press, democracy, and the like is higher than the well-being of countries that do not have such freedoms. Absence of legal restrictions on travel, religion, marriage, sex, and suicide has been found to be correlated with high subjective well-being (Veenhoven, 2000). Public acceptance of such freedoms is also important.

Justice. High subjective well-being is associated with the rule of law, low levels of crime, effectiveness and predictability of the judiciary, and the enforceability of contracts; no violations of civil rights; no corruption (e.g., the Berlin Transparency Index shows no corruption). In countries where public institutions are not corrupt, and people carry out their jobs efficiently, people tend to have higher levels of well-being than in countries where this is not the case.

Trust in Fellow Citizens. Those cultures that are high on trust in fellow citizens tend to have low levels of aggression, which should be related to well-being (Lim, Bond, & Bond, 2005).

Brotherhood. High levels of subjective well-being are found in cultures where there are satisfactory citizen–officials relationships. Additionally, tolerance of people who are different in race, social class, religion, and so on, or brotherhood, is also associated with subjective well-being and good health. Trust in people (no enemies) is desirable. Distrust reduces subjective well-being. Believing that you have many enemies reduces subjective well-being (Adams, 2005). In Africa, people who believe in magic are especially likely to distrust others.

When people volunteer to help others their health improves. *Time Magazine* (2005, p. A5) reported a poll that asked Americans, "What are your major sources of happiness?" "Contributing to the lives of others" was mentioned by 75% of the sample. Only relationships with children and friends (77% and 76%, respectively) were mentioned more frequently. These findings indicate that brotherhood is an important factor in happiness. In collectivist cultures people receive more social support than in individualist cultures (Triandis, 1995); however, people also have more obligations and fear that they may be criticized for not behaving according to the norms of their in-group. Thus, the picture is complex, and empirically it is individualism rather than collectivism that is most closely associated with subjective well-being (Diener, Diener, & Diener, 1995).

Security. Security that derives from a sound health system is also important. One of the problems with the American health system is that it is not available to everyone, and thus many people feel insecure, i.e., they fear bankruptcy.

Social Equality. Social equality is desirable. Other indices being equal, the countries that have more equality, such as the Scandinavian countries, have higher levels of subjective well-being than countries that have much inequality. Both gender and economic equality (small ratios of the income of the top and bottom 20% of the population) are relevant (Veenhoven, 2008)

In one study of homicide rates across 56 countries (Lim et al., 2005), in which Colombia had the highest and Japan the lowest rates, most of the variability was accounted by within-country economic inequality and by GNP per capita. It is probable that the same factors are relevant for aggression in general. The study also identified the factors that decrease aggression: democracy, human rights, freedom, and a more or less equal status of women.

Note that the emphasis on equality is consistent with much of original Islam, but the emphasis on the equal status of women is dismissed by Muslim fundamentalists as "inconsistent with the will of Allah." (Note the self-deception that they "know" the will of Allah!) Islam is a consequence of both the original cultures before the Prophet Muhammad was born, and the "revelations" of the prophet. The original cultures were "cultures of honor" (Nisbitt & Cohen, 1996). In these cultures men are fierce warriors, and women are second-class citizens. Most religious authorities among Muslims do not make a distinction between "culture" and "religion" and as a result confuse the two.

The evidence is very strong that within a country social pathology is strongly related to inequality (Wilkinson, 1996). One can see the effects of inequality also when a crisis occurs, as for example when hurricane Katrina hit New Orleans in August 2005. Looting and killing of innocent people took place. That is an index of social pathology. Inequality results in low societal cohesion, which in turn reduces the life expectancy of some of the members of society. In the United States there is a link between low socioeconomic status and poor physical and mental health (e.g., Brim, Ryff, & Kessler, 2004; N. Schneiderman, 2000), which is due to lack of affordable medical care, unhealthy behaviors, greater stress, lack of personal control, greater hostility, and depression, as well as to physical conditions such as pollution, toxins, crowding, and violence. Inequality is also seen in the discrepancies within the educational system. Private schools provide a superb education, but public schools are no longer the best in the industrialized world, as they were in the 1940s. In fact, American science and mathematics test scores, compared with scores of other industrialized countries, now show very poor performance. Similarly, in the United States, the medical care provided to the affluent is the best in the world, but the poor get care that is below the standards of Canada, Britain, or France. As a result the United States has higher rates of diabetes, heart attack, cancer, and the like than do those countries (*Journal of the American Medical Association*, 2006).

Equality is desirable, but there is complexity concerning the correct place, time, and amount. Equality should be proportional to competence. As Aristotle recognized, an incompetent person is not equal to a competent one (Kurtz, 1983). For example, a student is not necessarily equal to a professor when it comes to deciding the content of a course.

The degree of inequality in the world is reflected in some statistics (Korten, 1995). The richest one-fifth of societies produces 83% of the world's wealth; the poorest one-fifth produces 1.4% of it. This statistic may be even exaggerated, because within-country disparities in income are ignored. The rich live in neighborhoods that are totally segregated from the neighborhoods of the poor, so they do not see the condition of the poor. Across countries also there is much inequality. The world's 500 largest corporations employ .0005 of the world's population, but control 25% of the world's economic output (Korten, 1995).

In short, government policies that increase inequality, such as tax cuts for the rich, are immoral. They might be defended on other grounds, such as stimulating the economy, but when an action is good for one goal and bad for another we have to decide according to our values. Considerable research exists showing that cultures differ in the extent they value different goals (Schwartz, 1992). However, around the world one goal is less "respectable" than all others: seeking more power. Thus, humans learn to disguise their quest for power, and do so often by using various self-deceptions. For example, many religious authorities say they do what they do to "serve God." As is seen later, this can be an excellent mask for their search to increase personal power.

Satisfaction with the health system is lower in the United States than in Canada, Britain, Germany, and Japan (Deaton, 2007). The statistics indicate that the so-called "socialist health systems" deliver more satisfaction, health, and longevity than does the American health system.

Low Rates of Lethal Accidents. Few lethal accidents and the presence of social security systems are correlated with subjective well-being. A related factor is a sense of control over one's life. Religions provide this sense of control, and that is the reason I support a religion that uses the common ethics of the world's religions, and allows each religious group to practice its traditions.

Nature Is Kind. High levels of well-being are found in countries that do not experience many earthquakes, hurricanes, floods, droughts, and so forth. Of course, members of cultures have little control over these factors. If they happen to live in an environment with frequent earthquakes and volcanic eruptions, their subjective well-being suffers, but it is not their fault.

Individualism. Across countries, individualism has been found to be associated with higher levels of well-being than collectivism, even when GNP per capita is controlled statistically (Diener et al., 1995). Even in collectivist cultures, such as Korea, defining the self as autonomous (which is a definition of individualism) from groups is associated with well-being (Suh & Koo, 2008). Also in collectivist cultures one has many obligations and is constantly concerned that one will not be a "good member of the in-group." Such concerns can reduce subjective well-being.

Peace. Countries that are not in conflict with other countries show high levels of well-being. The absence of peace is often associated with cultural disintegration, which increases mental illness (Marsella & Yamada, 2007).

Individual Factors. Research shows that certain individuals have higher levels of well-being than others. There is a "happy personality" (DeNeve & Cooper, 1998). Subjective well-being is especially high among individuals who do not show "repressive defensiveness," which is the tendency to deny the existence of threatening information. Of course, that is related to self-deception, so that much self-deception is associated with unhappiness. DeNeve and Cooper also found that subjective well-being is high among those who trust others, are emotionally stable, extraverted and agreeable, hardy (react in an optimistic way and actively cope with stressful life events), and socially competent. Those who have mostly positive emotions are healthier and live longer than those who have mostly negative emotions, such as fear, worry, sadness, anger, guilt, and shame (Nettle, 2005). Negative emotions are all consuming, whereas positive emotions are less focused. This can be traced to our evolutionary history. When wild animals chased our ancestors, the negative emotions were all consuming. They could not afford to think of anything other than escape. But when hunting prey, the animal's positive emotion of a prospective meal was less focused.

People who feel empowered are more likely to be mentally healthy (Marsella & Yamada, 2007) than those who do not feel that way. Empowerment requires frequent experiences of mastery over the environment (Bandura, 1989).

The activities that humans engage in can increase their sense of well-being. Tasks that are challenging and require skills and concentration, have clear goals, provide immediate feedback, allow people to get deeply and effortlessly involved, provide a sense of control, allow the individual to forget about the self, tend to produce more well-being than nonchallenging pleasures, such as looking at TV or eating chocolates (Seligman, 2002). Seligman provides the example of a man interested in minerals, who spends the whole day studying a particular crystal. He does not realize that he has forgotten to eat because he is so involved in studying that crystal that time has stopped. People who have such intensive interests are likely to be high in well-being, and cultures that allow people to have such interests and to spend their time engaged in them are cultures in which the average well-being will be high.

Bertrand Russell, the major 20th-century philosopher, published *The Conquest of Happiness* (1930, reissued in 1971). He argued that individuals who show "zest" are moderately interested in many aspects of life, give and receive affection, do meaningful, productive work, have many vocational interests that challenge the mind, are likely to be happy. Benefiting others and understanding when to be resigned to insurmountable realities can increase happiness (Berumen, 2006). Note that the last point overlaps with Buddha's view that one must not have excessive needs. Epicurus (341–270 BCE) (2002) said, "A man contented with little can hardly possess a greater good" (Charleton, 1926, p. 62). Lao-Tse recommended swimming with rather than against the stream.

Other factors that have been found to be associated with well-being include having a purpose in life (hence the proposed goal of life presented earlier is important), personal growth, and self-acceptance. Good physical health (note that there is a circular causation: happy people are healthier and healthy people are happier), a good job, good marriage, enough education, a good fit of culture and personality, a personality that is open to new experiences, extraversion (e.g., Nettle, 2005), conscientiousness, feelings of environmental mastery, and optimism are also helpful. Furthermore, people who have opportunities to compare themselves favorably with others have a wide circle of friends and acquaintances, receive much social support, are not experiencing much stress, and belong to a like group have high subjective well-being. Laughter also promotes good health.

Well-being is higher among religious individuals (Argyle, 1999) primarily because they receive more social support and their relationship with God is similar to the relationship of nonreligious persons with friends and relatives. Religion also increases the sense that one can control uncertainty (see chapter 5) and that is associated with greater happiness. Additionally, people in very rich societies have too many options, and that is confusing. Religion provides some "no-nos," and that simplifies life. Living the life that people want to live also increases their subjective well-being (Cantor & Sanderson, 1999). Each culture has specific tasks and goals that are considered especially valuable. When individuals have an opportunity to

engage in appropriate tasks and to reach such goals they experience especially high levels of subjective well-being.

Diener interviewed some very rich Americans and found that they were
only slightly happier than average Americans (*Time Magazine*, 2005). Furthermore, the children of the rich are often in trouble. Luthar (2005) found
that upper-class children in America might manifest elevated tendencies
toward substance abuse, anxiety, and depression, in relation to average
Americans. The authors trace these behaviors to excessive pressure for
achievement and to isolation (both literal and emotional) from parents.
People who are exposed to commercials and advertising and have a lot
of money have more desires. But the empirical evidence supports the
Buddha—those with few desires are happier. Those who have a lot of
money and use it to help others are much happier than those who use
it to satisfy their own desires. Research supports Buddhism, because subjective well-being is high in countries where people do not have high expectations and requirements for material resources (Diener & Suh, 2000).

Seligman (2002) and his associates studied the ancient Greek philosophers, as well as the Christian, Jewish, Buddhist, Korean, and Indian
sacred texts. They also examined Confucius, Lao-Tse, and Benjamin
Franklin. They found that there was agreement that certain "virtues" were
universal—wisdom and knowledge, courage, love and humanity, justice,
temperance, spirituality, and transcendence. The purpose of life I advocated earlier is consistent with this list. To know ourselves means that we
are wise; the nothing in excess principle is consistent with temperance. To
help as many humans as possible reach good health, longevity, and subjective well-being while the environment is protected (or improved) means
to love humanity as well as justice. A goal that is greater than we are is the
essence of spirituality and transcendence.

Clearly, to promote the purpose of life advocated above we need to
minimize aggression. One definition of aggression is "coercive control
exercised against another" (M. Bond, 2004). Aggression takes many forms,
from war, terrorism, pogroms, holocausts, inquisitions, ethnic cleansing,
to bullying in schools, random shooting, homicide in the streets, and do-
mestic violence. The world includes much that is undesirable. One purpose of life is to reduce the undesirable parts as much as possible. An
ingredient that is common to all those detrimental social behaviors is
the selfish quest for power. Much of this quest is based on various self-
deceptions. We can start reducing this factor by making people aware
of the role of the selfish quest for power in human affairs and by developing norms that increase altruism. Altruism is helping others even
when this is somewhat costly, and when one does not expect any benefits
from it.

Some of the factors mentioned here as consistent and inconsistent
with good physical and mental health are correlated with each other
(sometimes they are correlated negatively). We do not know yet the

relative importance of these factors as determinants of well-being. That will require a large research project.

How to Maximize Good Physical and Mental Health

This is a vast topic that cannot be covered in this book in any detail. Interested readers should consult Baum, Revenson, and Singer (2001); Solovy, Rothman, and Rodin (1998); and Taylor, Repetti, and Seeman (1997). Furthermore, there is evidence that the factors that contribute to subjective well-being also contribute to good health. For instance, social class is strongly linked to health. The best predictor of good health is the number of years that the parents of a person owned their house (Sheldon Cohen, on NPR, March 27, 2008).

There is a literature that makes the case that good health and longevity require that people be interconnected. Social support is crucial for good health (Taylor, 2007). Receiving emotional support (compassion, encouragement, compliments, etc.) is highly desirable, whereas loneliness is undesirable. Although there are cultural differences in these relationships (Uchida, Kitayama, Mesquita, Reyes, & Morling, 2008), for our purposes they are important in most cultures. Humans have a need to belong (Baumeister & Leary, 1995). Impressive research exists that shows that people who are integrated into social systems, by having many social roles such as spouse, parent, in-law, child, family member, close neighbor, friend, workmate, schoolmate, volunteer, congregation member, are able to withstand the stresses of everyday life better than those who are not well integrated. The more multiple roles a person has the longer that person is likely to live (S. Cohen, 2004).

A good diet, such as that of the island of Crete (Simopoulos & Robinson, 1999), which consists of large quantities of fruits and vegetables, and uses olive oil, has been shown to lead to good physical health. Moderate amounts of exercise each day, such as 40 minutes of walking, have been proven to be beneficial, and even to keep the IQs of older samples reasonably steady (Kramer, Colcombe, McAuley, Stalf, & Erickson, 2005).

Hypertension, which can lead to stroke, heart and renal failure, and blindness, is not taken seriously by 75% to 90% of patients diagnosed with it. They fail to take their medications regularly because the lack of obvious symptoms allows them to not feel sick, often leading them to forget to take their medications (Alcock, 2000, p. 59). The self-deception of believing there is nothing wrong enables them to ignore the reality that can be revealed only by actually measuring their blood pressure.

A Buddhist perspective is also helpful. The Buddha was very much aware of self-deception. He argued that "we almost never see things the way they are in themselves, but our vision is colored by whether we want them or not, how we can get them, or how they can bring us profit" (Armstrong, 2001, p. 74). He developed the skill to see things as they really are.

The Buddha wanted to be "enlightened," that is, to see the world with the utmost accuracy, and without the desires that distorted his vision. Nirvana was reached when the fires of desires were extinguished, at which point one can be truly free because nothing can stress the individual.

The Buddha saw that everything is in constant change, a view that was also espoused by Heraclitus, who said that one cannot step into the same river twice, because the river will be different the second time. Thus, the Buddha, with impeccable logic, argued that there is no point being too attached to anything (person, opinion, object, even life itself) because everything will change. That view was also advocated by other Greek philosophers, in addition to Heraclitus, who suggested that the virtuous life involves freedom from passions (*apathia*) and nondisturbance (*ataraxia*) by passions (Haybron, 2008).

The "self" is constantly changing. Opinions that are "right" today may be "wrong" tomorrow. The Buddha dismissed many questions asked by his followers as "useless speculations" (Rahula, 1959). For example, whether life exists after death is a useless speculation. The Buddha favored the extinction of illusions and had a truly "scientific" attitude toward understanding the world, which allowed him to be tolerant of most beliefs. He believed that most people fool themselves when they see the world. He even used stronger language by saying that they are mentally ill (Rahula, 1959). He had astonishingly accurate views consistent with the views of modern psychology. Buddhist prayer is not like the prayer of deist religions. It is simply paying homage to the memory of the Master who showed the way. He was also a strong believer in the "nothing in excess" view emphasized throughout this book. The Buddha also stressed the advantages of reaching *nirvana*, which includes low stress and reduces the probability of heart attacks (Marmot & Syme, 1976). Stress is very undesirable for health (Averill, 1973; Henry & Stephens, 1977; Meaney 2000).

However, note that this version of Buddhism is not present in most contemporary Buddhist societies because as the words of the Master were transmitted from person to person they were distorted and acquired some of the prejudices (e.g., celestial beings) that existed in the cultures of those who transmitted them. Bartlett (1932/1950) examined this phenomenon experimentally by having participants repeat an American Indian story. As the story went from person to person it became shorter and conformed to the cultures (typical ways of thinking, prejudices) of those who transmitted it.

Ideally, we want a world where people are safe and secure, able to become what they are capable of becoming, feel competent and valuable, and are well connected with family, friends, and their community. Spirituality is reaching for something greater than we are. As I mentioned in the preface, spirituality is an aspect of religion, and I fully endorse those aspects of religion that are not self-deceptions.

In short, I have the bias of wanting to see the world realistically, but I also believe that humans are spiritual beings, and spirituality requires that we have a purpose that "stretches us" that is much greater than we are. As long as we have such a purpose we will always be interested in the world, and active in pursuing that purpose, and that is good for our mental health.

Seeing the world with moderate self-deceptions and in optimally complex ways should also be beneficial. Moderate self-deceptions can include myths and art. Armstrong (2005) traced the history of the use of myths by humans starting with the Paleolithic period (20,000–8,000 BCE), when most of the myths were related to hunting, through the Neolithic period (8,000–4,000 BCE) when they were mostly linked to agriculture to the contemporary world where myths are no longer used as much, but art has taken their place. Armstrong argued that important poems, such as T.S. Eliot's "The Waste Land," play the role that myths played in previous ages. I believe that we need art for good mental health. Whether it is great music, like Bach or Beethoven, paintings, like a Picasso, dance or opera, plays or fiction, we need contact with such activities for our mental health.

Longevity

Good health and high subjective well-being are related to longevity. In the United States, upper-class males have a life expectancy of 80 years, whereas lower-class males have a life expectancy of only 71 years (NPR, March 27, 2008). There may be additional factors, such as serenity and low stress. Why do the citizens of Andorra, a small country in the Pyrenees located between France and Spain, live so long? One can imagine little pollution, serenity, and low stress as probably relevant, but perhaps there are other factors, as well. For example, Andorra gets its water from glaciers that have many minerals. It would be interesting to compare water supplies in different regions with longevity.

Social Cohesion

Social cohesion increases life expectancy. Those samples in different parts of the world that receive much social support, which is common in "collectivist cultures" (see chapter 3), have, other things being equal, lower levels of blood pressure, morbidity, mortality, cardiovascular disease, cancer, and respiratory illness (Uchino, Cacciopo, & Kiecolt-Glaser, 1996). Social cohesion even benefits the endocrine and immune systems. In short, it is a factor that lowers mortality.

In a study in which the American states were the unit of analysis, the correlation between low levels of inequality and high life expectancy was high (.86). This is traceable to very different longevity for the upper classes

(80 years old) and the lower classes (71years old; NPR, 2008). The Japanese have one of the highest life expectancies in the world. They are also homogeneous and have one of the lowest levels of inequality among the rich countries.

In the highly socially integrated community of Roseto, Pennsylvania, the heart attack rate per 1,000 inhabitants was about 6, whereas in a matched, not especially well-integrated community (similar distribution of age, cholesterol levels, weight, exercise, and smoking rates) in Pennsylvania the rate was 9.5 (see Triandis, 1994, for details). Even the rich residents of Roseto drove inconspicuous cars and wore the same clothing as the less affluent. They did not want to stand out. The same is true in many Scandinavian countries, where sticking out is in poor taste. Only 2% of Swedes desired very high social status, compared with 7% of Americans and 25% of Germans (Triandis, 1995).

In cohesive communities no one is left behind, resulting in low stress. The adrenal gland is not too large in such places, so we can even see differences in the physiology of the residents. Social cohesion is generally beneficial for all kinds of indices of social pathology (Naroll, 1983). In the United States, and much of Western Europe, lifestyle involves competition and perceived inequality, which generates more creativity, but is also associated with stress (Henry & Stephens, 1977), and social pathology (poor mental health, high crime, delinquency, homicide, and divorce rates). Stress reduces life expectancy and increases the chances of cardiovascular disease. Thus, the choice seems to be to "stick it out and live a successful, stressful, but shorter life," or "blend in and live a calm life for a long time." Fortunately, in many cultures people have a choice of lifestyle. This discussion should not be assumed to recommend selecting a lifestyle with small challenges. There are studies showing that people in highly responsible, challenging jobs experience less stress than their subordinates. Airline pilots are not usually stressed. Challenging jobs can be enjoyable and often result in happiness; dull routine jobs often produce more stress.

PROTECTING THE ENVIRONMENT

This topic is not discussed in detail here because it is complex, and Gore (2007) provided a good discussion. However, it may be that mankind's most extreme self-deception is that we can stop global warming (Jenkins, 2008). Jenkins said that to hold carbon dioxide constant we must eliminate the equivalent of 11,000 coal-burning plants. But the planet, at this time, has only 800!

How can we continue increasing our GNP by 3% per year and keep the carbon dioxide constant? China is building about 350 new coal-burning electricity-generating plants per year. How can China continue growing its economy without additional power?

Jenkins claimed that to avoid catastrophic damage to the planet we must not go beyond 450 parts per million in greenhouse gasses, and today we are at 384 and growing. To avoid the catastrophe, we need several drastic changes, *at the same time*:

1. Shifting the fuel efficiency of 2 million cars from 30 miles per gallon to 60 miles per gallon.
2. Doubling the energy efficiency of appliances and buildings (use of insulation, etc.).
3. Sequestering the carbon in *all* power plants.
4. Increasing the use of alternative fuels.
5. Building 2 million wind turbines.
6. Doubling the number of nuclear electricity-generating plants.

There are serious doubts about Jenkins' recommendations because, for instance, the increased use of alternative fuels raises the price of foods, and plunges millions into hunger. My only mantra is the "nothing in excess" principle. Let us not think that any of these solutions will be a panacea, but moderate amounts of these solutions may be viable. More research is need.

Is there the political will to do moderate amounts of what Jenkins recommended? I do not think so.

2

Information Processing

Biased reasoning is very common among humans (Plous, 1993). Nisbett and Ross (1980) reviewed extensive laboratory work indicating the shortcomings of human information processing. For example, they showed that humans persist in adhering to a theory when the number of exceptions to the theory exceeds the number of confirmations. Data are influenced by theory, and sometimes adherence to the theory precludes observations of blatantly contradictory data. People make erroneous generalizations from small samples of data, not realizing the unreliability of small data sets. People are poor judges of covariation and make many errors in judging covariation and in making predictions. Most humans are sure that they see the world objectively. When others see it differently they are rejected as being biased (Pronin et al., 2002), "stupid," or even "crazy" (Rokeach, 1964). Recall that the Soviets put those who opposed communism into psychiatric hospitals.

Balcetis and Dunning (2006) argued that people often see what they want to see. When presented with an ambiguous figure such as 13 that can be seen as a B or the number 13, those who have been motivated to see letters see it as a B, and those who have been motivated to see it as a number see it as such. When hoping to see a letter, 72% did so; when hoping to see a number, 61% said it was the number 13. In many other experiments, with different kinds of ambiguous figures, and different kinds of methods, similar results were obtained.

Kunda (1990) showed that individuals arrive at the conclusions they wish to arrive at, although the phenomenon has some limits. Pronin, Gilovich, and Ross (2004) reviewed a large number of studies indicating that people have the illusion that they see the world realistically, and when others see it differently it is because they are uninformed, biased, or idiosyncratic. Rokeach (1964) described an amusing case. He recorded the conversations of three people in a psychiatric hospital, each of whom believed he was Christ. One example: "How can he be Christ when I am Christ? He is crazy."

Pronin et al. (2004) reviewed numerous biases, such as the tendency for people to see themselves as better than average, to ignore the effect of halos, and to underestimate the amount of time required to complete a job. Liberals see the media as biased against liberals and conservatives see them as biased against conservatives. People treat their introspections as decisive data, while doubting the way other people report seeing the world.

Dunning (2001) concluded a review of the way motivation influences social cognition with this statement: "Thus, scanning the social psychological literature over the decades, one sees ample empirical support for the three motives to seek out information, to make sure it is favorable, and to insure that it is consistent with prior beliefs" (p. 365).

A number of environmental and situational factors also influence the way people see the world. For example, studies have shown that mood, information overload, time pressure, alcohol, task difficulty, and many other factors influence perception (see Paulhus & Suedfeld, 1988; Strachman & Gable, 2006). Humans tend to confirm their point of view by selecting only the evidence that supports it. A typical way to make an undesirable event acceptable is to belittle or exaggerate its importance. For example, if a perpetrator hurts a victim, the perpetrator is likely to say "it was a minor thing" but the victim is likely to exaggerate its importance. Often the perpetrator sees many antecedents that can excuse the actions, whereas the victim sees only the event. For instance, the Crusaders in the Holy Land ignored the atrocities they committed and paid attention only to the task of protecting the European pilgrims. They pointed to increased trade after the Crusades and to cultural exchanges. Few people in Europe today think about the Crusades. On the other hand, Muslims have felt victimized by them, and still resent them. Some fanatics, like Osama bin Laden, are even now talking about avenging them. In short, victims distort memories to exaggerate them, whereas offenders minimize or even eliminate the memories of unpleasant events.

Humans have a tendency to confirm their preconceptions, stereotypes, expectations, and theories. The essence of self-deception is found in wishful thinking, which is quite common. The probability of desirable events is overestimated and the probability of undesirable events is underestimated (this is known as the "wishful thinking effect"). Humans tend to maintain the meanings they hold of specific events (Heine, Proulx, & Vohs, 2006). For example, when an individual is faced with a deck of cards, he or she expects to find certain cards. If a black queen of hearts is present, it is not seen as black, but as red. More generally, humans reinterpret anomalies so that they are no longer anomalies.

Humans also have a tendency to use nonmaterial beliefs such as "fate," "God," "luck," "chance," "just reward," and "just punishment" to explain everyday events. In a series of experiments done in both the United States and India, Pepitone and Saffiotti (1997) found a strong link between such beliefs and descriptions of everyday events. For example, the event that a person missed a plane, which later went down at sea and all lives were lost, was attributed to fate (29%), God (20%), luck (38%), and chance (13%). One scenario described a social worker who devoted 20 years of her life to helping the underprivileged, and then received an anonymous multimillion-dollar contribution to build a health clinic. This was perceived as due to "just reward" by 88% of the United States and 84% of the Indian samples. In short, such nonmaterial beliefs make sense of life events, and humans feel good when they hold them. One can easily exaggerate the meaning of concepts that are invalid. Self-deceptions, such as "royal blood," "afterlife," "paradise," "omniscient," "omnipotent," and "omnipresent" carry much surplus meaning, and many nonsensical associations.

Some other concepts often have dubious meaning, such as "the most beautiful (greatest, strongest, most exciting) in the world." Usually, the person who uses such concepts does not have evidence about the distribution of the entity throughout the world. Concepts can acquire several additional meanings. For example, the "sacred" can refer to material objects (crucifix), time (Sabbath), space (mosque), event (birth, death), cultural products (music), people (saints, cult leaders), psychological attributes (meaning), social attributes (caste), and roles (work; Pargament, Magyar-Russell, & Murray-Swank, 2005). Anything that is sacred can become desecrated. Thus, much human conflict can be traced to an insult or dishonor that one group inflicts on another by desecrating something important to that group.

Humans also have the "illusion of permanence" (Baumeister, 1991), that is, they think that most entities are more permanent than they really are. Belief in the afterlife is a consequence of this illusion. Humans believe that they are more permanent than they really are, and therefore invented the concept of the "soul" to help them be permanent and even eternal. The illusion of permanence has many undesirable effects. For example, modern Turks have the illusion that they are very similar to the Turks of 100 years ago, and thus feel defensive about the Armenian "genocide," which the rest of the world considers "a fact." Repressing negative information is inconsistent with good mental health. Modern Turks would be less stressed if they saw the Ottomans (Turks of 100 years ago) as very different from contemporary Turks. What happened in 1915 is water under the bridge, and contemporary Turks have had nothing to do with it. Similarly, modern Japanese refuse to put in their history books information about the Japanese atrocities in China, such as the rape of Nanking (Chang, 1997), assuming that the Japanese of 1935 are the same as the Japanese of 2008. Yet, most Japanese have had nothing to do with these acts. If they saw themselves as different from the Japanese of 1935, which in my view is quite true, they would not carry the burden of suppressing the information about these atrocities, which is psychologically undesirable (unhealthy). Repression is a defense mechanism that is inconsistent with good mental health.

Overconfidence in our judgments is another cognitive bias. Overconfidence is, of course, temporarily satisfying, although disastrous in the long run. There are both individual differences and cultural differences in overconfidence. Those with unusually high levels of self-esteem tend to be overconfident. In experiments carried out in the United States, people usually were 70% to 85% correct when they felt 100% sure of a decision. Studies of medical decisions show that even when the actual probability of a correct diagnosis is 10%, physicians feel 90% confident in their diagnosis. That is, of course, an example of self-deception. This high level of confidence is not found among weather forecasters because they receive more frequent feedback. The more frequent the feedback, the better "calibrated" is the decision maker. High levels of calibration mean that there is a good correspondence between the subjective and the actual probability of being correct.

People sometimes ignore information that could improve their performance (Abelson & Levi, 1985). This phenomenon has been described as "motivated irrationality" and "defensive avoidance." People also tend to ignore base rate information. For example, if presented with the information that there are 70 lawyers and 30 engineers at a party, and that a particular individual who is at the party is good at mathematics, people are likely to think that this individual is an engineer, when the base rate of the people present at the party makes it much more likely that the person is a lawyer. Only if lawyers are never good in mathematics can this choice be justified.

The co-occurrence of events leads to misremembering them in the direction of the stereotypes that are present in the culture. Commitment to a prior decision increases the chances the decision will be seen as "correct." Stress decreases the scanning of information, so people under stress are especially likely to make wrong decisions. If an activity leads to undesirable consequences, people who are committed to the activity see little connection between the activity and the consequences (Abelson & Levi, 1985).

Cognitive illusions are of many kinds. For example, in one study (Rosenthal & Jacobson, 1992), randomly chosen teachers were told that their pupils had unusual potential for intellectual growth. Eight months later these pupils showed significantly greater gains in IQ than did the remaining children who had not been singled out for their teachers' attention. In short, the researchers created a "reality" that was entirely in the heads of the teachers, but it had important consequences for their pupils.

Humans are prone to errors in judgment and to poor decision making. We are easily taken in (Bruner, 1986), and have many illusions and fantasies. Gullibility is widespread so that too many people are foolish, irrational, imprudent, or impetuous in their conduct (Kurtz, 1983). Gullibility is helped by the desire for mystery, drama, and excitement. The enormous success of computer games should be instructive. Millions of people, all over the world, spend several hours a week immersed in computer games (Castronova, 2005). They live in a fantasy world, and have trouble distinguishing the game from reality. Castronova suggested that these virtual lives take precedence to the detriment of the real-world lives of many players. Some players believe that the "real" world is the game, and they are on earth just to play, eat, and sleep. One South Korean man died after a 50-hour game session. The success of the casinos in the United States is also an indication that many people prefer their fantasies ("I will become rich") to reality ("the house always wins, otherwise it would not be in business"). In short, we are susceptible to many errors and biases, some of which can be traced to the stimuli we are processing, whereas others have been shaped by our cultures, and/or our cognitive, emotional, and memory systems.

Taylor and Brown (1988) provided an excellent review of experimental work on self-deception. Their work shows that overly positive self-evaluations, exaggerated perceptions of control, and unrealistic optimism are normal among humans (at least in the United States). Positive illusions are consistent with good mental health, according to Taylor and Brown, because there are positive correlations between having these illusions and a positive sense of self, satisfying social relationships, caring about others, happiness, the ability to set goals and sustain the motivation and persistence to achieve them, the ability to cope effectively with setbacks and change, and productive, creative work.

E. Langer (1975) found that humans have the "illusion of control." They perceive the probability of their success as being higher than the objective probability generated by experimenters. Our judgments depend on the stimuli we have been exposed to in the past. There is a large body of research (e.g., Helson, 1964) showing that if we have been exposed to several heavy weights when we are subsequently asked to judge the weight of an object of moderate weight we will call it "light." Conversely, if we have been exposed to many light weights first, the very same object will be perceived as "heavy." This so-called "level of adaptation" phenomenon is ubiquitous, because it applies to every kind of judgment. For example, research by C. Sherif, Sherif, and Nebergall (1965) showed that extreme

Republicans see a moderate statement such as "Although it is hard to decide, it is probable that the country's interests will be better served if the Democratic presidential and vice-presidential candidates are elected in November" as very pro-Democratic. Similarly, extreme Democrats see the same statement as an inadequate endorsement of their candidate. Conversely, extreme Democrats see this statement with Republican substituting Democrat, as very Republican.

People see patterns in random data. Gods, spirits, witches, luck, and so forth are needed to explain what is scientifically explicable by the concept of randomness, which is one of the most difficult and sophisticated concepts in existence. Humans have great difficulties dealing with randomness, and the world makes a lot more sense to them if some entity makes it tick. To understand how religion works, it is important to examine the perception of randomness. Experiments show that people are not good at dealing with randomness: They see random events as nonrandom, and when asked to generate randomness they overdo it.

People often see what they wish to see, and believe what they wish to believe, which of course is the essence of self-deception. They often attribute to others characteristics that they themselves have (e.g., if they are angry they see that other people are angry). People frequently make biased estimates of the beliefs and habits they share with others. This so-called "false consensus effect" (Kruger & Clement, 1994) results in our thinking that others share our beliefs to a much greater extent than is in fact the case. For example, in 1945, Ho Chi Minh, the Communist leader of Vietnam, stated, "50 years from now the United States will be [a] Communist [country]" (Tuchman, 1984, p. 244). As 1995 has passed and the United States is not Communist, this can be considered a self-deception on Ho's part. Religious fundamentalists do not think that everyone in the population shares their beliefs, but they overestimate how much their beliefs are shared by the general population. Interviews with incarcerated terrorists indicate that some of them thought that "everybody was joining" the terrorist organization (J. Post, Sprinzak, & Denny, 2003, p. 173). Bin Laden and Zavahiri, the major masterminds of the 9/11 attacks planned these actions not only to destroy the West, but also to arouse the Arab masses against their governments (Kepel, 2004). They clearly overestimated how much the ordinary Muslims would agree with their actions, and in fact lost prestige when their later actions resulted (2002–2003 in Saudi Arabia and 2005 in Jordan) in the murder of Muslims.

In this book I emphasize especially two aspects of defective information processing:

1. Cognitive simplicity, which is a serious defect when the situation is complex.

2. Self-deception, which is seeing the world according to our needs, wishes, and hopes rather than according to the way it is.

COGNITIVE COMPLEXITY

H. L. Menken suggested, "For every complex problem there is a solution that is simple, neat, and wrong" (cited in Richardson, 2006, p. 203). That is, cognitive simplicity often leads to wrong decisions.

When thinking about any of the major problems of the world, one necessarily deals with a system of variables—sociocultural, economic, political, philosophic, religious, and aesthetic. If one examines only a small part of this system one necessarily does not reach an optimal decision.

Cognitive simplicity–complexity is an individual-differences variable corresponding to cultural simplicity–complexity. Cultures differ from simple (e.g., hunters and gatherers) to complex (e.g., information societies). Hunters and gatherers live in bands of about 50 people, so the number of relationships among these people is small; in information societies one is interacting with millions of people, in the same city or on the Internet. The number of relationships is enormous. The number of roles in simple societies is small (hunter, gatherer, various family roles). Information societies have, according to the *Dictionary of Occupational Titles*, about 250,000 jobs.

Humans are cognitively simple when they are children, but become more complex as they have more experiences. Cognitive simplicity can be seen in the case of bin Laden and his vision of a world where everyone becomes a Muslim. What could be simpler? Who wants 100,000 religions (Wallace, 1966) anyway?

The educational system can result in different levels of cognitive complexity. An educational system that is didactic, where the teacher tells the pupil "this is the way the world is," and there is no discussion, is likely to result in cognitive simplicity. On the other hand, a "constructivist" educational system that requires pupils to argue both sides of an issue, and emphasizes openness to new experiences, creativity, and exploration is likely to result in cognitive complexity (Johnson & Johnson, 1993).

However, it should not be assumed that cognitive complexity is desirable in all situations. Gladwell (2005) showed that when predicting whether a person who has chest pain and a normal electrocardiogram is having a heart attack physicians need to know only if the pain felt is unstable, if there is fluid in the patient's lungs, and if the patient's systolic pressure is below 100. A myriad of other bits of information just causes confusion and noise that should be avoided. Thus, the commonsense idea that the more information the better is not always correct. Suedfeld and Tetlock (2001) pointed out that Hitler's pronouncements in the Munich Conference were simpler than Chamberlain's statements, but most analysts would agree that Hitler came out ahead in this case. Complex decision makers are often seen as indecisive, wishy-washy, and slow to act. Related to cognitive simplicity is the tendency toward cognitive closure (one stops looking for more information). Closure can be an advantage only when an early conclusion is in fact correct.

My own conclusion is that moderate complexity is desirable, in most situations, but one needs to take the situation into account. There are situations where simplicity is an advantage (e.g., a simple mathematical problem) and situations where complexity is highly desirable (e.g., a sociopolitical issue).

Research shows that cognitive complexity is related to moderate attitudes toward political issues, as well as to low prejudice toward minorities (Hall & Crisp, 2005), whereas extreme attitudes are associated with cognitive simplicity (Tetlock, 1989). In world politics, cognitive simplicity often results in errors and biases (Tetlock, 1989, 1998). Cognitive simplicity often reflects a closed mind (Kruglanski, 2004). In fact, a number of desirable attributes are associated with cognitive complexity, such as tolerance for ambiguity, low dogmatism, low right-wing authoritarianism, and wisdom (Suedfeld & Tetlock, 2001) and suspending judgment until more information becomes available. Enjoying thinking, resisting jumping to conclusions, and appreciation of the point of view of others are generally desirable in most situations.

Cognitive complexity can be examined along three aspects (Schroder, Driver, & Streufert, 1967):

1. Discrimination: does the person see a number of shades of the concept? (e.g., different political parties).
2. Differentiation: does the person use many dimensions when discriminating among concepts? (e.g., many dimensions for discriminating among political parties).
3. Integration: does the person see many relationships among these dimensions?

Another way is to examine (Crockett, 1965) the number of constructs or ideas and the number of relationships among the constructs, which are often organized hierarchically (e.g., living beings, animals, dogs, poodles).

Complexity is different from domain to domain (Burleson & Caplan, 1998). A person may be complex in one domain, and not in others. In a hunting culture, for instance, individuals are likely to be very complex about animals, plants, hunting tools, and the like, but simple in most other domains. Domains such as social relationships, economics, politics, religion, geography, education, philosophy, music, and aesthetics are independent of each other, so that a person may be very complex in one, perhaps music, and know nothing about the others. In fact, I remember a good pianist, in the middle of the 1945 revolution in Greece, when the

Communists tried to take over the country, asking me: "What is EAM?" (EAM was the name of the Communist political movement that was trying to overwhelm the government.) It is incredible that in the middle of a revolution someone would not know the names of the parties in the conflict.

Serious study of one of these domains is likely to increase the cognitive complexity of the domain. Neglect of a domain is likely to decrease the cognitive complexity of thinking about it. As we become cognitively complex we start by using more differentiated categories. Some of the categories may be perceived together with their opposites, forming a dimension (e.g., good–bad, strong–weak, active–passive). Sometimes these dimensions form higher order structures that are integrated (e.g., active musical themes are good), so that a complex hierarchy of levels of abstraction among the categories may be formed.

The more developed the cognitive system, the greater the number of categories that are related to each other, and interconnected in complex ways. For example, a child may know "my house" versus "outside my house." As the child develops geographical knowledge, he or she can identify buildings, cities, countries, continents, and begin seeing attributes of each and how they are related to each other. Eventually, attributes of economic geography may be linked to population statistics, migration rates, health and longevity statistics, crime rates, suicide rates, and so on. Research of the cognitions of experts, such as chess masters, shows that they have numerous models of chess games in their minds (i.e., high complexity), so that they can look at a chessboard and in seconds identify the type of game and the best move to make. This explains how they are able to play simultaneously with scores of moderately good chess players and win most of the games.

Individuals who are cognitively complex quickly discriminate phenomena in a given domain, recall information relevant to that domain quickly, organize schema-consistent information quickly, notice, recall, and use schema-inconsistent information, and resolve discrepancies between schema-consistent and -inconsistent information with some ease. However, it is important to remember that cognitive complexity is unrelated to intelligence, such as IQ, or academic achievement. There are very intelligent people who are cognitively simple. Complexity is a matter of "cultivation" of the mind, not of speed of learning or execution of cognitive tasks.

Most cognitive activities, inferences, judgments about what causes what, impressions we have of other people, retrievals of information, memories, integrations of new and old information, figuring out how others feel about an issue, evaluating others, and so on depend on the relative simplicity or complexity of our cognitive system. Cognitive complexity is relevant for understanding how people acquire, organize, and integrate information. The ability to produce sophisticated appropriate behavior requires a good deal of cognitive complexity.

The complex way of thinking develops during childhood. When a child grows up in a cognitively simple environment, he or she is likely to develop a simple way of thinking. By contrast discussions around the dinner table that explore both the positive and negative aspects of issues are likely to lead to cognitive complexity. Additionally, feeling impotent, marginalized, excluded, or denigrated increases arousal. Arousal results in relatively simple thinking.

An *intensive* emotion, such as passionate love (Hatfield, Rapson, & Martel, 2007) or hate or fear (Gore, 2007), is likely to make a person cognitively simple. Passionate love has been associated with dizziness, confusion, intoxication, and delusion (Hatfield et al., 2007). Fear has confounded al-Qaeda and Saddam Hussein (Gore, 2007). Uncertainty has the same effect as fear. It makes people cognitively simple, and extremist (Van den Bos, Van Ameijde, & Van Gorp, 2006). Negative emotions such as fear, and those associated with fighting and fleeing, narrow the perceptual field, so people become more cognitively simple. Positive emotions, such as those associated with playing and exploring, broaden the perceptual field and make people more cognitively complex (Fredrickson, 2008). Cognitive complexity allows people to discover the "good within the bad."

An authoritarian teaching style, as found in *madrassas* in Muslim countries, results in cognitive simplicity. My hypothesis is that cognitive simplicity explains, in part, why there is so much violence in the Muslim world. When a simple mind is insulted the first thing that comes to mind is revenge. If a weapon is visible it will be used. The eye for an eye and a tooth for a tooth way of thinking is widely in use in that part of the world. But as Gandhi pointed out: "Soon the world will be blind and toothless" (Zakaria, 2008, p. 147). My hypothesis is that monotheism is associated with cognitive simplicity. This is most clear in Islam; in Christianity cognition is a bit more complex because of the trinity. In India, where there are 100,000 gods (Zakaria, 2008), there is the most complexity.

SOME APPLICATIONS OF COGNITIVE COMPLEXITY

Many commentators discuss the "mystery" of so many young Muslims becoming "radicalized" in Britain and Canada. These are largely well-run, welcoming societies where blowing up subways and public buildings makes no sense. However, the phenomenon can be explained by considering cognitive simplicity. If a Muslim cleric convinces these young men that their religion is under threat, they are likely to become cognitively simple (arousal increases cognitive simplicity), and hold only one simple idea: blowing up an important part of the society. Muslim identity has two important elements: honor and Islam (Gregg, 2005). The threat to one of these identities overwhelms the cognitive system.

Cognitive simplicity also occurs when a politician is afraid that he or she will loose an election. Fear results in arousal, which increases cognitive simplicity and then the politician has only one thought: How can I get elected? As a consequence, no creativity in solving the country's problems can be exhibited because most creativity requires cognitive complexity.

How can a society overcome cognitive simplicity? As seen in the last chapter education, debate, travel, examination of both the pros and the cons of an issue, developing a mindset that is critical and doubts any simple solution can be an antidote. I discuss simple and complex cultures in chapter 3. There is some correspondence between complex cultures and complex ways of thinking (Bieri, 1966; Harvey, Hunt, & Schroeder, 1961; Triandis, 1971, 1994, 1995).

There are a myriad of positions that individuals may take on this dimension of simplicity–complexity, with the majority falling in the middle of the dimension while few people use extremely simple or extremely complex ways of thinking. People with a simple way of thinking tend not to examine their beliefs critically, so they are less likely to catch their own self-deceptions. Also, they try to fit a complex reality into a simple framework, and that is likely to result in defective information processing. Thus, it is likely that in simple cultures people faced with a complex problem will make more errors in information processing and will have more self-deceptions than in complex cultures.

Religiosity tends to be associated with rural, simple cultures more than with urban, complex ones. The reduction of cosmology, biochemistry, and evolutionary theory to a simple concept, such as "God," as an explanation of why and how humans were created, is an example of cognitive simplification, widely favored in simple cultures. Fundamentalist religions display simple cognitive styles, such as "I have the truth," and "you are totally wrong."

As discussed earlier, one aspect of cognitive simplicity is that different entities are placed into the same category. For example, in June 2004 five members of Doctors Without Borders were killed in Afghanistan. Their killers claimed that they were "American spies." Did they really see them as spies, which would indicate that they saw humanitarian and military organizations as belonging to the same category, or did they just say that to justify the murders? We cannot be sure, but given other examples of cognitive simplicity in that part of the world the first possibility seems likely.

The second attribute of cognitive simplicity is the number of dimensions needed to understand a phenomenon. Using only one dimension when judging an entity, reflects cognitive simplicity. For example, someone who murders a doctor who performs abortions only considers that the doctor performs abortions, and ignores all other attributes of the physician, such as his bedside manners, his role as father, citizen, and supporter of the fine arts, and so on.

Acceptance of abortion is a more complex position than prohibition of abortion, because acceptance says "too bad that the fetus has to be killed, but it is not the state's business to tell women what to do in this intimate situation." Prohibition says "it is bad, period." The cognitively simple see abortion in theological terms, forgetting that the world is overpopulated, resources are limited, overpopulation is modifying the environment, and there is excellent research showing that mothers of unwanted babies are likely to be cold and rejecting, and such childrearing is related to delinquency, and even criminality (Rohner, 1986). Rohner (2004) summarized the attributes of children who have been rejected by their mothers as follows: they are high in

(a) hostility, aggression, passive aggression, or have problems with the management of hostility and aggression; (b) dependence or defensive independence, depending on the form, frequency, duration and intensity of perceived rejection; (c) impaired self-esteem; (d) impaired self-adequacy; (e) emotional unresponsiveness; (f) emotional instability; (g) negative worldview.

Consistent with this and my previous points, among those who supported the availability of abortion, 70% voted for Gore; 74% of those who wanted abortion to be illegal voted for Bush (*The Economist*, 2003).

Bin Laden provides another example of cognitive simplicity when he states, "I am doing God's work." He attacked without consideration of the impact of his actions on innocent people, and whether the attack would result in a crusaders-like conflict between the West and Islam. He has simple megalomaniac hopes, such as making the whole world Moslem of his particular sect. Al-Qaeda offers an example of cognitive simplicity. Their leaders issued a statement at the time they had bombed the United Nations building in Baghdad, "justifying" the action with various arguments including that the UN had "stolen" Muslim territory, referring to the UN's help in freeing East Timor from Indonesia. They saw Indonesia as "Muslim territory," ignoring many complexities including the facts that the population of East Timor is mostly Christian, it was a Portuguese colony and historically not linked to Indonesia until after World War II, and the Indonesian army had oppressed the population. Furthermore, parts of Indonesia (Bali) are Hindu, about 5% of the population is Christian, and about 4% is Buddhist. Thus, the concept of a "Muslim territory" is flawed. In any case, many Muslims believe that the West is trying to suppress Islam (Tahir, 1996). This is a cognitively simple self-deception. What the West wants is an end to terrorism.

The reality is that the modern world is extremely diverse, and simple thinkers find the competition from different religions and philosophic positions threatening. Especially objectionable are the values of the West, which stress tolerance for deviation from norms. For example, in the West now one can leave a religion without getting severely punished. Muslim fundamentalists believe that punishment for apostasy (defection) must be severe and public (e.g., the defector must be killed, preferably by stoning). This simple way of thinking is very common around the world, and some elements of it can be found among fascists, Communists, as well as fundamentalists of all religions (Buruma & Margalit, 2004).

The Documentation Center in Nürenberg, Germany, contains documents about the Nazi period. I selected a few of the statements I saw there to illustrate cognitive simplicity: "Mein Führer, you are Germany." "One people, one Führer, one Reich (Germany)." Hitler consolidated the top three offices of the German state in his person, thus creating more simplicity. Most analysts also believe that some aspects of the simple way of thinking were frequent among Gaullists, Maoists, the Khmer Rouge of Cambodia, al-Qaeda, and members of cults (e.g., the 900-plus followers of the Reverend Jim Jones who killed their children and committed suicide in Jonestown, Guyana, on his orders). Jones attracted members to his cult on the basis of fantasies about doing good work, like the Peace Corps. Whole families joined and shared the self-deception that they were doing something valuable. Then the cult moved to Jonestown, Guyana, an agricultural commune in which Jones exercised total control of the information reaching the members. Tapes of his speeches were broadcast 24 hours a day and individuals were prohibited from living with their relatives. All information came from Jones, thus maximizing cognitive simplicity, and no new information or exchanges of doubts about what was going on, was likely to reach the members. Interviews with members who managed to escape from Jonestown indicate that many of the activities were coerced, and the suicides were made possible by appeals such as "they are coming to kill us; it is better to commit suicide and die with dignity." There is a parallel between the thought control of bin Laden and Jim Jones. In both cases only information generated by the leader reaches the members of the organization. In both cases suicide is required, and the explanation of why it must be undertaken is given by an ideology that makes sense to the members, in an environment where contrary information is not available.

In groups like Jones' cult or al-Qaeda, people focus on a worldview organized around a simple ideal. They stress the "purity of thought" that is consistent with total agreement with one set of norms, that is, where all agree with an authority (e.g., Jones, bin Laden). Often, they value the simple life and go back to an image of the world as it was many centuries ago. They stress religious rage, and focus on a high ideal that is a single entity, such as the Volk of the Nazis, the purity of the Aryan race, total equality, God, Allah, the Führer, or the emperor. The ideal they seek can be a one world under Islamic (*Shari'a* law), or under communism, or some other ideology. They do not realize how regressive these ideas really are. As early as 1744, Vico (1744/1970) identified three stages of the evolution of cultures—divine, heroic, and humane. The divine required submission to the authority of gods; the heroic submission to the aristocracy; the humane submission to human-made laws. Thus by advocating return to *Shari'a* law Muslims attempt to return to a very early stage of human evolution.

To achieve this great ideal the simple thinkers need heroes, and often show megalomania. They strive for grandeur. Self-sacrifice, discipline, austerity, individual submission to the collective good, worship of the divine, emphasis on instinct rather than reason. Thinking and feeling the same way as everybody else results in "mental clarity." It is notable that such simple thoughts can be found in many settings, such as in bin-Laden, the Khmer Rouge Communists, the Nazis. Hitler argued that it is important to have one and only one important idea; otherwise the public becomes confused. He used anti-Semitism like a hammer used to accomplish all tasks. The masses of the German people, like people in all countries, were cognitively simple and understood the cognitively simple message. Furthermore, cognitively simple individuals sometimes view heroic death (e.g., Hitler in the Berlin bunker) as the highest human aspiration. They reject the nothing in excess principle that I advocate throughout this book, because they associate it with mediocrity, and find it unbecoming to a "hero."

Some people with a simple worldview think of Western culture as too complex. They see it as mechanical, materialist, dehumanizing, decadent, and characterized by moral laxity and mental confusion. There are too many choices. Instead of one kind of mustard, consumers may have access to 20 varieties, and that is confusing, even objectionable. They see Western cultures as too "loose," punishing crimes inadequately, instead of cutting the hands of thieves. They see it as having "messy institutions" emphasizing civil liberties instead of doing what the leader specifies; free-market economics, instead of central planning; democracy (many sources of power) instead of dictatorship (one source of power). They see it as focused on commerce, artistic freedom, leisure, personal safety, wealth, and power. Furthermore, they say the West is extremely arrogant as well as mentally confused (if one has more than one idea one is confused!); it consists of admirers of messy things like jazz, and is characterized by greed, depravity, and decadence. This contrasts with simplicity in the form of a grand vision, sacrifice for one noble cause. In the case of Islam, the establishment of only one faith all over the world would result in eternal peace (according to bin Laden).

The cognitively simple despise intellectuals because such people tend to have many angles, many doubts, too many "it depends." Instead of rationality the simple thinkers emphasize soul, instinct, and intuition. They feel that what they advocate is intuitively and obviously correct, and requires no further discussion. The contrasting worldview is cognitively complex. The complex worldview is found among cosmopolitans who live in cities, are multicultural, and sophisticated in the arts and sciences. Science is international and uses reason, not intuition. The soul is just a hypothesis. Cognitively complex people are often materialist and support liberalism, individualism, humanism, and rationalism.

The cognitively simple tend to live in rural, simple settings and see the city associated with loneliness, the indifference of bystanders, and as an arrogant challenge to God. Furthermore, the simple see the complex as bourgeois (unheroic, worried about personal safety), and as emphasizing not only reason but also feminism. For the simple, women belong in the home, breeding heroic men who will lead the society to the one perfect world condition. Women who have a job are too complex, and threatening.

However, even educated people can think in cognitively simple ways. Consider the reaction to globalization. Korten (1995) pointed out that in the West after 1970 political decisions became fragmented as a result of sound bites on television and the increased specialization of political analysts. Thus, people tend to pay attention to changes in the GNP per capita but ignore changes in the environment or in civic society (crime rates, divorce rates, depression rates) that are correlated with the economic changes. Cognitive complexity requires consideration of a balance between the forces of government, market, and civil society. The GNP increased but there are fewer secure jobs, less decent housing, and less access to clean water and food uncontaminated by chemicals. A complex evaluation of a society would examine (a) GNP per capita, (b) subjective well-being, (c) longevity, and the (d) compatibility of human actions with the preservation of the environment.

Greenspan (2007) is very complex in analyzing economies, but he paid no attention to depression rates, and other aspects of mental health. He provided a good example of high complexity in one domain, but simplicity in others.

The elites are delighted with globalization, whereas the unskilled are enraged. Downsizing is seen as "good" no matter what it does to the lives of the people who become unemployed. Korten presented data that over a period of 30 years, as many professional jobs were developed in the West, among bank employees, insurance, stockbrokers, tax collectors, and accountants, as jobs were lost among unskilled manufacturing workers. Across countries, the GNP has gone up, but social pathology, such as drug abuse and prostitution, has also increased (e.g., 500,000 new child prostitutes in southeast Asia each year). Analysts count the number of billionaires per country, not the number of hungry people. One billion people are hungry, the soil is getting depleted, and water is in short supply. As there is more insecurity the image of political leaders has deteriorated. The more economic activity there is the more garbage has to be stored in poor countries (France sells garbage to Africa) or next to the houses of the poor.

Corporations no longer fully control their destiny because market forces shape their future. Greed is now widespread (e.g., Enron, etc.). Nonproductive mergers and acquisitions make money for the paper-pushers, but do not increase the availability of goods for the poor and hungry. After mergers and acquisitions there were 2,000 cases of "new owners" who "stole" $21 billion from the company pension accounts of the corporations they acquired (Korten, 1995). The World Bank is supposed to help poor countries get out of poverty, but a single dinner provided to the directors of the bank costs $200 per person (Korten, 1995). Contrast this with the child in Alabama who said that he only had breakfast "sometimes," could not afford the 35 cents required for lunch, and so sat on the side, feeling ashamed and crying. For me that is emblematic of globalization! It also shows how even educated people can focus on one aspect of a problem and ignore the other aspects (i.e., use the central mechanism of self-deception).

Another overly simple political judgment is to think that there is nothing in between totally free markets and communism. Actually, there are many in-between political systems, where the amount of government control of the economy is small, medium, or large. Adam Smith (1784/1976), in *The Wealth of Nations*, presented a theory of wealth, but most "users" of the theory forget his complex qualifications. In short, they deal with it in a more cognitively simpler way than he did. Smith specified that his theory would work *only* if the buyers and sellers were small so that their decisions could not influence the market price. Thus, he did not visualize the giant corporations of this century that can monopolize the market. Smith was totally opposed to monopolies, to trade secrets, to intellectual property, and to unrestricted greed, such as the multimillion-dollar bonuses many executives receive as a reward for "downsizing" (i.e., firing) workers to save the company money (Korten, 1995). Similarly, the cognitively simple see only our present health system and "socialist" health systems and nothing in between

Extreme cognitive simplicity in a complex culture is related to poor mental health. However, we need research to establish how extreme must the simplicity be to affect mental health. We know that black-and-white thinking is related to dogmatism (Rokeach, 1960), prejudice, fascism (Adorno, Frenkel-Brunswik, Levinson, & Sanford, 1950), communism

(Eysenck, 1978), and the like. However, it is unclear that such beliefs constitute psychopathology. They are probably within the range of ordinary variation of cognitive functioning.

SELF-DECEPTION

Errol Morris (winner of the 2002 Academy Award for best documentary, for the *Fog of War*) joked this way: "God sent Adam and Eve out of Eden, but he felt a bit bad about it. So, he gave humans the gift of self-deception. This way, while it is miserable outside Eden, nobody notices."

The tendency to sample the positive and ignore the negative information in the environment is the essence of self-deception. The accentuation of the positive is especially likely to occur when a person is in a good mood, and the avoidance of negative information is especially likely not to occur when a person is in a negative mood (Tamir & Robinson, 2007). Passionate love includes the perception of positive information about the loved person, and the suppression of negative attributes of that person (Hatfield et al., 2007). It is often associated with delusions, fantasies, and the like.

This tendency toward self-deception is likely to take many forms. For example, the "self-serving bias" (D. Miller & Ross, 1975) is the tendency of humans to take more responsibility for their successes than for their failures. Baumeister (1998) reviewed numerous empirical studies that indicate that humans discover flaws in information that is unfavorable to themselves, minimize the amount of time for processing information that is unfavorable to themselves, selectively forget their failures and remember their successes, compare themselves to those who will make them look good, search their memories for favorable self-traits, think that their good traits are unusual and their faults common, shift the meaning of ambiguous traits in their own favor, and dismiss criticism as biased and due to prejudice. When a trait is supposed to lead to success many humans tend to think that they have it! Pittman (1998) concluded, "Motivation can intrude to bias beliefs, interpretations and conclusions" (p. 566). There is also experimental evidence that people pay attention to culture-congruent information while ignoring culture-incongruent information (Hwang, Jung, & Haugtvedt, 2006).

Self-deception is ubiquitous in human life. Albert Camus (1956) put it this way: "After prolonged research on myself, I brought out the fundamental duplicity of the human being. Then I realized, as a result of delving in my memory, that modesty helped me to shine, humility to conquer, and virtue to oppress" (p. 84).

It is important to know that all humans deceive themselves, some more than others. Self-deception is so widespread that most humans are unaware of it. It is like oxygen. Breathing occurs without effort or thought; so does most self-deception. I propose the hypothesis that it is desirable for people to learn to identify their own self-deceptions. That is, it is desirable for us to learn to examine our judgments and try to identify and "control" our self-deceptions. For example, some years ago I was nominated for a prize given to psychologists who have done good research on both sides of the Atlantic. I did not get it, and my first thought was that it was anti-Americanism that gave the prize to two Europeans. But after mature thought, I realized that this judgment was just a self-deception on my part.

Closely related to self-deception is self-justification. Tavris and Aronson (2007) presented it by using Festinger's (1957) theory of cognitive dissonance to explain how it works. Cognitive dissonance is a state of tension that occurs when an individual holds two contradictory cognitions (attitudes, beliefs, opinions, percepts). For example, suppose there are two courses of action, A and B, and an individual has chosen Action A. Then all the positive elements of A and all the negative elements of B are pleasant and are likely to be perceived, and all the negative elements of A and the positive elements of B are dissonant with the individual's behavior, and are likely to be ignored, if possible. People are also likely to construct additional elements that support Action A, and if they encounter any elements that support Action B they are likely to find them inadequate or flawed.

A number of sociopsychological phenomena, such as ethnocentrism ("My culture is perfect and has no faults; other cultures are 'good' if they are like my culture"), groupthink (Janis, 1982; "The opinions of powerful people are important and my own criticisms of these opinions might not be worth mentioning"), and stereotyping ("I know for sure what these people are like, while the evidence that this is not so can be ignored") can be seen as special cases of self-deception.

SOME MORE EXAMPLES OF SELF-DECEPTION

The diversity of the phenomena that are self-deceptions is immense. I show here that it occurs in almost every domain of everyday life. Humans see their personality much more positively than do objective observers (Funder & Colvin, 1997; Grams, 1997).

Diamond (2005) provided an interesting example of self-deception. In a narrow river valley below a high dam, pollsters found that the people who reside immediately under the dam, who are certain to drown if the dam bursts, are not concerned about the dam bursting. Those who live a few miles downstream are very concerned, and, as expected, the farther they live from the dam the less concerned they are. It is anomalous, of course, that those who live immediately under the dam are not concerned.

Obviously, they deny that the dam could burst. Presumably, they focus on the positive elements of their residence and ignore the negative.

Many policemen believe that criminals can be identified in a police lineup. If the police lineup "works" the case is solved, and their job is done. However, the evidence that police lineups identify criminals correctly is negative (Tredoux, Meitssner, Malpass, & Zimmerman, 2004). By sampling the positive information (it works) and ignoring the negative information (it does not work) they provide an example of a self-deception.

A friend of mine is clearly overweight, but she says she feels just fine and does not need to do anything about it. The consequences of obesity are well known: increased risk of cardiovascular disease, cancer, and diabetes and lower life expectancy. My friend continues to eat French fries and cream pies, despite the evidence. She is deceiving herself. There are at least two beliefs: I feel fine and do not need to lose weight/I am overweight and should do something about it. My friend pays attention to the first belief and ignores the second. In the case of self-deception people pick the belief that is most agreeable; consistent with their needs, wishes, and desires; and ignore the other one. When my friend goes to a restaurant the menu may feature a large number of heart-healthy dishes, but she opts for pasta Alfredo and skips the spinach salad. Clearly, she could see the healthy items on the menu but selects the unhealthy. The process occurs automatically; in other words, she does not spend a lot of time deliberating whether to attend to this or that belief. In most cases, people are not even aware that there are several beliefs, but automatically zero in on the one that is most consistent with their wishes.

The Bay of Fundy, in Canada, includes a wonderful phenomenon that draws many tourists. The tide is the highest in the world, and amounts to as much as 62 feet. The water rushes in with a bore of 3 to 6 feet in height. The Bay lies between the provinces of New Brunswick and Nova Scotia. The literature I saw in New Brunswick referred to the Bay as "belonging" to New Brunswick; the tourist information in Nova Scotia mentioned that it "belongs" to Nova Scotia. I suppose if one pressed the authors of these texts they would admit that the Bay is shared by both provinces, but they prefer to think that the Bay belongs to their province. This is pleasant, but harmless. So, there is nothing wrong with a little self-deception in this case, as long as it makes people happy. That is true of many self-deceptions. In fact, there is a literature that explores the conditions under which self-deceptions are adaptive (Snyder, 1989), and the consensus is that *minor* self-deceptions are quite adaptive. D. Wilson (2002) reviewed evidence that stress increases the probability of a heart attack. If negative information is stressful, self-deceptions that reduce the stress must be considered adaptive.

A good example of people believing what they like to believe is the attack on Darwin's theory of evolution. One member of a Texas board of education objected to it because it teaches youngsters that they are no better than vermin (reported in the press, February 2004). Because the board member does not like the implications of the theory, he rejects it. The Discovery Institute has been trying to introduce into biology classes the ideas accepted by the Religious Right, such as creationism. Creationism is primarily a phenomenon prevalent in the so-called "Red States" that is ridiculed by biologists all over the world. Its supporters start with the assumption that the Bible's description of creation is valid. That is a self-deception that is especially attractive to cognitively simple people. To deal with the origins of life one needs a vast amount of information, from astronomy, biochemistry, genetics, molecular and cellular biology, paleontology, physics, physiology, and zoology. It is summarized in Sagan (1980). It is simpler and more pleasant to just say "God created it."

The latest version of creationism is "intelligent design," and that version purports to have nothing to do with religion. But the court in Dover, Pennsylvania, in 2005, found that those who support it are religious, and they may have the self-deception that it will get accepted in schools despite the constitutional separation of church and state. Both creationism and intelligent design are nostalgic returns to the pre-12th-century way of mixing religion and the explanation of natural phenomena, and have much in common with the Islamic fundamentalist attempt to return to the simple life of the 7th century. E. Wilson (2006) said, "The evidence for Intelligent Design, however, consists solely of a default argument" (p. 166). To put it more simply, there is no evidence for it, only argument, fantasies, self-deceptions. The proponents need a God so they insist that there is one, without evidence in support of their position.

Self-esteem is very highly valued in America (Baumeister, 1997). Perhaps all humans are susceptible to the tendency to see themselves as better than they really are, but in America people are especially likely to have an unrealistically good opinion of themselves. A survey of 1 million high school seniors found that 70% thought they were "above average" in leadership ability compared with other high school students, and only 2% thought that they were below average. In terms of ability to get along with others, all of the students thought they were above average (Gilovich, 1991). The mathematics says that only 50% can be above average. The Japanese appear more modest, more realistic, and may deceive themselves less than Americans. But apparently this difference occurs because the norm in Japan is to present oneself as more modest than is the case in the United States (Kurman, 2003). Specifically, although Americans tend to have a very good opinion of themselves, the Japanese tend to be self-critical (Heine, Lehman, Markus, & Kitayama, 1999; Sedikides, Gaertner, & Taguchi, 2003). Self-deceptions often improve human self-esteem, and self-esteem can function as a barrier against stress and anxiety (Hobfoll & Leiberman, 1987), and thus reduces the probability of depression. In short, self-deception can be motivated by reductions in stress and anxiety.

Furthermore, self-deception occurs in different domains, such as our self-concept; our beliefs about our social relationships; our beliefs about our economic, educational, or political systems; our thoughts about our culture or religion; our aesthetic judgments; and so on. Research has not indicated yet the optimal points in each domain when the amount of self-deception corresponds to excellent mental health. We do not know as yet how to calibrate self-deception in each domain in order to obtain optimal results.

Organizations sometimes behave in ways that guarantee self-deception. If they fire those who disagree with the views of the "boss" and give medals to those who agree, they create self-deception. A good example is the Bush Administration. Treasury Secretary Paul O'Neill was fired for arguing that a tax cut was unaffordable; economic adviser Larry Lindsay was fired for saying that the Iraq war will cost $200 billion. In fact, the Iraq Study Group Report (Baker, Hamilton, & Eagleburger, 2006) estimated that it will cost $1 to $2 trillion; a 2008 book claims that the cost will be $3 trillion. Army General Eric Shinseki was retired early for arguing that several hundred thousand more troops would be necessary in Iraq. At the same time CIA Director George Tenet, who did not object much about the way the Bush Administration "cooked" the data concerning the presence of weapons of mass destruction in Iraq, received the Medal of Freedom (Alter, 2005).

In many situations people avoid getting "bad news." That situation must also be included in the conception of self-deception because it involves motivated selective perception. For example, in Botswana the incidents of AIDS are very high. Those who avoid being tested for HIV do not wish to face reality, and this must be considered a self-deception. Conversely, selecting only positive information, regardless of what one does with negative information, must be considered a self-deception.

The TV networks make most decisions in ways that they believe promote the public good (Welles, 1986), when in fact they stimulate sex and violence. Summarizing several studies Wood, Wong, and Chachere (1991) concluded that children who see much violence in the media behave more aggressively in spontaneous social interactions than children that have not seen much violence. The managers of TV networks and the producers of such shows must be aware of such studies. But their self-concept would be threatened if they thought that their work increases social pathology. On the other hand, sex and violence increase their profits. It is convenient to pay attention to thoughts about the improvement of the bottom line and ignore the unpleasant aspects of the reality that one is hurting the public good.

Ethnocentrism is a universal attribute of cultures (Triandis, 1994), because we start life by only knowing our culture. It is natural that most people place their culture in the center, and consider other cultures "good" to the extent they are like their own culture. With such limited information people make poor judgments. For example, King Sargon II of Assyria, who ruled between 721 and 705 BCE from his royal palace in Khorsabad, Iraq, asserted that he was "King of the Universe!" The ancient Greeks considered Delphi the center of the world, and the Romans accepted this view and in turn passed it on to the European languages. Thus, the parts of the world to the east of Greece are called the Middle East and the East, and the parts to the west of Greece are called the West. The Chinese called themselves the "Middle Kingdom." In most languages the name of the tribe corresponds to "the people," or as Herskovits (1955) said, "The ethnocentrism of non-literate peoples ... is manifest in many of the names whose meaning in their respective languages signifies 'human beings'" (p. 356), which makes outsiders not quite human.

Campbell and LeVine (1968) and Brewer and Campbell (1976) showed that those who are ethnocentric define the norms and traditions of their culture as "natural" and "correct" and those of other cultures as "unnatural" and "immoral." They perceive their own norms as universally valid, and "what is good for us" as "good for everybody." They think of their own values as "obviously correct." They think that it is natural to cooperate with members of their in-groups, to do favors for their in-group, to be proud of the in-group, and to feel hostility toward out-groups. Those who travel widely are somewhat less ethnocentric. A member of a Florida school board provided a splendid example of ethnocentrism: he commented on the desirability of the inclusion of some material on multiculturalism in the school curriculum in this way: "That is fine, as long as the children learn that American culture is the best in the world in every way." An extreme example of ethnocentrism is the position of a Moslem cleric who advocates that anyone not praying five times a day (as is required for Muslims) should be put to death (*The Economist*, 2006).

In December 2003, as Saddam Hussein came out of his spider hole, he said in English to the American soldiers: "I am the president of Iraq, and I want to negotiate." The first statement was probably a legalistic claim, but the second is clearly a self-deception. The Americans were not going to negotiate. He probably had two beliefs: "I want to negotiate" and "I might be shot." He chose the belief that was more agreeable.

When students made predictions about whether they would act in a socially desirable way they made more rosy predictions than when they predicted how other people would act in the same situation (D. Wilson, 2002). Social desirability biases are very common, and psychologists have devised elaborate schemes to get around them.

Frank Terpil became a terrorist entrepreneur after he fell from grace at the CIA. He sold torture equipment to Idi Amin in Uganda and weapons to other unsavory characters. He thought of himself as "doing business" and satisfying "consumer needs," with a company called Intercontinental Technology. His self-deception was explicit when he said "If I really thought about the consequences all the time, I certainly wouldn't have been in this business. You have to blank it out" (Moghaddam & Marsella, 2004). In short, he consciously chose not to pay attention to the consequences of what he was doing, so as to see himself as an "ordinary businessman." Most of the people in the arms trade—former diplomats, military personnel, intelligence officers, money raisers for terrorists, and so on—probably have similar self-deceptions. They usually are engaged in only one of the dozen activities from the manufacture to the sale of the weapons, so that they are not thinking of the total picture of how much harm will be done with these weapons. Such harmful self-deceptions are nevertheless probably consistent with good mental health.

Australian aboriginals believe that they will be reincarnated after death and return to earth as Whites (Lévy-Bruhl, 1910/1966). This is a good example of how a wish becomes a belief.

There are many examples of detrimental self-deceptions. An analysis (Trivers, 1988) of the final 30 minutes of Air Florida Flight 90, in 1982, showed that its crash was caused by a pattern of self-deception on the part of the pilot, which allowed him to minimize and deny many signs of danger around him. He avoided unpleasant information, and thus killed himself and others.

The casino gambler must know that the house makes a profit. Therefore, on average, logically, it is inevitable that he will lose some money. Maybe he gambles for fun with a limited sum of money. That is fine. But often he gambles to the point of suicide and that is clearly undesirable. In the latter case he hopes and also believes that he will make money. We see here two contradictory ideas: the house makes money/I will make money. Self-deception involves paying attention to the belief that is consistent with one's wishes and ignoring the other.

In gambling situations, there is no such thing as a person being lucky in the long run. There is a bell-shaped distribution of outcomes, and the most frequent outcome will be losing some money (because the house has to make money). As in any distribution of outcomes some will be "good" and some "bad." If the person focuses on the good ones she will think that she is lucky. But luck is in the head, not out there. Luck has validity only *after* the events that can be described as involving luck. Luck cannot be used to *predict* events. There is empirical evidence that gamblers think only of the outcome (I will win millions) and ignore the associated probability (which may be one in a million; Baumeister, 2005). In short, self-deceptions prevail.

Empirically, capital punishment has been shown not to be effective in preventing crime, yet its supporters have the self-deception that it does prevent crime. They feel good because something is done to reduce crime, ignoring the fact that sometimes it kills innocent people. Not only that. Some people change completely when they are in jail for years, and the state puts to death a person who is different from the one who committed the crime. Countries that use capital punishment cannot join the European Union. There is no evidence that crime rates are higher in Europe than in countries that execute large numbers, such as China and the United States.

Most Americans avoid thinking of the detention of Japanese-Americans during World War II. We like to think of our society as just, and that was not a just treatment of our fellow citizens.

The placebo effect makes people believe that a useless pill is doing them some good. They focus on feeling good and avoid thinking that they spent money for a useless pill.

In the 18th and 19th centuries, physicians used vigorous bleeding of their patients. They had the self-deception that they were helping their patients. In fact about half the patients died. But the physicians noted that the other half of the patients survived, and they congratulated themselves for using this highly effective technique.

People believe that religiosity decreases crime. Empirically there is no relationship between religiosity and crime rates, but it makes people feel good to have something they can offer as a means of crime reduction.

Many older men have the self-deception that they are desirable sex partners of young women.

In many parts of the world girls are deceived to believe that they will get a good job in "the city" or in another country. The reality is that many end up in houses of prostitution.

A French physicist by the name of Blendot believed that he had "discovered" the N-rays. This was very soon after Roentgen had discovered the x-rays. The best French physics journal rejected the paper of an American physicist who indicated that he could not replicate Blendot's experiment. The paper was eventually published, and the world of physics learned that the N-rays were not "real," but Blendot went to his grave believing that he had discovered them. The rejection of the paper by the French journal is a case of self-deception. The editor of this journal did not want to accept negative information about an "important" French discovery (Gratzer, 2000).

Another example from physics was presented by William Feynman (Nobel Prize, 1965) in a commencement address at the California Institute of Technology in 1974. He mentioned that the famous physicist Millikan measured the charge of an electron slightly incorrectly, because he used the incorrect value for the viscosity of air. For many years subsequently physicists who obtained a different value fooled themselves by questioning *their own work*, whereas the ones who found a similar value did not look into their own work very closely. In other words, when our perception of "reality" fits our expectations we do not question our percepts, but when it does not fit our expectations we tend to question our perceptions.

In Puccini's opera *Madame Butterfly* a 15-year-old Japanese girl expects the return of her American husband who will take her to America, where they will live happily ever after. She had the self-deception that her husband was true to her, refusing to pay attention to clues that he did not perceive his marriage to her as legitimate.

In a charming story, Dostoyevsky (*A Nasty Story*) describes a pompous general who walks by the house of one of his subordinates at 1 in the morning and remembers that the subordinate is getting married. He has the self-deception that the subordinate will be delighted if he "honors" the wedding with his presence. So, he interrupts the wedding festivities, and the guests do not know what to do with him. He then has the self-deception that they will be delighted to hear a lecture about the glory of Russia, and of course the whole situation is a disaster, but he keeps drinking and thinking well of himself and of how he has "honored" the bride and groom with his visit.

People sometimes explain a personal failure by pointing to the "bias" of some group against them. That is very satisfying because they are not to blame for the failure.

In the case of unrequited love, the lover typically ignores signs that the other person is not in love. One woman said, "I was blind to this fact for a long time because I refused to admit that I slept with someone who cared less for me than I cared for him" (Baumeister, 1993, p. 173).

The Catholic Church insists on celibacy for its priests. This is an unnatural requirement. The self-deception is that men can live all their life without sex. In fact, the data indicate that only 2% of priests achieve celibacy, and 8% are celibate "with some failures." The rest masturbate in large numbers, or have heterosexual (30%) and homosexual (15%) relations (Sipe, 2003). One belief is that priests will not have sex; the other that priests do have sex. The first belief is consistent with the church ideology so it is sampled, while reality is ignored. Sipe (2003) concluded, "The church is at a pre-Copernican stage of understanding regarding human sexuality" (p. 323). A survey of 5,000 priests by *The Los Angeles Times* found that most "try but do not succeed" (p. 53) to be celibate.

In most cultures, selflessness is a virtue (Essock, McGuire, & Hooper, 1988). Thus, it does not serve people's interest to present themselves to others as selfish. That requires self-deception. Individuals attempt to convince themselves that they are generous, benevolent, and altruistic, when much of the time they are selfish. The self-deception makes it possible for them to like themselves and to present the best front to others who then like them. This increases the chances that they can procreate, and thus serves social evolution.

This is only part of the story. The other part is avoidance of pain. Many studies (Golman, 1985) indicate that humans shift their attention away from painful or anxiety-producing stimuli. When a lion attacked the African explorer David Livingstone, he later reported that he felt detached from the pain produced by the lion's bite. Similarly, in many clinical situations humans shift their attention away from anxiety-producing stimuli, which, although helpful, is an aspect of self-deception.

Tavris and Aronson (2007) provided numerous examples of self-justification, which, as mentioned earlier, is closely related to self-deception. People often believe that their judgments are correct when in fact the evidence is inconsistent with this belief. For example, police officers often think that they can tell who is lying, when in fact they cannot. To support their judgments they plant evidence, and they lie to the people they interrogate. Police falsification of evidence even has a name: *testilying*. Some police officers believe that they *never* interrogate innocents so it is natural that they find most people they interrogate guilty. This is very serious because it keeps innocent people in prison and allows guilty people to remain free.

In fact, when a Predictor X is used to predict a Criterion Y, unless the correlation of X and Y is 1.00 there will always be false-positives and false-negatives. In the human sciences, correlations of 1.00 simply *do not exist*. When a variable is correlated with itself (test–retest reliability) the correlation is almost never more than .98. Thus, the idea that one can predict with infallibility is foolish. From the point of view of good mental health the correct attitude is that of Thomas Edison. Edison replied to a person who lamented his 10,000 failures to find the right ingredients for the filament of an incandescent light bulb, by saying "I successfully discovered 10,000 elements that don't work."

The examples of Tavris and Aronson (2007) include psychiatrists who believe that recovered memories are valid, physicians and judges who believe that they are above conflicts of interest, prosecutors who are certain that they have convicted the guilty party, spouses who are certain that their interpretation of events is the right one, and nations who are certain that their version of history is the only one that is correct.

In short, self-deceptions occur in a wide range of situations, and can be found in fictitious as well as real events, in science as well as in art, in medicine, and in almost every walk of life.

MISCELLANEOUS ISSUES ON SELF-DECEPTION
Measurement of Self-Deception

Tendencies toward self-deception can be measured. Paulhus (1998) developed a scale with items such as "My first impressions of people usually turn out to be right" and " I am very confident in my judgments." Clearly, people who agree with such statements are sampling positive information about themselves and do not sample negative elements such as "I sometimes make mistakes."

Another way to measure self-deception is to content analyze statements made by a person and compare them with known facts.

How Much Self-Deception Is Desirable?

Many psychologists have argued that good mental health consists of seeing the world the way it is (M. Jahoda, 1958). According to this view the president of Iran, Mahmoud Ahmadinejad, who claimed, in December 2005, that the Holocaust was a myth, is mentally sick. However, I am not sure. Very religious people live in mythical worlds, and this man is supposed to be very religious. Such people see the world the way they would like it to be (i.e., are very high in self-deception), but that does not automatically make them mentally sick. More information is needed about other kinds of behavior before that conclusion can be firm. However, his pronouncements (that there are no homosexuals in Iran, a statement he made at Columbia University on September 24, 2007, and Israel will be wiped off the face of the earth, made in 2005) suggest that he has many cognitively simple self-deceptions and thus he *may be* mentally ill.

Extreme accuracy in perceiving the world is found among people who suffer from depression (Alloy & Abramson, 1979). They are "wiser but sadder" than others. Extreme self-deceptions (e.g., believing that one is God) are inconsistent with mental health, but some self-deception is good for mental health (Kitchens, 2003). There is ample evidence that *a bit* of self-deception, at the individual level, is desirable. Some data indicate that positive illusions permit patients with cancer to live better and longer (Taylor, 1998a). In recent studies, patients with AIDS who thought they could beat the disease lived 9 months longer than patients who were not as optimistic. When self-deceptions are switched off, as happened for those who became paranoid about a second terrorist attack after 9/11, mental health is not optimal. In short, both no and extreme self-deceptions are inconsistent with good mental health.

Baumeister (1989, 1991), after reviewing such findings, suggested that optimal psychological functioning requires some self-deception, but too much or too little self-deception is associated with poor mental health. I talked to Shelley Taylor about this and she told me that empirically she did not find evidence consistent with Baumeister's suggestion. Thus, this topic requires further research.

There are many examples indicating that self-deceptions are useful. An excellent example of the utility of self-deception can be found in *The Wild Duck*, a play by Henrik Ibsen (1950). Hjalmar has the self-deception that he has a wonderful family, consisting of a wife and daughter. He also has the self-deception that he will become a great inventor. His close friend, Gregers, returns to town after 17 years. Gregers has an Oedipus complex, hatred for his father, and knows that his father had an affair with Hjalmar's wife prior to Hjalmar's marriage. He believes that revealing this "truth" to Hjalmar will be good for him because that will place his marriage on a "solid basis." Truth is better than self-deception is the key idea behind Gregers' decision to tell Hjalmar about his wife's affair. Circumstances reveal that Hjalmar's daughter was conceived during the illicit affair. The truth, in this case, shatters Hjalmar's self-deceptions of the happy home, and the great inventor, and leads to a series of dramatic episodes, including the daughter's suicide. In the last act a neighbor comments, "Take the saving lies from the average man and you take his happiness away, too." In short, there are circumstances when it is best to let people have their saving lies.

Optimal health, adjustment, happiness, and performance arise when people overestimate themselves slightly. But departure from the "critical margin of illusion" results in depression or in "crazy" beliefs. Golman (1989) agreed that some self-deceptions are helpful to individuals, but he argued that they are most unhelpful to the collective. Individuals may have happy lives because of their self-deceptions; but collectively ignoring the fact that they live in a world where some fanatics believe that an atomic holocaust will make it possible for them to go to "paradise" while their enemies will go to "hell" is a lethal self-deception. Similarly collective self-deceptions about the planet's population trends and the environment are very dangerous. Too often our illusions work too well, so that we ignore what is wrong with the planet.

While extreme self-deceptions (e.g., I am God) are most undesirable, we need not avoid all self-deceptions. It is good for people to think that they are better than they are. It makes them able to deal with criticism. There are many benign self-deceptions that can be very useful. For example, when a businessman undertakes a risky investment, an analysis of the situation may suggest that he has the self-deception that he will succeed.

As long as there is a modest probability of success, he should make the investment. Research has shown that successful entrepreneurs take risks that have neither very low nor very high probabilities of success. Modest probabilities are desirable, which reminds us of the "nothing in excess" wisdom of ancient Greek and Chinese philosophers.

A modest amount of self-deception is good for our adjustment. An example comes from a study of marital satisfaction. O'Rourke and Cappeliez (2005), studied 400 people who were 49 years or older and had been married for 20 years or more. They measured "marital aggrandizement," which they defined as the tendency to reject negative information about one's marital history. That fits the definition of self-deception. Additionally, they measured marital and life satisfaction. They found 208 people (more than half their sample) who were "idealists" characterized by high marital aggrandizement, and satisfaction with marriage and life. They were moderately high in self-deception and that was associated with satisfaction. Thirty-six people were "distraught," characterized by low marital aggrandizement, and dissatisfaction with marriage and life. Thus, this sample lacked self-deception and was dissatisfied. Additionally, 156 people showed very little lack of marital aggrandizement, and were only slightly dissatisfied with their marriage and life. The authors labeled them the *realists*. Thus, this sample was low in self-deception and slightly dissatisfied. In short, the participants who did not show any self-deception were distraught; the participants who showed some self-deception were slightly dissatisfied; those who showed a fair amount of self-deception were quite satisfied. In other words, at least in the marital domain, the greater the self-deception the more satisfied are the participants. This study did not provide data about very high levels of self-deception but one would guess that people with such levels would have trouble relating to their social environment.

Children often have cognitively simple self-deceptions (Dawkins, 2003), but they are usually harmless. However, adults who have cognitively simple self-deceptions in politics, religion, and terrorism can harm others, and sometimes the consequences are lethal (as seen in chapter 4).

Humans high in self-deception perceive threatening situations as less threatening than they really are (Tomaka, Blascovich, & Kelsey, 1992). That could be helpful, but it could also be lethal. Complexities such as cultural differences do exist, but on the whole humans tend to overestimate the desirable and that sometimes has undesirable consequences.

Most humans have the self-deception that the way they see the world is "real" (Pronin et al., 2004). But the evidence is very strong that what they see is in part due to the stimulus they are looking at and in part due to their cognitive, emotional, and memory systems. For example, when a group of people is asked to estimate the temperature in a room, if the thermometer shows 70 degrees Fahrenheit, the average judgment is likely to be close to 70, but there will be some people who will judge the temperature to be 80 and others who will think that it is 60. To take a more interesting example, researchers have constructed statements that were as neutral as possible, neither conservative nor liberal. When these statements were presented to conservatives they saw them as liberal; when the statements were presented to liberals they saw them as conservative. I review later many more examples where judgments are not accurate. Yet most people believe that what they see is objectively there, immutable, eternal, unchanging. Of course, it is much more agreeable to think that what we see is really as we think it is, than to doubt our perceptions. But that is because we have a tendency toward self-deception.

In all cultures people see the world the way they want it to be rather than the way it is. For example, they have stereotypes about age, gender, nationality, race, religion, occupation, and so on. Such stereotypes sometimes have a kernel of truth (Lee, Jussim, & McCauley, 1995), but they are mostly inaccurate. The self-deception is that people think they understand the behavior of others, which is pleasant, when in fact they do not. Interpersonal conflicts and misunderstandings develop that reduce the mental health of both those who have the stereotype and the targets of the stereotype. In conflict situations people see the common elements between the two parties as part of their own position, and the elements that are not common as more different from their own elements than they really are. In any case, we need to see self-deception in the context of normal psychological processes, because all of us are likely to engage in self-deception.

The basic mechanism of self-deception is attention to the pleasant and avoidance of the unpleasant. Even 4-month-old infants show this tendency. An experiment by Diane Montague (see Wingert & Brant, 2005), described in *Newsweek* in 2005, shows that the tendency starts when humans are very young. She played peek-a-boo with these babies. She began peeking around a cloth with a big smile on her face. Predictably, the babies were delighted and stared at her intently—this is the time-tested way to tell if the baby is interested. On the fourth peek, she emerged with a sad look on her face. The babies looked away, and did not look back even when she began smiling again. Refusing to make eye contact is a classic baby sign of distress. The experiment showed that babies look at pleasant and avoid unpleasant faces. Similarly, humans tend to believe in the "good old days" because, as is seen later, they tend to remember the pleasant everyday events better than the unpleasant.

When another person says, "the world is this way" we need to ask: Is the perception especially pleasant for the one who holds this view? What is the empirical evidence that might be used to test this idea? Is there convergence across multiple observers, from very different cultures or backgrounds? Such questions will help us identify the other person's self-deceptions, and we might be able to say: "the emperor has no clothes!"

The Role of Ignorance

There are false beliefs that can be traced to ignorance rather than to selective perception. A person who thinks that the world is flat usually simply does not know enough about it to make the correct judgment. That is not a self-deception in the sense that I use the term in this book. Just looking outside the window and seeing the flatness of the image does not involve distorted perception due to wishes or needs. On the other hand, there are some religious people who even when shown pictures from outer space continue to think that the earth is the center of the universe. Now it is the religious framework that is protected, and there is a wish as well as a need to see the world that way. That is a self-deception. The smoker who does not know that smoking may lead to cancer does not have a self-deception. But the smoker who is shown the data and insists that one can prove anything with statistics is protecting an addiction.

All Illusions Are Not Self-Deceptions

Humans experience many illusions. For example, a large number of illusions (e.g., psychology texts show a number of them, such as the Müller-Lyer illusion, where two equal lines are seen as unequal) have been discovered in visual perception and in cognition but they are not self-deceptions. Self-deception is a phenomenon of *motivated* selective perception; the perception must be self-relevant. When a patient with cancer thinks that he or she will live a long life (Taylor, 1989) that is certainly self-relevant, or when Hitler thought that a counterattack against the Russians would change the course of the war in April 1945 that was also self-relevant, and clearly a self-deception.

Cultural, Collective, and Individual Self-Deceptions

I mentioned earlier that humans often adopt a cultural belief that was generated by a self-deception. Institutions often perpetuate cultural self-deceptions, such as that there is something "holy" about the king, that a "holy" book is the actual word of God, that there is something mythical about the correctness of a law. Humans often engage in collective self-deceptions, such as the extraordinary speculation of 1637, known as "tulipomania," when some paid as much as 2,600 Dutch guilders for a single tulip bulb. Thousands were bankrupted when the tulip market burst. In stock markets, to the extent that people buy to meet their desires though a bubble is about to burst, they exhibit a self-deception. In short, some self-deceptions are cultural (i.e., widely shared by members of a culture), and others collective (held by a group) or individual (held by only one person).

Parallel to the self-deceptions that occur within a person there are collective self-deceptions that occur when people disagree within a group. Again positive elements are selected and negative elements are rejected. The majority in the group wants to see the world in a certain way, because of their ambition, anxiety, status-seeking, face-saving, illusions, or prejudices. Yet a minority warns them against seeing it that way. The prototype is the story of the Trojan horse. According to the *Odyssey*, the Greeks besieged Troy for 9 years with little effect, until Odysseus devised a ruse. They constructed a wooden horse that could house scores of Greek warriors and left it before the gates of Troy with a sign indicating it was dedicated to the Goddess Athena. Then they departed from Troy until they were out of sight. A large debate occurred among the Trojans. The majority wanted to bring it into the city and present it to Athena, to obtain her protection. A minority, including Capys the Elder, Laoccoon, and Cassandra, warned that the horse was a trick and should be destroyed. The majority won and the horse was brought into the city. During the night the warriors crept out of the horse, opened the gates of the city, and the returning Greeks destroyed the city. Tuchman's analysis of such follies, when the majority decides in favor of an action that is against its best interests, suggests that the lust for power is often a major factor. "Government remains the paramount area of folly because it is there that men seek power over others—only to lose it over themselves" (Tuchman, 1984, p. 382). Her examples include the follies of the renaissance popes (1470–1530) who provoked the Protestant Reformation, the British loss of America, and the American fiasco in Vietnam. The Trojan example also reminds us that religion can lead to folly.

Megalomania in Self-Deceptions

There is an element of megalomania in many self-deceptions. Bin Laden thinks of himself as being in the footsteps of Mohammed, the founder of his religion, and he aspires to become the Caliph (leader) of Islam; President Bush talked with God (Mansfield, 2003) who told him to attack Iraq. In the Netherlands, Mohammed Bouyen, who killed Theo van Gogh, the producer of a film critical of Islam, said in court, "I acted in the name of my religion." One of the suicide bombers of the July 7, 2005, attack on the London underground stated on an al-Qaeda video, taped some time before his suicide, that he will do what Allah commands by attacking those who suppress, attack, and torture Muslims. Bin Laden exaggerates in many of his statements. Thus, he said that Americans "occupy" Arabia, and killed 1 million Muslims. Therefore, it is "God's command" to kill Americans (B. Lewis, 2003). The jihadists also have the megalomania that God has enemies and needs their help (B. Lewis, 2003). As long as people have such gross self-deceptions, terrorism will continue. We need to educate children, while they are still young, by telling them to be vigilant of megalomania and self-serving fantasies. Self-deceivers should understand that they have no right to hurt innocents by being inspired by fantasies.

Antecedents of Self-Deception

Humans are capable of perceiving trillions of stimuli (e.g., our eyes can discriminate 7.5 million different colors; see R. Brown & Lenneberg, 1954), but they can process only few (7 plus or minus 2) independent pieces of information (G. Miller, 1956) at one time. Our senses can detect 11 million pieces of information per second (D. Wilson, 2002), but we cannot pay attention to that much information. When we are confronted with trillions of stimuli we deal with them by using categories. But the categorization processes introduces biases. For instance, the way we perceive categories depends in part on how the categories are grouped. Suppose I ask you: Are Budapest and Prague to the east of Vienna? You might be tempted to say "Yes" but the correct answer is "No." Prague is to the west of Vienna. However, by the way I asked the question I placed Budapest and Prague together and also many people think of Budapest and Prague as being together in "Eastern Europe." In short, when these two cities are grouped together there is likely to be an error in perception.

Self-deception is especially likely when the situation is ambiguous or vague, and when people have a strong need (Robinson & Riff, 1999). The need motivates them to self-deceive, and the ambiguity of the situation makes it easy to do so. Robinson and Riff found that self-deception is especially high when it concerns future events.

Categories have emotional loadings—some are "good" and some are "bad." Evaluation is the most important aspect of stimuli (Osgood, May, & Miron, 1975) and is most likely to be perceived when humans have to make judgments under stress or in a limited time (Paulhus & Suedfeld, 1988). Paulhus, Graft, and Van Selst (1989) showed that the more information in the environment the more likely people are to use positive responses.

When confronted with many stimuli, humans select those that are most useful, pleasant, and intense or least undesirable, and avoid those that are unpleasant, offensive, disgusting, or anxiety-producing. They consciously perceive the pleasant and avoid the unpleasant. Erdelyi (1974) reviewed evidence that in perception humans select pleasant and avoid unpleasant information. Humans tend to perceive what is pleasant and what is intense. Matlin and Stang (1978) also reviewed much empirical work that supports this view. Specifically, on the first two pages of their book they list 23 generalizations, such as

- People seek out the pleasant and avoid the unpleasant. For example, they avoid looking at unpleasant pictures.
- People are more accurate in recalling pleasant life experiences than in recalling neutral or unpleasant life experiences.

Furthermore, they argue that extremely pleasant or unpleasant experiences are processed equally accurately. Performance is optimal when the stimuli are both pleasant and intense, next best when the stimuli are unpleasant and intense, and worst when the stimuli are neutral (neither pleasant nor unpleasant nor intense). Nevertheless, there are some conditions when unpleasant stimuli are perceived quickly (perceptual vigilance). This happens when survival depends on the perception of these stimuli. Certainly, if a tiger is attacking those who have the self-deception that "all is well," they will not be around to be counted!

The selection of positive and the avoidance of negative information are not always deliberate (i.e., conscious). Some of this selection occurs outside of consciousness in the "adaptive unconscious" (D. Wilson, 2002). D. Wilson contrasted the adaptive unconscious and consciousness. The former is the more primitive system that evolved first in human evolution. It detects patterns, is concerned with the here and now; it is fast, unintentional, uncontrollable, effortless, and sensitive to negative information. It is the kind of system that detects a poisonous snake that is attacking us. The latter system developed later in our evolutionary history, and is more likely to use checks and balances, take the long view, be slow, intentional, controllable, and effortful, and sensitive to positive information. It is the system that allows us to tell that it is not a snake but just a stick that looks like a snake. The unconscious system is crude and makes a lot of mistakes. But the conscious one also makes mistakes, namely by increasing the chances of self-deception.

Holmes (1970) instructed his students to keep a diary of pleasant and unpleasant experiences for 1 week, and to rate each experience according to pleasantness and intensity. One week later the students recalled the experiences and rated them according to their pleasantness and intensity at that time. The students recalled a large percentage of the pleasant experiences. They also recalled more experiences that were originally rated as intense. Thus, both the pleasant and the intense experience were recalled.

Our memory system is designed so that the probability of self-deceptions is high. For example, in an experiment by Jersild (1931), students were asked to list the pleasant and unpleasant experiences they had during the previous week. Three weeks later they were asked to list these experiences again. They remembered 46% of the pleasant and only 32% of the unpleasant experiences. Adverse or threatening events are responded to by minimizing or even erasing the memory of the event (Taylor, 1991). But in perception, negative events receive a larger weight than positive ones. The longer the time interval between the event and the recall, the greater is the difference between the recall of pleasant and unpleasant events. The intensity of unpleasant experiences decreases more than the intensity of the pleasant, and that is reflected in the way experiences are recalled (Holmes, 1970). These findings explain why people believe that things were better in the past (the good old days) than they are now.

In short, selective perception is the essence of self-deception, and self-deception tends to be very pleasant. Of course that is not always so. The husband who has the self-deception that his wife is faithful, when there is much evidence that she is not, has suppressed the undesirable evidence and that is an uncomfortable state. Baumeister, Brotslavsky, Finkenauer, and Vohs (2001) presented evidence that negative elements are more powerful than positive ones. Thus, suppressing the negative elements requires much effort. In any case, much self-deception may be caused by our effort to avoid unpleasant truths. This sometimes is done quite consciously. Furthermore, information that is inconsistent with the cognitive schema that people have about who they are is very likely to be ignored (Gilbert & Cooper, 1985).

Studies of human attention (Treisman, 1969) find that humans restrict the number of inputs they analyze, or the dimensions they analyze, or the items (critical features) attended, or the results of the perceptual analysis that controls their behavior. Only a few elements are stored in memory. Thus, there is ample opportunity for the selection of pleasant elements, whereas unpleasant elements can be ignored.

Even in situations where and when individuals perceive both the pleasant and unpleasant stimuli, if they act on the basis of only the pleasant ones they are deceiving themselves. In some situations, processing a lot of information is difficult or unlikely. Specifically, people who are tired, under time pressure, highly aroused (e.g., very hungry, thirsty), or subjected to extremely disagreeable noise are not capable of processing much information. That increases both cognitive simplicity and the probability that they will attend only to the pleasant stimuli and ignore other stimuli, and thus they are likely to use self-deception. For example, those who are extremely hungry are likely to see an R in the street as a restaurant rather than a restroom!

Westen, Blagov, Harenski, Kilts, & Hamann (2006) argued that humans process emotional stimuli unconsciously. They slant the representation of those they like and care about in positive directions, and those they dislike in negative directions. Their judgments are influenced by several emotions simultaneously, which pull their cognitions in different directions. They process cognitions and emotions in parallel (like two computers set to work in parallel, one processing the emotions and the other processing the cognitions), and at some point the two computers "talk to each other," and the emotions often overwhelm the cognitions.

Westen et al. presented several empirical studies of decision making that show that emotions often overwhelm cognitions. For example, a community sample was asked to judge whether an Abu Ghraib prison keeper accused of mistreating prisoners should be able to subpoena Secretary of Defense Donald Rumsfeld and President Bush to obtain exculpatory evidence. Their judgments did not reflect legal reasoning but were simply determined by the way they felt about the issue (i.e., their party affiliation and their attitudes toward human rights and the military).

Often, our high self-esteem is not justified (Baumeister, Campbell, Krueger, & Vohs, 2001, 2003). But in some cases it is justified as, for instance, in the case of George Washington. When he was rejected by the British after applying to become a British officer, he did not believe that there was something wrong with himself; instead he just thought that the British were stupid. Imagine what would have happened if he had been accepted as a British officer. The American Revolution may not have succeeded. However, few humans have the qualities of George Washington. Thus, their overly positive self-evaluations are generally not justified objectively. Nevertheless, such self-evaluations are helpful in facing criticism. In most cases, threatening information passes through filters that make it look inconsequential. In feedback experiments, humans perceive the feedback in a self-serving manner (Taylor & Brown, 1988).

Quattrone and Tversky (1985) demonstrated the choice of the more pleasant stimulus in an experiment by with Stanford students. The students "cheated" during an experiment and selected behaviors that were supposed to be associated with a long life, over behaviors that were supposed to be associated with a short life, although these designations were simply experimental manipulations and had no implication about longevity.

Self-Deception Is Universal in Human Affairs

This point was made very clearly by Taylor (1988, 1989). Bruner (1986) stated that humans are so easily taken in that they could be called *homo credens*. Murphy (1975) discussed the "too-muchness of reality." Humans need blinders to protect themselves from fear, danger, and threats. They achieve protection by paying attention to their desires rather than to reality. In fact, "we have two ways of ordering reality: the way of science and the way of personal desires" (Murphy, 1975, p. 8). Murphy quoted Nietzsche, in *Beyond Good and Evil*, as follows: "My memory says I did it. My pride says I could not have done it, and in the end my memory yields" (p. 39).

Cognitive Simplicity and Self-Deception

There is a relationship between cognitive complexity and self-deception. Paulhus and Suedfeld (1988) provided a discussion of how the selection of cognitions may take place. They used cognitive complexity theory (see Harvey et al., 1961) and focused on two aspects: *differentiation* (the number of separate viewpoints or dimensions considered by the individual) and *integration* (the degree of reconciliation of the various points of view). Very low complexity is reflected in no differentiation or integration. Moderate complexity includes differentiation. Maximum complexity includes both differentiation and integration. They argued that emotional arousal reduces the complexity of information processing. This reduction increases the importance of evaluation in making judgments. Any threat or time urgency triggers fast-rising arousal, which reduces complexity, before other information is processed. "Dynamic complexity" is adaptive and defends the individual from threats. They review experiments that support this theory. The argument is that when people are under stress there is a reduction in cognitive complexity, an increase in the role of evaluation, and then negative information about the self is most likely to be rejected, and thus self-deception is likely to be high. These effects occur on representations in working memory, leaving untouched long-term representations, so that when the threat is reduced the individual may gain access to the information that was not attended to when the individual was under stress. In summary, the more cognitive complexity there is, the less self-deception is likely to occur. Thus, from this theoretical point of view, self-deception is especially likely to occur when people are under threat, have very little time to consider the situation, or experience a high information overload. Many factors that increase arousal, such as noise or fatigue, also decrease our information processing capacity, and thus increase the probability of self-deception.

How Is Self-Deception Related to Mental Health?

Previously it was discussed that optimal mental health may require some self-deceptions, although self-deceptions are dangerous for the health of the planet. "Positive illusions" are helpful. For example, men who have been infected with the HIV virus, who had the illusion that they would live a long time, experienced a less rapid course of the illness (Taylor, Kemeny, Reed, Bower, & Gruenewald, 2000). Positive illusions have been found to be beneficial in several U.S. studies as well as studies in Japan (Toyama & Sakurai, 2001) and in the Ukraine (Kitchens, 2003).

What are some of the ways in which self-deception and mental health are related? Taylor, Collins, Skokan, and Aspinwall (1989) argued that normal mental health is associated with a self-aggrandizing bias, allowing people to receive criticism without being devastated. Personal control and optimism are minor self-deceptions that help mental health. Mental health can be indexed by measures of happiness, number of social bonds, creativity, persistence, and effective coping. These attributes are found among those who are optimistic and have a good opinion of themselves and a sense of personal control. Of course, unrealistic optimism is a major self-deception. It has been shown that people in individualistic societies are higher on this attribute than people in collectivist societies (Chiu & Hong, 2006), thus individualists may have more self-deceptions in this domain than do collectivists.

On the other hand, too positive a self-assessment can lead to careers in which the person is not successful, may result in the pursuit of and persistence in tasks that are uncontrollable, may have the consequence of ignoring legitimate risks, and may result in failures to prepare for life's catastrophes. Negative information about the self (e.g., criticism received from family or friends) is often useful, but the individual needs to be able to use it without becoming depressed. This can be done by accepting that one has "pockets of incompetence" or by filtering out some of the negative information.

A number of self-deceptions are inconsistent with good mental health. For example, a disaster may be the result of believing that some undertaking will be successful because of divine intervention, such as by wearing a "sacred shirt." Baumeister (1989) reviewed studies of the Ghost Dance movement among First Americans. It was initially effective but then it evolved in the belief that they could conquer again the lands lost to Whites, a classic self-deception. The Khmer Rouge had the self-deception that they could become independent of the West, and could develop an agricultural society that would be food-self-sufficient. Their leaders started with modest goals, but kept raising the production goals. Those local officials who were not able to meet the goals were executed. Then, the other officials exaggerated their production. The top leaders asked them to deliver the rice, but to do that they had to starve their subordinates, who produced even less, and so on until the whole scheme became a series of deceptions and executions. Numerous examples from revolutions, the 1929 depression, and so on led Baumeister to argue that there is an "optimal margin of illusion" and when people expect outcomes to be higher than this standard there is failure, and when outcomes are lower than the standard people become depressed.

In summary, humans have tendencies toward cognitively simple self-deceptions. Cognitive simplicity requires less effort, and self-deception allows them to see themselves as "good." Even criminals see themselves as good. Thus, self-deceptions protect their self-esteem and give meaning to their existence.

The chapters that follow explore some of these ideas in greater depth. The next chapter examines the influence of culture on information processing.

3

Fooling Ourselves Across Cultures

Almost everything human shows individual differences. For instance, our internal organs are not all the same size. Size follows the bell-shaped curve, where the most frequent size is of a given value and smaller and larger sizes are less frequent. Extremely small and extremely large sizes are rare. Cognitively simple self-deceptions also are distributed according to the bell-shaped curve.

Mahmoud Ahmadinejad, Iran's president, proclaimed during a speech at Columbia University in September 2007, "Iran has no homosexuals." He also said that the Holocaust did not occur, and that Israel will be wiped from the face of the world. Three self-deceptions suggest high susceptibility to self-deception. It is unclear at this time whether this is the result of culture or personality. In any case, it suggests that some people are unusually high in self-deception.

Both culture and personality differences are traceable to biased tendencies to sample information from the environment. There are differences in the availability of certain constructs to cultures and individuals, there are differences in the accessibility of the constructs, differences in the applicability of the constructs in particular settings, and also differences in the way the constructs are organized (Mendoza-Denton & Mischel, 2007). It seems likely that individuals and members of various cultures will have different tendencies to sample positive and avoid negative information, and that will result in individual differences in self-deception rates. There is a need for research that will explore this matter in detail.

In different domains, such as on personal or public matters, self-deception is likely to be greater in some cultures than in others. This chapter explores such individual differences.

CULTURE

The conceptualization of culture is by no means a simple matter. There are hundreds of definitions (Kroeber & Kluckhohn, 1952), but for our purposes let us say that "culture is to society what memory is to individuals" (Kluckhohn, 1954, p. 921). It includes what "has worked" in the experience of a society, so that it was worth transmitting to future generations. There is also some consensus among anthropologists (Borowsky, Barth, Shweder, Rodseth, & Stolzenberg, 2001) that Redfield's (1941) definition of culture as "shared understandings made manifest in act and artifact" (p. 1) is a good one.

Elements of culture are shared standard operating procedures, unstated assumptions, meanings, practices, tools, myths, art, kinship, norms, values, habits about sampling the information in the environment, and shared meanings. Dawkins (1989) called the elements of culture *memes*. They could include a word, tune, idea, clothes, fashions, ways of making pots, and so on. The essence of a meme is that is a replicating entity. Cultural evolution involves the transmission of memes from generation to generation. For example, the meme for god is very likely to be transmitted because it occurs first when children have not yet developed critical faculties, in other words, "faith" develops before people have developed critical faculties. Faith means "blind trust in the absence of evidence" (Dawkins, 1989, p. 198).

Because perception and cognition depend on the information that is sampled from the environment and are fundamental psychological processes, the meme that influences the sampling of information is of particular interest for our discussion of self-deception, which is a consequence of selective perception.

Cultures develop conventions for sampling information from the environment, and also for weighing the sampled elements. For example, people in hierarchical cultures are more likely to sample clues about hierarchy than about aesthetics. People in individualist cultures, such as those from north and western Europe and North America, sample with high probability elements of the personal self (e.g., "I am busy," "I am kind"). People from collectivist cultures, such as those from many parts of Asia, Africa, and South America, tend to sample mostly elements of the collective self (e.g., "My family thinks I am too busy," "My co-workers think I am kind"; Triandis, 1989).

Consequently, the self-deceptions of people from individualist cultures will be mostly about individuals (e.g., "I have wonderful attributes"). The self-deceptions of people from collectivist cultures will glorify their in-groups (e.g., "My family is the most honorable in the country"). When individuals become disappointed with life they cannot have the self-deception that they have wonderful attributes, and then they may become depressed. The rates of depression in the individualist segment of the world are alarmingly high, and it is notable that when people from col-lectivist cultures arrive in individualist cultures their rates of depression are low but begin to increase the longer they remain in the individualistic culture. The third generation of these immigrants has the same depression rates as the general population of the individualist culture. There is also evidence that the highest suicide rates are in some individualist cultures (e.g., Austria, Hungary, and Sweden; Eckersley & Dear, 2002). Suicide at times is an escape from self (Baumeiseter, 1990), and that is especially rel-evant in individualistic cultures. One factor that may protect collectivists from suicide is that failure is not personal but shared. Many decisions of collectivists are taken after extensive consultations with the in-group, and if the decision turns out to be bad the whole in-group shares the blame.

Cultures emerge in specific ecologies (geographic features, resources, climate, how to make a living in a particular environment). For exam-ple, if there is fish in the environment people are likely to become fish-ermen; to have beliefs, norms, and values that are related to fish; to have myths about fish; to eat fish; and to give special meaning to fish. The tra-ditions that emerge from the ecology eventually become elements of the religions and other elements of culture. The cultures that emerge in dif-ferent parts of the world often reflect the availability of flora, fauna, and other resources, as well as historical factors, such as migrations, wars, rev-olutions, and inventions (Whiting, 1994).

The way ecology determines culture is illustrated by the role of a mete-orite in shaping Islam. A meteorite called Ka'ba was located in Mecca in pre-Islamic times, and was worshiped by the local population. Local mer-chants took advantage of its presence to provide services to the caravans that frequented Mecca. In pre-Islamic times there were images of numer-ous gods depicted on this stone, including that of Jesus and his mother Mary (Jannoulatos, 1975/2001).

The ancient Arab tradition of worshiping the Ka'ba became incorpo-rated into Islam, and became the fifth pillar of this faith. Muslims are supposed to visit Mecca, and participate in the so-called *hajj*, at least once during their lifetime. This includes the worship of the Ka'ba. Numerous rituals are associated with the hajj. The believers must be clean, should have cut their hair and nails, should not have had sex, and should put on their white robes no less than 10 miles before they reach Mecca. Women should be totally covered. The ritual requires circling the Ka'ba seven times. Ideally, the pilgrims should kiss or at least touch the stone. At a given moment they are supposed to say, speaking to God, "I am present and awaiting orders." After that, they are supposed to run seven times between the hills of Safâ and Marva. They are then supposed to walk to Arafa, which is a few hours walk from Mecca, where they wait until sunset, "before the eyes of God." Upon returning from Arafa they must collect 49 stones that they must throw at a monument in the city of Minã, recalling the stoning of the devil by Ismael. (Incidentally, it is at this point where several hundred pilgrims died in February 2004, when they were trampled to death.) Finally, on the 10th day of the 12th month they are supposed to sacrifice an animal remembering the sacrifice of Abraham (Jannoulatos, 1975/1981).

In short, starting from ecology (i.e., the availability of a meteorite), an elaborate cultural ritual has developed that is one of the five pillars of Islam.

Cultures differ on a number of dimensions. The most important are discussed here.

Complexity

The greatest contrast on this dimension is found between hunter–gatherers and information societies. Chick (1997) considered the size of settlements as the most important index, because hunter–gatherers usually have bands of about 50 to 200 individuals, whereas information societies have megalopolises with millions of inhabitants. Nomadic, agricultural, and industrial societies are between these two extremes. GNP per capita is also an index of cultural complexity. Other indices may include the percent of the population that is urban, the size of cities, personal computers per capita, and so on. The simplest way to think about this dimension is to contrast a village with a cosmopolitan city, like London, New York, or Tokyo. Villages usually have many individuals who think alike, whereas a city like New York has every variety of different ways of thinking, languages, religions, races, social classes, and so on.

There is little inequality in hunting–gathering cultures. Because food cannot be preserved for a long time (no refrigeration), it is not possible to accumulate wealth. The greatest inequality is found in societies where inventors are financially successful and become differentiated from their peers. Cognitive simplicity contrasts with cognitive complexity the way rural settings contrast with metropolitan areas.

However, the rural–urban contrast is only one factor. Another factor may be religion. Monotheism is more cognitively simple than polytheism. It is not surprising that the most peaceful period in history, from the point of view of religious wars, was during the Roman Empire (Gibbon, 1963).

Cognitive simplicity–complexity parallels cultural simplicity–complexity. It is obvious that illiteracy, which is an index of cognitive simplicity, is more common in the simple than in the complex cultures.

However, we need to pay attention to each cognitive domain. Hunters are likely to be extremely complex in domains relevant to hunting—plants, animals, animal traces, scents, means of hunting, such as bows and arrows. Some simple cultures have an enormously complex knowledge of their ancestors. At the same time, they are likely to have little complexity across domains, such as history, anthropology, physics, chemistry, and the like. Given that the modern world is very complex, cognitive simplicity is generally undesirable and is likely to be associated with defective information processing.

Lévy-Bruhl (1910/1966) discussed the way people in simple cultures think by using the term *mystical thinking*. By this he meant a "belief in forces and influences and actions which, though imperceptible to senses, are nevertheless real" (p. 25). Such people pay attention only to concrete entities (what they can actually see or hear), but attribute unfortunate events (e.g., death, illness) to imperceptible forces, such as witchcraft, a bad spell, or an evil spirit. In complex cultures we might use a myriad of diseases and ways in which a person might die from illness or from an accident. In simple cultures there is just one or very few, undesirable forces. For example, when a member of the Ovambi tribe (west Africa) was preparing an ox for work, the ox put out the man's eye. The locals said that the "man who had lost his eye had been bewitched" (Lévy-Bruhl, 1923, p. 47). In simple cultures there is no concept of randomness, which is a complex idea. Everything occurs because of a force, such as witchcraft. The seen and unseen world is one and the same, indicating cognitive simplicity. Omens are important indicators of future events. Practices such as the "evil eye," divination, the dreading of the dead, ordeals (judgments of God), follow the laws of magic outlined by Frazer (1968). That is, they reflect the laws of similarity and contact (see chapter 5 for details). Success is not attributed to the self, or to good instruments, but to favorable supernaturals. In simple cultures they dislike the unknown, which will complicate one's cognitive system. In complex cultures, people test their beliefs by looking for objective evidence. In simple cultures, they do not use the concept of contradiction (Lévy-Bruhl, 1923), so they do not use such tests. They use no abstract generalizations, which are part of a complex cognitive system (see chapter 2).

Authoritarian leaders are often culturally and cognitively simple, and are attracted to simple rural environments. Note that Hitler hated Berlin, which he wanted to change to a completely different entity, and his ideal place was on the Bavarian Alps in Berchtesgaden. Mao mobilized his Red Guards, who came mostly from rural China, to bring down the cities. His followers went after intellectuals, who represented complexity and the city. Similarly, the Khmer Rouge attacked Phnom Penh, turning its schools into torture chambers, killing 2 million people. In Serbia the intellectuals who could avoid serving in the army left the country, and the Serb Army, consisting mostly of peasants, attacked Sarajevo, a cosmopolitan city, famous for its libraries, museums, universities, cafes, learning, and trade.

In the Middle Ages in Europe, the secular and the sacred were often combined in the person of the king or emperor. That was a simpler societal form than modern democracies. When Louis the XIVth said, "I am the state" he was accurate—he combined the legislative, judicial, and executive functions of the state, and dominated the religious establishment. As societies evolved the various political functions became independent. There was separation of church and state in America, thanks to the efforts of Jefferson, among others. Cognitively simple thinkers such as bin Laden advocate no separation of mosque and state. The American Constitution established the independence and equality of the three branches of government. When the three branches of government have equal power there is more complexity and less abuse of power or corruption. When the executive has more power than the other branches of government there is abuse of power (e.g., Russia) and corruption (e.g., France, Italy). For example, in France politicians who have been convicted sometimes stay out of prison, and are even at times reelected. Similarly, in Communist countries the party dominates all branches of government and there is both abuse of power and corruption.

Tightness

In tight cultures, many norms are present and they are imposed tightly. In loose cultures, deviation from norms is tolerated (Triandis, 1994). Such tolerance is found in relatively heterogeneous societies (where several normative systems are present), where people do not depend much on each other, and where population density (e.g., opportunity for surveillance) is low. Rural Thailand is considered a loose culture. The expression "mai bin rai" (never mind) is used frequently. Thailand is at the intersection of two major cultures—India and China—and thus there are different norms about "proper" behavior. One must tolerate behavior that is not "proper" because too many people behave that way. In Thailand, when people do not do what is "correct" other people just smile. They smile more than in any other culture I have ever visited.

Indian culture is quite tolerant (Zakaria, 2008), and the religion is very complex. Zakaria said that the best way to characterize it is that its guiding principle is *ambiguity*. When there is ambiguity the society is necessary loose, because one cannot punish a transgression that is ambiguous. However, it is important to remember that tightness–looseness depends on the domain. In the case of transgressions involving the caste system, the society is tight.

An open frontier is related to looseness (Triandis, 1994, 1995). As satellite television and the Internet spread, people become aware of more different ways of "correct" behavior, and that reduces the attraction of very strict (tight) norms or religions. On the other hand, as more options (choices) become available, people may become more tight or religious in order to get some guidance concerning how to behave. In short, when there are too few or too many choices the culture may be tight.

When people depend on each other, it is important that they do what is expected of them, otherwise social life may become chaotic. When people's behavior is apt to be observed by others, it is more likely that people will behave the way they are expected to behave. Thus, in such cases the culture is tight.

A clue about a culture's tightness is the percentage of the population that is left-handed. In very tight cultures less than 1% is left-handed; in loose cultures it is as high as 15% (Dawson, 1974). Another clue of tightness is that there are rules about a myriad of behaviors, most of which are not allowed. Two examples can be given: traditional Japan and extreme Islam. In Christian monasteries also, the culture is very tight.

The Japan of the 19th century was very tight (Edgerton, 1992). It had hundreds of rules about how to smile, bow, and be polite. Even today, Japanese live in fear that they will not act properly (Iwao, 1993), and they tend to criticize teenagers for minor deviations from "proper" behavior, such as having too much suntan, or curly hair, or the "wrong" (e.g., social class) accent (Kidder, 1992).

Muslims are now generally tighter than the populations of the West, although there are variations of tightness–looseness in both Islam and the West. As per the earlier description of the hajj, one sees very elaborate rules, norms, and traditions. Deviation from these norms is punished. The Taliban is a good example of a very tight culture. This group developed hundreds of rules: You cannot listen to music or view television. You must not smile. You cannot fly kites (a traditional pastime in that culture associated with "fun" and "freedom"). You must wear certain clothing, and so on. Deviation from such norms was severely punished through executions and lashes; for example, 100 lashes to a woman walking in the street with a nonrelative. I return to this construct in the discussion of religion and terrorism because it appears that very tight cultures are likely to generate more terrorists. The West was tighter 60 years ago than it is now.

A Web site, which may or may not be representative of the majority of Islam (www.islam-qa.com), provides answers to Muslims in many cultures because the site can be read in English, Indonesian, Chinese, Arabic, French, Hindi, or Spanish. The answers are extremely puritanical. My Muslim friends tell me that this site is not providing "normal Islam" information, but it is very difficult to determine precisely what is "normal." In any case, a check of this Web site shows that there are many rules and most behavior is not permitted (*haram*). Incidentally, the structure of these prohibitions is very similar to the rules found in a summer Bible camp (Hood, Hill, & Williamson, 2005), where the campers are not allowed to do many things. So the tight rules are not found only in a Muslim setting. They also occur in Christian or any fundamentalist setting.

One example from this Muslim Web site is that stoning is the prescribed punishment for writing a letter to the opposite sex. Tightness is also indexed by the specificity of the norms. The Tabligh, a Muslim minority group in India, specifies that one must dress like the Prophet, sleep as he did on the ground, and on one's right side (Kepel, 2004). Some Muslims prohibit others from wearing a tie because it is the symbol of the cross (Kepel, 2004). Even "excessive laughter" is prohibited in some circles (Manji, 2003).

The greater tightness of Islamic cultures is in contrast to the looseness found in the West. America had a much tighter culture in the 1950s than it does in the 21st century. Much of the opposition of religious conservatives to current trends is a reaction to the greater looseness of 21st-century culture, as indexed by tolerance for sexual behavior previously considered unacceptable, teenage pregnancies, single-parent families, mounting divorce rates, high levels of crime, widespread drug use, and pornography and violence in the media. Islamic fundamentalists object to the looseness of the West even more than American religious conservatives. In my opinion they are right in objecting to some of our looseness. For example, our tolerance for violence in the mass media is scandalous, when there are more than 1,000 well-done studies showing a link between viewing violent behavior and acting violently (e.g., Richards, Bond, & Stokes-Zoota, 2003).

In high uncertainty avoidance or tight cultures, people are more certain of their religious beliefs. In loose cultures, people can tolerate different religions. In tight cultures, for example, fundamentalist Christianity, Islam, Judaism, Shinto, only a few "truths" can be accepted. Low uncertainty avoidance cultures have religions such as Buddhism, Taoism, and Hinduism (there is one truth, it has many names) that are more mystical, where there are many contradictory beliefs, and whether something is good or bad depends on the context (the situation). Dialectical thinking is common in such cultures (Peng & Nisbett, 1999). When inconsistency is tolerated, people can accept different religions. In New Delhi, India, there is a temple where all religions can be practiced. Gandhi was respectful of all religions, although fundamentalist Hindus objected to his position, and Hindu extremists assassinated him.

Categories are more "accessible"; that is, more likely to be used in information processing and decisions, when they are frequent in the environment and when they have been used recently. In Muslim cultures, for instance, the word *God* is used with great frequency and "God willing" occurs in almost every sentence. Thus, we can expect that God will be involved in most information processing in Islam. Because God is a wish (Farazza, 2004), as seen in chapter 5, it is a self-deception, and thus self-deception is very common in Islamic cultures. For example, during the Arab–Israeli war, the Egyptians insisted that American military forces supported Israel (Glenn, 1981). They had no evidence for their assertion, but it fitted their self-concept that they were "great warriors," which only a superpower could defeat.

It is likely that self-deception is higher in tight than in loose cultures. In tight cultures, people must act according to the group's norms, which at times use very high standards. But few people can reach such high standards of "correct" behavior all the time. It is likely that on many occasions people who deviate from a norm will see themselves as "good enough" when in fact their in-group will not think that they are good. Thus, they will pay attention to their self-evaluations, which are positive, and ignore the evaluations of others, which are negative, so they will be using a self-deception. Research is needed to test this idea, however. The situation in which an individual has a good self-opinion, whereas others have a bad opinion of him or her may be quite general, and is likely to involve self-deceptions. I suspect that it is very common in human affairs.

One explanation of terrorism is that tightness results in some Muslims feeling that they are not "good enough Muslims." When there are a lot of rules that must be followed, it is only human that individuals will break some of them. When this happens, the Muslims believe they are no longer good. At that point, they become more receptive to a suggestion by members of terrorist organizations who tell them that they will be superb Muslims if they blow themselves up. Chapter 6 on terrorism discusses that the "package" of rewards that is supposedly associated with "martyrdom" is extremely attractive to cognitively simple self-deceivers, and includes the elimination of all previous "sins."

Collectivism

Collectivism is extremely high in cultures that are simple and tight (Carpenter, 2000; Triandis, 1994). However, these relationships are not strong, so that the three dimensions (simplicity, tightness, collectivism) must be kept separate. In one study that examined 186 cultures, the most collectivist culture was the Mbuti pygmies of the Congo; the most individualist culture was the Ibos of Nigeria. Although the Ibos are more complex than the Mbuti, they certainly are not as complex as the western Europeans or Japanese. Many empirical findings about this cultural attribute have been presented in Kitayama and Cohen (2007).

Few cultures are collectivists in every domain. Mao's China was collectivist in social relations, religion, economics, politics, education, and aesthetics. But clearly, in recent years China has developed more individualist patterns in aesthetics and economics, and is changing in some of the other domains.

The essence of collectivism is concern for the effect of one's actions on other people. That is, people in such cultures are *allocentric*. Their social relations include a strong component of adjustment to other people (Kitayama, Duffy, & Uchida, 2007). Individuals feel linked to a collective (e.g., family, tribe, religion, social class, country, athletic team). People think frequently of the effects of their actions on the collective. They are especially sensitive about losing face (Ho, 1976). They share their successes and failures with the collective. For example, when an athlete wins an Olympic medal, the citizens of a country might experience it as their own win, and the athlete is likely to emphasize that his or her coach contributed to the win. The mindset of collectivists is to connect and integrate, to assimilate figure and ground, self with others (Oyserman & Lee, 2007). They see the world using an outsider's perspective; that is, how do members of my in-group see the world? (D. Cohen & Hashino-Browne, 2005).

A prototype of collectivist cultures can be found in theocratic societies, such as in monasteries. If the hypothesis that there is more self-deception in simple/tight cultures is supported, then it follows that there would be more self-deception in collectivist than in individualist cultures. However, in all cultures we expect to find self-deceptions. As mentioned earlier, in collectivist cultures the self-deception will be about the in-group (e.g., "My family has been the most respected in this community for three centuries," "My country is glorious") and in individualist cultures the self-deceptions are more likely to be about individuals (e.g., "I have wonderful attributes").

The self-concept of people in collectivist cultures has much social content (e.g., "I am a member of this family," "I am an uncle"), but when people from such cultures move to individualist cultures they increase the number of personal attributes they use to describe themselves (e.g., "I am an introvert"; Altocchi & Altocchi, 1995; Fiske et al., 1998; Ma & Schoeneman, 1997).

As suggested previously, there are personality attributes that correspond to collectivism and individualism, called allocentrism and idiocentrism, respectively. There are allocentrics and idiocentrics in all cultures, but their proportions differ. Furthermore, allocentrics in individualist cultures are "misfits" because they do not find enough interdependent relationships (unions, communes); idiocentrics in collectivist cultures seek to leave the culture and move to an individualist culture, where they will not be pressured to behave as specified by some in-group. Allocentrics in collectivist and idiocentric in individualist cultures have optimal mental health. The "fit" between culture and personality is consistent with good adjustment and mental health (Ward, Bochner, & Furnham, 2001). People who have been exposed to multiple cultures often have both the idiocentric and the allocentric models in their cognitive system and use one or the other depending on the situation (Hong, Morris, Chiu, & Benet-Martinez, 2000).

A person can switch from one perspective to another if placed in a particular situation. For example, Trafimow, Triandis, and Goto (1991) randomly assigned students to two conditions: think for 2 minutes either about what you have in common with your family and friends or what makes you different from your family and friends. After an interpolated task the participants were given the Twenty Statements Test (Kuhn & Mc-Partland, 1954), which requires the completion of 20 statements that begin with "I am . . . " Those who received the collectivist prime (same as family) provided sentence completions that were more collectivist (e.g., "I am a member of this group"; "I am an uncle"). Those who received the individualist prime (different from family) provided sentence completions that were more individualist (e.g., "I am busy"; "I am hard working"; "I am a music lover").

Allocentrics in general emphasize interdependence, sociability, and family integrity; they take into account the needs and wishes of in-group members, feel close in their relationships to their in-group, and appear to others as responsive to their needs and concerns (Triandis, 1995).

But allocentrics are more ethnocentric than idiocentrics; they have very positive attitudes about their in-groups and quite negative attitudes about their out-groups. These tendencies usually result in self-deceptions that favor the in-group, and put down the out-group. Allocentrics will also believe that they are very different from their out-groups when in fact they are not that different. Idiocentrics will have the self-deception that they are unique and unusual even when they are quite ordinary. Idiocentrics tend to be more dominant while allocentrics are more agreeable, more easily embarrassed, and are higher in affiliation than is the general population.

I hypothesize that collectivists will tend to think that their in-group's successes are real and widely known, whereas their in-group's failures are of little importance.

- They will discover flaws in information that is unfavorable to their in-group.
- They will spend little time processing information that is unfavorable to their in-group.
- They will selectively forget the failures of their in-group and remember mostly the successes of their in-group.
- They will compare their in-group with groups that will make their in-group look good.

- They will search their memories for desirable characteristics of their in-group.
- They will tend to think that the good attributes of their in-group are unusual and important and the faults of the in-group are common and unimportant.
- They will shift the meaning of ambiguous traits of the in-group to the advantage of the in-group.
- They will dismiss criticisms of the in-group as due to prejudice, racism, and other cognitive biases.

There are many kinds of collectivist cultures. One important distinction is between vertical (much attention to hierarchy, status) and horizontal (emphasis on equality) collectivist cultures. Vertical collectivist cultures (e.g., an Indian village; in this country the Mormons) are traditionalists and emphasize in-group cohesion, respect for in-group norms, and the directives of authorities (Triandis, 1995). For example, only the "president" of the Mormons can have a revelation that changes the doctrine, and in consultation with his 12 "apostles" he can change doctrines in a radical way (e.g., polygyny was the rule until the top authorities decided that it was no longer desirable). Ordinary members of this church do not have a say on how things are run.

In collectivist cultures, in-groups are often at loggerheads with each other, but there is harmony within the in-group. There is cohesion within narrow in-groups, such as the family, or the church. Traditional China is also vertical collectivist, but modern China has pockets of individualism. Similarly, in India, Bangalore will have many subcultures that are individualist.

Vertical collectivism (VC) is correlated with right-wing authoritarianism (RWA; Altemeyer, 1996; Triandis & Gelfand, 1998), a tendency to conform to authority (R. Bond & Smith, 1996) and to endorse conventionalism. Both VC and RWA are correlated positively with age and religiosity, and negatively with education and exposure to culturally diverse persons. Horizontal collectivist cultures (e.g., the Israeli kibbutz) emphasize empathy, sociability, and cooperation. Every member has the same duties and members can decide how the in-group is to run.

In collectivist cultures people have an unrealistically positive view of their in-groups—family, tribe, political party, religion, educational institution, and so on. Additionally, because in vertical collectivist cultures people tend to believe whatever the authorities of the culture believe, when these authorities are high in self-deception, then the population is also likely to be high in self-deception. In short, in vertical collectivist cultures there is likely to be a high correlation between cultural, collective, and individual self-deceptions.

We see people boasting about their group in some situations and about themselves in other situations. In short, the situation interacts with the personality tendencies to produce different kinds of self-deceptions. The importance of the situation is suggested by a study (Chatman & Barsade, 1995) in which allocentric and idiocentric students were randomly assigned to a simulated collectivist or individualist culture and their level of cooperation was measured. The most cooperation occurred among allocentrics in the collectivist culture; in the other three cells cooperation was relatively low. In short, the situation frequently controls what people will do (Ross & Nisbett, 1991).

In collectivist cultures people are interdependent with their in-groups (family, tribe, nation, etc.; Markus & Kitayama, 1991), see positive attributes linked with "us" and slightly negative attributes linked to "me" (Chiu & Hong, 2006), give priority to the goals of their in-groups (Triandis, 1990), shape their behavior primarily on the basis of in-group norms (Suh, Diener, Oishi, & Triandis, 1998), and behave in a communal way (Mills & Clark, 1982) within the in-group. Even when dissatisfied with their in-group they are not likely to leave it. For example, allocentrics who are dissatisfied with their jobs and organizations are less likely to try to find a new job than are idiocentrics (Wasti, 2002). When perceiving and communicating, collectivists use the context of the stimuli more than do individualists (experimental evidence in Chiu & Hong, 2006). Specifically, they communicate indirectly (more emphasis on nonlinguistic cues, such as posture, eye contact, position of the body, level of voice; and more circumlocutions; Holtgraves, 1997). Ambiguity in communication can be functional in a collectivist culture, where clarity in communication may result in a break in interpersonal relationships or sanctions from authorities (Lin, 1997).

A related phenomenon is that collectivists stress how something was said rather than what was said. (See the example of the Iraqis misunderstanding Secretary Baker's message in 1991 that the United States will attack them if they do not move out of Kuwait, in chapter 1.)

There are numerous experiments that show that collectivists focus on the context, whereas individualists focus on the content of a message or stimulus complex (e.g., Nisbett, 2003). In one laboratory experiment, in which fish were swimming in an area that had rocks and plants, collectivists paid more attention to the rocks and plants than did individualists. The latter paid much attention to the central focus of the stimulus complex (i.e., the fish) and more or less ignored the context.

As a result, Westerners and East Asians see situations differently. For example, East Asians often see the history of an event (context) as more important than the event itself, and believe that others also view the history as more important than the event. On the other hand, people from the West may ignore the history and may believe that others also ignore the history. For example, during the negotiations between the Chinese and the British about the future of Hong Kong, the Chinese kept bringing up the history of how Hong Kong became a British colony, and the British argued that this was irrelevant, and the task in hand was to determine the future of the colony (Kwok Leung, personal communication).

Important values among collectivists are patriotism (e.g., sacrifice for the nation), bravery (e.g., taking chances to protect the in-group), loyalty (e.g., sticking with the in-group no matter how unpleasant), and self-sacrifice (e.g., doing what helps the in-group even when it is costly to self). Among Chinese collectivists, filial piety (e.g., taking care of one's parents, even when that is very costly) is traditionally a very important value.

Collectivism is high in cultures or subcultures that

1. are homogeneous in their norms,
2. are lower class,
3. are insular (where people have not been exposed to other cultures),
4. are high in stability; little social change,
5. have many old people (e.g., Trommsdorff, Mayer, & Albert, 2004),
6. have many large families,
7. have people who experience common fate with their in-group,
8. have people with strict religious upbringing, and
9. have people who lack exposure to the modern mass media, such as Western-made television (e.g., McBride, 1998; more references in Triandis & Trafimow, 2001).

Roccas (2005) reported that the values of very religious persons emphasized self-restriction, order, and resistance to change, and de-emphasized hedonism, and independence in thought and action. This pattern corresponds to collectivism. Triandis and Singelis (1998) found that collectivists were more influenced by religion during their upbringing than were individualists. In short, collectivism and religion may be closely linked, although more research on this point would be helpful.

A defining characteristic of people in collectivist cultures is their notable concern for relationships. For example, Ohbuchi, Fukushima, and Tedeschi (1999) found that collectivists in conflict situations are primarily concerned with maintaining relationships with others, whereas individualists are primarily concerned with achieving justice. Thus, collectivists prefer methods of conflict resolution that do not destroy relationships (e.g., mediation), whereas individualists are willing to go to court to settle disputes (Leung, 1997).

Interpersonal relationships and saving face are more important in collectivist than in individualist cultures, thus there will be more self-deception in collectivist cultures. Saving the other's face often requires one to exaggerate the good qualities and ignore the bad qualities of the other, and people may do so without even being aware of doing it. In collectivist cultures, the ideal is to have harmonious relationships within the in-group.

An important aspect of collectivism is that behavior is often very different when the other person is a member of the in-group or the out-group. When the other person is a member of the in-group the actor is often self-sacrificing, going much beyond what is necessary to help and support the in-group member. By contrast, when the other person is a member of the out-group the actor can be cruel, and act as if the other is an animal or a devil. Thus, in international negotiations, collectivists perceive the relationship as a battlefield (Chu, 1991). One can take advantage of the opponent. However, one does not necessarily want to win all the battles. It is enough to win most of them.

In short, in collectivism there is a strong contrast in the behavior toward members of the in-group and out-group (Triandis, 1972). For example, the Tacospans native people of Mexico are very content and peaceful when they drink with members of their in-group, but are insulting and fight when they drink with members of their out-group (MacAndrew & Edgerton, 1969). This sharp distinction between in-group and out-group behaviors is not found in individualism. In collectivism, the greatest contrast is between in-group and out-group; in individualism, it is between "me" and "all others" (Iyengar, Lepper, & Ross, 1999). Collectivists use one morality for behavior within the in-group and another for behavior toward the out-group. Thus, it is okay to lie and cheat if one is dealing with a member of the out-group, but not if one is dealing with a member of the in-group (Triandis et al., 2001). Collectivists use the concept of collective responsibility; thus it is okay to punish a whole group if one person from that group misbehaves. For example, punishing the parents of a criminal makes sense to collectivists. The sharp distinction between the behavior toward the in-group (which often involves self-sacrifice) and out-group (which sometimes involves killing) found in collectivism has been found also in studies of terrorism. Terrorists from collectivist cultures are more likely to target and kill large numbers of foreigners (Weinberg & Eubank, 1994). Terrorists from individualist cultures are more likely to target property within their culture.

Individualism

The essence of individualism is independence and distance from collectives. One does one's "own thing" rather than being concerned with the effects of one's actions on others. Thus, people in such cultures are idiocentrics who focus on influencing, rather than adjusting to, others. The mindset of individualists is to pull apart and separate, to contrast figure and ground, self from others (Oyserman & Lee, 2007). They see the world through an insider's perspective (D. Cohen & Hashino-Browne, 2005). In individualist cultures, one's successes and failures are individual events, not shared with others. Individualism occurs in cultures that are complex and loose, but again the correlations are not strong, so it is necessary to keep complexity, looseness, and individualism separate. Many empirical findings about this cultural attribute have been presented in Kitayama and Cohen (2007).

At the cultural level of analysis (where data from many cultures are used in the analysis), individualism is the opposite pole of collectivism. Within culture, however, the two attributes can be independent of each other (Triandis & Suh, 2002). Thus, idiocentrism and allocentrism, the personality attributes that correspond to the cultural patterns, are independent qualities, and people can be high or low on both of them. Those who are high on both behave one way or the other depending on the situation. As mentioned already, allocentrics in collectivist situations are especially cooperative. But allocentrics in individualist situations or idiocentrics in any kind of situation are not particularly cooperative. A simple way of thinking about individualism and idiocentrism is to consider the behavior of many Hollywood stars whose social relationships are in constant flux. They do what they consider to be fun, at the moment. For example, when Arty Shaw met Lana Turner they decided to get married that night! No consultations with parents or friends were required. The trend continues. Britney Spears married Jason Allen Alexander in Las Vegas, but the marriage lasted only 55 hours because they discovered that they had different interests! The marriage was annulled 2 days after it took place.

An important aspect of individualism is that individuals are expected to determine their own identity. They do not have to take their identity from group memberships. By contrast, in collectivism one's identity is determined by group memberships. Individualists use dispositional attributes (attitudes, beliefs, personality) to explain the behavior of other people more often than do collectivists. They see personality as relatively stable and the situations as variable; collectivists see the person as malleable, ready to fit into different situations, and the situation as relatively stable (Norenzayan, Choi, & Nisbett, 1999). Individualists make the fundamental attribution error more frequently than do collectivists (Fiske et al., 1998). This error is detected when researchers ask observers to explain the causes of the behavior of a person and also ask that person the same question. Individualists use internal factors (which they assume are relatively stable) such as attitudes, beliefs, and personality as the causes of behavior. The person usually does not use external factors, such as norms, roles, and group pressure, as the explanation. Collectivists usually give external factors as the explanation, which they see as relatively stable, and thus do not make this error as much as do individualists.

Individualists have a very positive self-concept (Heine et al., 1999), and are very optimistic (Lee & Seligman, 1997), whereas collectivists prefer to be modest and are not too optimistic. Individualists see failure as being the result of the difficulty of the situation, and rarely attribute it to themselves. If they fail they manage to maintain a positive self-view by using various self-deceptions.

Idiocentrics in general emphasize self-reliance, competition, uniqueness, hedonism, and emotional distance from in-groups. They value creativity, power, artistic talent, intelligence, persistence, and wisdom, all of which are attributes of individuals. They also value equality, human rights, democracy, individuality, freedom, and uniqueness more than is the case in collectivist cultures (Triandis & Suh, 2002). Idiocentrics tend to have a better opinion of themselves than do allocentrics. In fact, allocentrics, even in individualist cultures, tend to be self-critical (Heine et al., 1999).

In vertical individualist cultures (e.g., U.S. corporate cultures), competitiveness is high and one must be "the best" in order to climb the corporate ladder. In horizontal individualist cultures (e.g., Australia and Sweden), hierarchical differentiation is de-emphasized, and the emphasis is only on self-reliance, independence from others, and uniqueness (Triandis & Gelfand, 1998).

People in vertical individualist cultures are especially likely to deceive themselves about their own qualities. We saw in earlier chapters that Americans tend to think that they have extremely positive personal qualities. This self-deception is more common in individualist cultures than in other kinds of cultures. More specifically, people in individualist cultures have person-linked self-deceptions (e.g., "I am extremely intelligent") that are more extreme than people in collectivist cultures. That is, they exaggerate positive aspects of themselves. They see their abilities and skills as much above average. They take a lot of credit for their successes, and when they fail they blame the environment or the difficulty of the task. They hold unrealistic views about their ability to control the environment, and are overly optimistic. They desire more choices (e.g., six kinds of mustard) than people in collectivist cultures (who are usually happy if they have only one kind of mustard). This can lead to the perception that people in all cultures desire many choices. The value of choice depends on the culture (Iyengar & DeVoe, 2003).

Cultural changes toward individualism result in more well-being and more individual choices. These changes have important consequences for religious institutions that attempt to control the behavior of individuals. This is one factor that makes some religious authorities, especially the three religions of the book (Judaism, Christianity, and Islam), generally opposed to modernity. It means that if the masses become idiocentric the authorities will lose their power. This is especially relevant for understanding why fundamentalist mullahs consider the West an "evil."

People in individualist cultures tend to think that the causes of behavior are inside the person—attitudes, abilities, personality, and habits. People in collectivist cultures tend to think that the causes of behavior are outside the person—group norms, values, and pressures from group members (Triandis & Suh, 2002).

Emphasis on religion is negatively related to affluence. If one knows the country's level of affluence and its religion one can predict about three quarters of the variability on psychological variables (Hofstede, 2001).

Religiosity, which we argued might be associated with tendencies toward self-deception, is especially high in Africa and South Asia, and relatively low in East Asia. Some scholars inquired if religiosity is related to psychoticism (Francis, 1992). I do not think so. I think it is much more a matter of conformity to the norms of the society.

The American South is especially high in religiosity, whereas western Europe is relatively low in religiosity (Dogan, 1995). A Gallup International Survey (1977) found that in Japan only about 20% of the population takes religion seriously; by contrast 66% of the general population in the United States, and approximately 86% in India, take it very seriously. In another study, the percent of the population affirming strong religiosity was 97 in Nigeria, 85 in Poland, 79 in India, 71 in Turkey, and 65 in the United States, in contrast religiosity was high in small percentages of the population: 19 in Japan, 10 in Estonia, and 4 in China (Huntington, 2005). Although there is no empirical evidence on this point, as yet, it is very probable that the frequency of self-deceptions will be especially high in those regions where religiosity is high. Because most of these regions are also collectivist, we can expect to see many self-deceptions that glorify the in-group (e.g., caste, country, religious group) in cultures where religion is important.

Euthanasia is accepted in individualist cultures, especially in Switzerland and the Netherlands, but is definitely not accepted in collectivist cultures. It is seen as an individual right in individualist cultures (in most cases a way to avoid pain). Because it is the individual who is in pain, it is not the business of any group to interfere. Collectivists, especially religious ones, do not think that individuals should decide the end of life because that is the business of God. Although America is an individualist culture, on some issues, such as euthanasia, it is collectivist. But regional differences do exist. Vandello and Cohen (1999) showed that individualism is higher on the coasts and lower in the South, which may explain Oregon's position on euthanasia, which is not shared with the rest of the country.

A large study by Inglehart and Baker (2000) examined data from several countries and found two distinguishing dimensions. The first contrasted traditional authority with secular-rational authority. The traditional side emphasized the importance of God; whereas the secular side emphasized permissive attitudes toward sexual and other issues. This contrast, among

cultures, is positively related to individualism (more secular) and negatively to power distance (hierarchical cultures give more importance to
God). The second dimension contrasted survival (emphasis on money,
hard work) with well-being (leisure, friends, and concern for the environment). Northern European countries were high on both the secular and the
well-being dimensions. African and Muslim countries were on the traditional and the survival sides of the two dimensions. The other countries
fell between these two sets of countries. Affluence is related to both individualism and subjective well-being, and is negatively related to power
distance. In other words, hierarchical societies are less affluent than relatively egalitarian societies. Because external religions are related to self-
deception, it can be expected from this study that there will be minimal
self-deceptions in Scandinavia and maximal self-deceptions in Africa and
in the Muslim world.

The United States is high on individualism and looseness; however,
there are regional differences. The South and states with large Latino or
East Asian populations (e.g., California and Hawaii) are more collectivist
than the rest of the country (Vandello & Cohen, 1999).

Brewer and Chen (2007) developed a useful theoretical distinction between *relational* and *group* collectivism. This distinction is important for
researchers of this topic, but is not discussed here because it is not directly
relevant to the topic of this book.

Although humans in general sample positive and avoid negative information, there are individual differences. Some people emphasize pleasure
more than others. They seek achievement, advancement, and have high
aspirations. Others avoid pain and emphasize responsibility, obligations,
and security (Higgins, 1997). Aaker and Lee (2001) found that idiocentrics are more likely to seek pleasure; whereas allocentrics are more likely
to avoid pain. This suggests that there are two types of self-deceivers, the
first being more common in the West and the second kind more common
in the rest of the world.

Ethics and Culture

Allport (1950/1967) said, "But on the whole, in dealing with individual
cases, one is more impressed by the apparent separation of moral standards from religion than by their dependence upon it" (p. 74). In Taiwan and Japan, only 3% of the children attend formal religious classes,
whereas in the United States 69% do (Stevenson, 1991). Yet there is a lot
more crime (e.g., homicide) in America than in Taiwan or Japan (M. Bond,
2004). Of course, there are many confounds, such as the greater inequality
in the United States and the greater cultural diversity of the population.
Nevertheless, the two statistics are so drastically different that one cannot
ignore the evidence. Despite this empirical evidence, the public strongly

believes that morality and religion are closely linked. In one study, 69% of Americans said that "more religion" is the best way to increase moral behavior in America (Huntington, 2005). In 2007, a Pew survey asked whether one must believe in God to be moral. In that study, 57% of Americans answered yes, whereas in China, 72% answered no (Zakaria, 2008). In short, Americans think that "the more people believe what I believe the more moral they are," but that is a self-deception. The empirical evidence does not support this link. Dennett (2006) devoted an entire chapter to showing that no such link exists; however it is consistent with the wishes of most Americans that there be such a link. They pay attention to the way they like the world to be rather than to the way it is.

At the individual level of analysis also, the reality is that there are religious people who are criminals, and many irreligious people who are virtuous. Traditional ethics are more closely linked to self-deception than are modern ethics because the standards of traditional religions are often unrealistically high, requiring people to believe that they act in a virtuous way when they do not. For example, Roman Catholic priests are supposedly celibate, but in fact they masturbate frequently, and have many undesirable interpersonal relationships (Sipe, 1995, 2003).

Further evidence of a nonlink between religiosity and desirable aspects of societies is provided by Zuckerman (2006). He reviewed several empirical studies that show that the most religious countries (where large percentages of the population say they believe in God) are the least stable, peaceful, free, wealthy, and healthy. The most desirable societal attributes are found in Sweden, Denmark, Norway, Japan, and the Czech Republic, where on average about 70% of the population is agnostic. Irreligious countries have the lowest rates of infant mortality, homicides, illiteracy, and AIDS and HIV infection, and the highest gender equality. The only index on which they do not do well is on suicide rates. I believe that high suicide rates can be traced to excessive individualism, which is associated with high rates of wealth as well as competition. In individualist societies, people tend to feel alone, and when they think they are failures suicide is more probable than in societies where people are well embedded with others. There are complexities, of course, such as in collectivist cultures people may commit suicide because of "honor."

The strong empirical correlations between religiosity and undesirable attributes of a society suggest that failed societies are religious. Of course, correlation does not indicate causation. One might speculate that the relationship is reciprocal: when a society is a failure it is especially likely to cling to religious traditions so that people can have the self-deception that there is another world to which they will go after death to escape their undesirable circumstances; at the same time very religious societies do not use rational measures to improve their condition and expect supernatural help to improve their situation, so they do not become successful.

Pascal pointed out that what is moral on one side of the Pyrenees is immoral on the other side. Thus, when people move from one culture to another, they are likely to experience culture shock. In my opinion, the best advice to such people is to "do in Rome as the Romans do." Immigrants from collectivist cultures, such as Turkey, who move to individualist cultures, such as France or Germany, discover a new cultural morality. If instead of acting in Rome as the Romans do they insist on acting as they do in Turkey, they are likely to experience major psychological problems. These problems stem from the self-deception that their culture is "correct" and ignore information that the host culture has "good" elements. In many cases, the immigrants demand that their children follow traditional norms such as the prohibition against girls dating, or choosing whom they will marry. Their children, on the other hand, are exposed to peers from an individualist society. They insist that having a boyfriend is no sin, and that they should be allowed to choose their own spouse. Many tragic cases of parents abducting or even killing their own children because the child was "immoral" according to their definition of morality have been reported (e.g., Shweder et al., 2002). For example, in Britain a father and his two sons murdered a young girl's boyfriend in order to restore the family's "honor."

In one case, a Moroccan family living in Norway took their daughter to Morocco against her will in order to force her to marry a man of their choice. The daughter managed to get help from the Norwegian ambassador to Morocco, and Norway charged the father with abduction. The father had a heart attack and the Moroccan community in Norway rejected the daughter for disobeying her father. This was clearly a lose–lose situation where neither the family nor the daughter got what they wanted.

Governments that accept immigrants from other cultures should provide cross-cultural training (see Triandis, 1994) prior to granting a visa. The training should include a discussion of the way local and traditional ethics from the immigrant's country differ. Basically, the potential immigrant should be told, "If you choose to come here, you must expect that your children will accept our ethics, which are not like your ethics," and "you cannot take the position that our ethics are immoral," and "when you raise your children you must accept that it is okay for them to adopt our ethics."

It is a cognitively simple self-deception to assume that immigrants from any culture can live without problems in any other culture. The cultural distance between the two cultures needs to be considered. Cultural distance is measured by examining the following:

• The linguistic distance: Do they speak a language from the same language family (e.g., German and English)?

- Do they have the same family structure (e.g., the power of mothers and fathers is the same or different)?
- Do they have the same religion?
- Do they have the same level of education and social class?
- Do they have the same values (Schwartz, 1992, 2004)?

The greater the cultural distance the more unwise it is to accept immigrants. We know from studies of attitude change (Triandis, 1971) that the acceptance of another's point of view is a function of attitudinal distance. Small attitude distance results in accepting the views of the other; whereas large distance results in rejecting the other. The same is applied in this case, and it is naive and cognitively simple to assume that anyone can be integrated into any society without extensive training. The greater the cultural distance, the more intense the training should be before the person can be accepted. This view suggests that the Europeans have a good case when they refuse immigrants from Africa and other continents. But, they do not have a good case when they do not help the Africans make a living in their own countries. For example, Spanish fishing fleets have depleted the waters off Senegal, so it is not surprising that the Senegalese want to immigrate to Spain. The world is a complex system, and it is a cognitively simple self-deception that we can deal with one problem without taking care of the whole system of relationships.

Conversely, when people from individualist cultures move to collectivist cultures they need to adopt the local norms. Part of the training, for instance, would be to learn to communicate indirectly. One does not say "No" bluntly, but indirectly. The following anecdote makes this point.

> In Indonesia a lower-class boy and an upper-class girl liked each other, and the mother of the boy visited the mother of the girl, who served tea and bananas. Because tea and bananas are never served together, the answer was "No; a wedding is out of the question." The mother of the girl did not have to say "No," and thus the mother of the boy did not lose face.

Of course, this example tells us that the person must know in great detail the local customs, otherwise how could anyone guess that serving tea and bananas means "No"?

There is tremendous variability within the major religions such as Christianity or Islam. The variability in part reflects the cultures in which the religions flourish. Thus, for instance, Indonesian mysticism is more tolerant than Afghan mysticism, because Indonesia is not as tight a society as is Afghanistan. I offer the hypothesis that self-deceptions will be more frequent in the tighter than the looser cultures because in tight cultures sticking to the norms is more difficult, and people are likely to think that they are behaving correctly when in fact they are not, from the point of view of the in-group.

When people have a strong sense that they themselves determine their identity (i.e., who they are), as is characteristic of people in individualist cultures, they are more likely to seek sincerity and authenticity (Trilling, 1972). People who emphasize authenticity are more introspective, and thus they are more likely to identify their self-deceptions and eliminate them. By contrast, when people feel swept by traditions and obligations, as is more likely among people in collectivist cultures, they de-emphasize authenticity. This point is also consistent with the argument that self-deception is more frequent in collectivist than in individualist cultures.

Many observers have emphasized the importance of saving face in collectivist cultures (Hu, 1944). Moral persons behave as stipulated by their roles, in-group members, and society. If the individual deviates from such ideal behavior, there is loss of face, not only for the individual, but also for the whole in-group. In many collectivist cultures, morality consists of doing what the in-group expects (Triandis, 1972). When interacting with the out-group, it is sometimes considered "moral" to exploit and deceive. In other words, morality is applicable only to in-group members and depends on the situation. When cheating other people in such cultures people may have the self-deception that they are behaving in an ethical way, because they follow their culture's norms and they ignore the fact that these norms are unfair to others and would be condemned in many cultures.

Predictability

In some cultures there is more predictability than in others. For example, the more earthquakes, tornadoes, hurricanes, droughts, floods, and the like in a particular environment, the more unpredictable is life. Ethnic diversity will also increase unpredictability. On the other hand, a high standard of living, higher development of science, tightness, social security systems, and a law-and-order society are generally related to more predictability. Unpredictability is likely to result in more self-deceptions (e.g., the hurricane will do nothing to me). Such self-deceptions usually have a religious basis (e.g., God will help me).

Empiricism versus Ideology

Cultures differ also on the extent people make most judgments based on information that comes from experience as opposed to making most judgments based on information obtained from opinion or ideological sources, such as leaders, tribal chiefs, and gods. Self-deception is likely to be more common in the latter than in the former cultures.

MODERNITY

The affluent part of the modern world, which includes Western Europe, North America (minus Mexico), Australia, and New Zealand tends to be individualist and loose. Japan and segments of the population in cities around the world in developing countries also have modern perspectives, although the original cultures of Japan and most developing countries were collectivist, and traces of that pattern can still be found in many perspectives and behavior patterns in these countries. Globalization makes some parts of some countries affluent, individualist, and loose. But, as Newton argued, every force produces a counter force. Similarly, individualism produces tendencies toward collectivism, looseness tendencies toward tightness, and tightness tendencies toward looseness. Thus, in all societies there are counter forces generated by modernity, which increase cognitive simplicity, religiosity, fundamentalism (e.g., "I have the truth and will go to paradise, you are going to hell"), and tightness.

The essence of modernity is openness to new experiences and to the future, nontraditional thinking (less religiosity), and the structuring of life around the clock. Cultures differ in the way they deal with time. People in modern cultures pay much attention to time (Doob, 1971; Inkeles & Smith, 1974). They also tend to use time monochronically (i.e., dealing with one topic or person at one time rather than dealing with many topics and different people at the same time). Modern cultures compared with traditional cultures tend to make more of a distinction between work and social time, and tend to use clock time rather than event time (e.g., a meeting stops when the clock reaches a certain point rather than when the event is completed).

The fundamental conflicts in the 21st century, as outlined by Buruma and Margalit (2004), are between the cognitively simple and complex worldviews. Simple worldviews include collectivism with only one narrow in-group, tightness (everybody behaves the same way), and purity of thought. Complex worldviews include individualism (everyone does his or her own thing), looseness (deviant behavior is not punished), tolerance, and a messy (improvisation) society.

The 9/11 terrorists had multiple motivations. Subconsciously, I believe, they attacked complexity (people from many races, nationalities, creeds), in the service of the superpower, global capitalism, and globalization. They also hoped to excite Muslims everywhere to unite in a struggle against "the infidels" and toward the goal of a universal Islamic state (Kepel, 2004). Islamic law considers war against infidels, apostates, rebels, and bandits perfectly legal. According to some analysts, war can be waged until the whole world adopts the Moslem faith (B. Lewis, 2003). This is an example of an extreme cognitively simple self-deception. One pays attention to the dream of everyone having the same faith (a very simple world, consistent with the wishes of persons in Islam) and ignores all the difficulties of such a dream.

Some cultures (e.g., Tahiti; see Lillard, 1998) reject negative information more than other cultures. In Tahiti one is simply not allowed to be sad. Thus, these cultures are more susceptible to self-deceptions than other cultures.

In cultures where goods can be stolen easily (e.g., cattle or camels) and where there are only ineffective agents of law-and-order to catch the thieves, people develop a culture of honor (Nisbett & Cohen, 1996). Men are fierce (D. Cohen & Nisbett, 1997) to discourage the thieves. People in such cultures kill easily for honor; and are likely to develop militant religions, as practiced by some Muslims. These cultures emphasize patrilinear kin groups and collectivism. Their members have an extreme concern for reputation. Men are defiant of any constraint imposed by others (except older kinsmen). They are violent outside the kin group, distrust others, use guile, and have little sense of moral obligations aside from those toward kin, clients, and guests. But they are extremely hospitable, and have special bonds derived from the guest–host relationship. They see women as vulnerable, so they require that they be secluded and veiled (Fiske et al., 1998). It is obvious that the original culture of Arabia was a culture of honor, as were more or less all the cultures around the Mediterranean and in the triangle between Arabia, northwest China, and Indonesia. Cultures of honor are very different from modern cultures.

Modernity challenges fundamentalists because the modern viewpoint is tolerant and accepts all religions as equally valid. Fundamentalists consider their religion as the only valid one. For example, Islam considers the Qu'ran the only valid text. Furthermore, modernity often requires people to speak in English, but for some Muslims Arabic is "the language of God." (They claim that God dictated the Qu'ran to Mohammed in Arabic, thus the Qu'ran cannot be translated satisfactorily.)

Darwish (2006) provided an excellent description of Arab culture, and showed that it tends to be especially high in self-deception. Cognitively complex people have many identities, but cognitively simple people have only a few identities. When one of few identities is threatened that event is especially significant in the case of the simple, and likely to result in violence. The most important identity of cognitively simple Muslims is "I am Muslim and have the only truth." Modernity threatens this most important identity because it considers all religions equally valid. People whose central identity is threatened often become violent. For example, to call a macho man "a sissy" is to threaten his identity and will almost certainly result in violence. Islam developed in cultures of honor, and thus a threat to a Muslim's central identity is especially likely to result in violence. Globalization is similarly considered the enemy of Islam, because it is secular, and has an English-speaking emphasis. Thus, part of the enmity of the Muslim world toward the West is a reaction to modernity and globalization.

This chapter suggested that there are individual differences in the tendencies toward self-deception. We examined many cultural, demographic, ecological, situational, and personality factors that may increase the probability of different kinds of self-deceptions. The next three chapters examine self-deceptions in politics, religion, and terrorism.

4

Fooling Ourselves in Politics

Tuchman (1984) stated, "Wooden-headedness, the source of self-deception, is a factor that plays a remarkably large role in government. ... It is acting according to wish while not allowing oneself to be deflected by the facts. It is epitomized in a historian's statement about Philip II of Spain, ... No experience of failure of his policy could shake his belief in its essential excellence" (p. 7). In other words, Philip focused on the good aspects of his policy and ignored any information that criticized it. The mechanism of selective perception of positive and ignoring negative information is apparent.

Cognitive simplicity is also detrimental to good government. Louis the XIV of France is usually considered a master monarch, but his "One law, one King, one God" (Tuchman, 1984, p. 20) and "I am the state" statements suggest cognitive simplicity, which resulted in the downfall of the Bourbons two reigns later. Historians generally agree that canceling his grandfather's Edict of Nantes in 1685, which was a decree of toleration, and the persecution of the Huguenots marked the beginning of the end of that dynasty.

A spectacular example of cognitively simple self-deception can be found on July 14, 1769, the day the French revolution started, with the storming of the Bastille. King Louis XVI had only a one-word entry in his diary: "Rien" (Nothing)!

A Japanese survivor of the Hiroshima atomic bomb, interviewed by Deutsche Welle Radio in 2005, stated that the United States started the war with Japan. Apparently instead of focusing on Pearl Harbor, he focused on the oil embargo the United States had imposed on Japan. It is, of course, more agreeable to think that the "other side" started a war. In most wars each side thinks that the other is to blame for starting the war.

Numerous political ideologies contain cognitively simple self-deceptions. For example, the Communists believed that they could create a "Communist human" who will do what the state desires rather than what individuals desire. The Nazis believed that a world without Jews would be a better place. The Fascists thought that they could reconstitute the Roman Empire. Mao and Pol Pot had visions of totally rural societies in the 20th century. In America, there are politicians whose only concern is no new taxes. For nationalists, individuals must give all their energy to the nation.

More generally, totalitarian states control information so that they create self-deceptions. If there is no free press to present both sides of an issue, the probability that self-deceptions will develop is rather high. In the past 20 years, the U.S. press has not been sufficiently critical; thus self-deceptions were and are generated. The influence of commercial interests on the American press has reduced its effectiveness. Gore (2007) mentioned that a recent international study rated the American press only the 53rd freest press in the world. The lack of criticism found in the press resulted in 70% of Americans in 2003 believing that Saddam Hussein was responsible for the 9/11 atrocities, when there was no objective evidence linking him to those events. Americans felt better "knowing" who was responsible and felt able to do something about it. Thus, the public was overwhelmingly in favor of the Iraq war in 2003 because it did not have the right information.

Perhaps the best discussion of self-deception in politics is in Jean F. Revel's (1991) *The Flight from Truth: The Reign of Deceit in the Age of Information.* Revel argued that the truth is not the principal guide to action or to intellectual activity. He pointed out that humans do not use all available information when they make decisions. Instead they pay selective attention to the type of information. He provided many examples, ranging from Alcibiades' reckless expedition against Syracuse in 415 BCE, to Napoleon's catastrophic Russian campaign of 1812, to Hitler's attack on Russia in 1941. "History is full of examples of political leaders who ruined themselves and their countries by pigheaded insistence on pursuing insane projects despite expert warnings and a wealth of admonitory information" (p. xix). Thus, basically they focused on the positive information and ignored the negative.

When major calamities of the type discussed by Revel occur, detrimental effects are seen on the mental health of the corresponding countries, at least temporarily. A country that lost a war, for instance, must experience a form of collective poor mental health (sadness, pessimism, low subjective

well-being). In fact, even the events of 9/11 resulted in a kind of "collective paranoia" in the United States, which made possible the reelection of
George Bush despite the numerous errors of his Administration—starting
an unnecessary war; cutting taxes during a war, which caused a huge budget deficit; ignoring global warming, and so on.

Cerf and Navasky (2008) compiled a list of misstatements by Washington politicians and the American press, concerning the war in Iraq. I identified 77 self-deceptions, such as "I believe ... that the Iraqi people will
greet us as liberators" (Sen. John McCain, presidential candidate on March
20, 2003). One year later, a poll taken in Baghdad found that only 2% of
the people interviewed viewed the Americans as "liberators." "American consumers will have cheap gasoline for decades to come" (*San Francisco Chronicle*, September 29, 2002; Cerf & Navasky, 2008). Self-deceptions
were especially likely when the speaker used the words "turning point"
or "God."

The cognitively simple self-deception that the reconstruction of Iraq will
be similar to the reconstruction of Germany and Japan is characteristic
of people who have not studied cultural differences. When faced with
a cross-cultural situation, the default reaction is to assume that people
abroad are either "just like us" or "so different from us that they can never
be like us." The first position was more consistent with the wishes of the
Bush Administration, and explains its self-deception. A detailed analysis
of the views of the neocoms, who dominated the Bush Administration
(Kepel, 2004), shows that they ignored culture. They thought that the confrontation of the Cold War (U.S.–USSR) was identical to the confrontation
between Islam and the West. Of course, such simplification is pleasantly
satisfying because they can use the experience of the past to plot the policies of the future, but the lack of realism is of great concern. Culture makes
a difference. See the example in chapter 1 of the Iraqis being told in 1991
that America will attack them if they do not move out of Kuwait, which,
as a result of their culture, they understood as a message that America
would not attack.

Early in his first term, President Bush, in the face of much evidence,
said, "It is not clear that there is global warming." That was a cognitively
simple self-deception. He did not admit that there is a problem until July
2005, when the scientific evidence and the unanimity of opinion among
the leaders of the industrial countries made it impossible for him to defend that position. President Chirac of France, in a November 22, 2004, interview on C-Span, said, "The house is burning and we look elsewhere."
That is a classic description of self-deception.

The Arctic Report was presented by Dr. Corell, on C-Span in November 2004. It was produced by 300 top scientists from eight countries. It is a
1,200-page volume full of statistics that shows that by 2080 the Arctic will
be half its present size; Greenland will be so warm that half of it will be

always free of ice. Many Arctic animals, such as polar bears, may become extinct. Seawater may increase by 1 meter, submerging 20% of Florida, much of Bangladesh, many island countries, and so on. This will produce millions of refugees fleeing to higher ground. Already several coastal villages in Alaska have to be moved (at the cost of $100 million per village) because the sea is flooding them. The indigenous people of Alaska and other polar regions are already suffering from the loss of the animals that they used to hunt. The language of Alaskan natives does not have a word for "robin." But now these birds have appeared.

According to this report, the decline in the size of the sea ice started in 1960, and in the last 45 years 20% of it has melted. Scientists have a record of the ice for the past 400,000 years, and after 1990 the observations are outside the range of natural variability. Dr. Igor Knupnik, an anthropologist specializing in the peoples of the Arctic, appearing on C-Span, indicated that the natives reported that the "weather has gone wild" and their past knowledge of weather patterns is no longer valid. To reverse the pattern of damage, even if we stopped warming the globe right now, would take 1,000 years! A policy committee consisting of representatives of the governments that have an interest in the Arctic was convened to discuss policy changes. The U.S. State Department representative insisted that nothing be done until all the research on the subject has been completed. The predicted results of global warming are increases in the variability of the climate—more hurricanes, more rain and also more draught, substantial cooling of northwestern Europe. The self-deception is comparable to the self-deception of smokers, who say, "I am smoking and I am still healthy!" But the reality is that smoking kills, eventually. We have no idea of what the effects of the greater variability in the weather will do to agriculture, and whether there will be enough food in the 22nd century.

In contrast to Bush, Chirac argued that it is urgent for people to change their lifestyles and reduce their consumption of hydrocarbons. He put environmental concerns into the French Constitution. I wonder if the difference in levels of religiosity (96% of Americans believe in God, 12% of Frenchmen do), which can be seen as an index of willingness to see the world the way one wishes it to be rather than the way it is, may be a factor in the difference in the perceived urgency of the need to change the behaviors causing global warming.

Governments have a tendency to act so as to make a good impression on the electorate, even when what they do is totally ineffective. Presumably, they have the self-deception that what they are doing is useful. Some examples are as follows: The bombing of German cities during World War II was ineffective, and not cost-effective, although it did cost 25% of the entire British war effort. Dyson (2005) wrote that, as a statistician at the British Bomber Command, he reported to the British government during the war that the loss of pilots and planes, and the diversion of the planes from the front, as well as the failure of the bombing to reach its targets made the bombing not cost effective. But the British "were deluding themselves and also deluding the British public" (p. 6) about the effectiveness of the bombing. The Germans also had self-deceptions. "Hitler was out of touch with reality, sending his precious airplanes to London to break our windows instead of sending them to Russia where they were desperately needed" (p. 4). The Jim Lehrer program on NPR had interviews with two CIA former employees who resigned from the agency after determining that the recruitment policies of the CIA were ineffective. They recruited mostly White Americans who did not know any of the languages needed to fight terrorism. The top bureaucrats seem to have had a model that the CIA agent would invite the terrorists to lunch, and convince them to stop what they were doing! But the management was making a good impression by hiring a large number of agents.

Sister Ortiz (2007) was tortured in Guatemala in 1989, because she taught reading to Mayan children. Her torturers were several locals under the direction of an American called Alejandro (he spoke poor Spanish and excellent colloquial English). When she denounced the torture in the United States she was openly accused of being a liar by the attorneys of the Department of Justice (DOJ). This can be understood as a case of self-deception. The DOJ employees had the self-deception that "Americans do not torture." Anyone who undermines that perception must be a liar.

Bazerman, Baron, and Shonk (2001) showed how public policy is negatively affected by poor information processing. Most of their examples reflect simple self-deceptions or just cognitive simplicity. For example politicians and citizens often make decisions on the basis of simple criteria, such as "do no harm." Thus, for instance, because vaccinations are painful some people avoid them. Yet, the minor pain has large desirable consequences. They provide many examples when a small loss results in a large gain. A simple idea is that "competition is always good," yet competition among government agencies or charitable organizations is often bad. Thus, they show that cognitively simple errors are barriers to finding the wise tradeoffs necessary to resolve the complex problems facing governments.

In *Politics and the English Language,* George Orwell (1968) pointed out that politicians use certain words quite freely, and when these words are used there is a high probability that the politician is trying to deceive the electorate. The list of words that should be examined with considerable suspicion includes democracy, freedom, socialism, patriotism, realistic, and justice. These words tend to have several meanings that are difficult to reconcile with one another. For example, democracy implies "we have a good regime." Thus, all a country has to do to make a good impression is to call itself a democracy (e.g., we have the Democratic Republic of the Congo!). Years of civil war, corruption, and mismanagement can be covered up by these nice words. In his 2005 State of the Union address, the president used "freedom" 27 times, and "liberty" 15. What do these words mean to people whose life is threatened daily?

The danger of relying on labels, such as "democracy," can be seen when "democracy" results in incompetent government. We have seen in America arrogant incompetence in the way the Iraq war was conceived and conducted, in the emergence of Hamas, and in the self-deception by Iran's president, Ahmadinejad, who was supposedly elected democratically, that the state of Israel can be eliminated. By contrast, although Singapore is not a democracy its government is high in competence, and its people appear to be satisfied. We need to be critical of labels.

The Documentation Center in Nuremberg, Germany, contains documents of the Nazi period, including press coverage of Hitler's speeches, photographs, and films produced by his propaganda machine. For example, one can see how the *Chicago Sun Times* covered one of Hitler's speeches. During the 1933–1936 period, the most frequent words used by Hitler were "freedom" and "peace." The rallies held in Nuremberg, when 400,000 people assembled in a large stadium, were called "freedom rallies." This created the self-deception among Germans that Hitler was a leader they could support because he had such good values.

Some other words that need to be examined with suspicion, according to Orwell, are social class, totalitarian, science, progressive, reactionary, bourgeois, and equality. President Bush used the famous phrase "the axis of evil." But the dictionary definition of axis is "an alliance of nations that coordinate their foreign and military policies." There is no evidence that Iraq, Iran, and North Korea ever constituted an axis. In fact, Iraq and Iran fought against each other in a war (1980–1988). But who cares about accuracy? It sounds good!

Of course, Orwell was correct when he said that we must be suspicious, but let us state that we cannot get rid of these words. We must just be more careful than we normally are when a politician is using them. We should tell ourselves, "He may be trying to deceive us." We were told in 2003 that we have "liberated" Iraq. Is the chaos we produced liberation?

Especially important is to pay attention to the words "freedom" and "equality." Research (Rokeach, 1973) shows that the leaders of socialist democracies use these words with great frequency. Leaders of Communist states use "equality" frequently but not "freedom." Leaders of market economy democracies use "freedom" very frequently, but not "equality." The leaders of Fascist states use neither of these words. Thus, one way of classifying the political orientation of a leader is to count his or her use of these words. In the United States, Republicans use "freedom" (which means, let the big corporations do their own thing) very frequently, and "equality" almost never. The Democrats use both words, but the frequency of their use can tell us if they are on the left or the right side of the middle of the Democratic Party.

An example of detrimental self-deception was Stalin's "liquidation" of 20 million people. He thought that it was possible to shape human beings so that they would not give priority to their self-interests but to the interests of the State. His self-deception was that this could be done. If the citizens of the USSR could forget about their personal interests and only do what is best for the State, they would be doing what Stalin wanted them to do. This was a pleasant self-deception. Stalin also thought of himself as the State. Many leaders identified the State with the self. Louis the XIV said it best: "L'etat c'est moi" (I am the State).

A major problem in the least developed countries (LDCs) is corruption. It inhibits economic development in a major way. The *Berlin Transparency Index* is based on interviews with businessmen and diplomats concerning working conditions in a particular country. It ranks countries on the extent one needs to bribe officials to get things done. The least corrupt countries are in Scandinavia and also include Singapore. The most corrupt countries are in Africa. Economic development is correlated with this index. Collectivism is also correlated with it (Triandis et al., 2001).

In many LDCs, the individual in power takes the funds that have been provided by aid agencies for his own personal use. Much of the time this is to build a palace or a monument. One can visualize the kind of self-deception that might explain such behavior. The person in power who constructs a palace, for instance, might have two cognitions: the money should be spent for the purposes it was given/the palace will impress foreign visitors as well as my own people. The foreign visitor might feel more comfortable dealing with someone who lives in such a palace and that is so "important" and so "civilized"; my people will feel my power and do what I tell them to do. Clearly, given such beliefs, the wish-fulfillment pressures will make the latter cognitions the salient ones.

The crisis in Palestine reflects detrimental self-deceptions on both sides. The Palestinians deceive themselves if they think that sending martyrs to Israel will improve their lot. It is true that with 70% unemployment rates it is easy to find martyrs. But nevertheless, martyrs decrease the chances of a peaceful settlement of the conflict. The Israelis deceive themselves if they think that attacking the Palestinians with large bombs that kill women and children will stop them from sending martyrs. Former U.S. President Jimmy Carter (2007) provided a rational analysis of the Israeli–Palestinian conflict. He states that both sides are at fault. Some on both sides reject this analysis because they let their emotions control their reasoning. Some Israelis think that occupying Arab land is legitimate, and some Palestinians honor suicide bombers.

The self-deception that the martyrs will go to paradise is very attractive to people with a strong ideology who want revenge, or who want to protest some Israeli action. It is necessary for the Palestinian leadership to convince their young people that blowing themselves up is counter-productive. The tragedy is that respect for religion in the United States prevents exposing the fraud of the belief that paradise exists.

The Geneva Accords of November 2003, which were prepared after 2 years of discussion under the leadership of two former ministers, the Israeli Beilin and the Palestinian Rabbo, require sacrifices on both sides. That is the nature of a good agreement in a conflict situation! Carter (2007) characterized them as the best hope for a settlement of the Israeli–Palestinian conflict. Yet both sides lack the vision to embrace them.

Some Israelis disagree with the policies of their government and have realistic views about the peace process, but they face religious fanatics in their own country who firmly believe that God has "given" to the Israelis all the land between the Nile and the Euphrates rivers!

Palestinians are divided on the desirability of the existence of the State of Israel. However, unfortunately the U.S. press feeds us with stereotypes, such that Hamas is "never" going to accept Israel. True, there are Arabs who believe that, but reading Carter (2007), who talked with Hamas, one can get a different picture. Hamas says, "If there is an agreement that will be accepted in a referendum by the Palestinians we will recognize Israel." Granted, they probably do not think this is likely to happen, but at least they are open to that possibility. In any case, there are Arab States that do accept the existence of Israel, and even have diplomatic relations (e.g., Egypt, Jordan) with it. The trouble with stereotypes is that they do have a grain of truth (Lee et al., 1995). But it is only a grain, and in general stereotypes are invalid. In my opinion, the Geneva Accords are the best hope for that region.

In November 2003, terrorists bombed an apartment complex in Riyadh, Saudi Arabia, killing 18 Moslems. It probably was the wrong target. That particular building housed employees of American corporations in the past. The people who were killed were Arabs working in Saudi Arabia. It is interesting to see the Internet justifications of this terrorism (*The Economist*, 2003). The terrorists stated that the 18 victims were FBI agents. Other Internet messages stated that the CIA or the Mossad (Israeli security service) staged the bombings in order to undermine support for the jihadists. This is also what some Arabs said after the 9/11 terrorist attacks (Kepel, 2004). When two beliefs are incompatible, people *invent* beliefs that reduce the incompatibility. Clearly, the beliefs "I am a Muslim" and "I killed Muslims" are incompatible. The inventions eliminate the cognitive conflict. Was this a self-deception that makes it possible for the leaders of the terrorists to justify their action? Or was it an intentional deception to justify the action? It is most probable that these are intentional deceptions, although in the case of a few people they may have been self-deceptions. The distinction between self-deception and deception is sometimes very difficult.

The military–industrial–congressional complex provides another example of how deception and self-deception are interrelated. F. C. Spinney, on Bill Moyers' NOW program, in July 2003, estimated that between 1995 and 2002 the Pentagon spent $1.1 trillion unnecessarily. But the accepted wisdom is that the more we spend on defense the safer we are (Self-deception 1). Pentagon officials think that getting one more military system, even if it is not totally clear that it is needed, is good because it strengthens our defensive capabilities (Self-deception 2). Congressmen get more pork for their constituents when military expenditures are approved, and they also get money from the defense industries in support of their reelection. They undoubtedly think that voting for a large Pentagon budget increases our national security (Self-deception 3). The defense industries are getting contracts that provide jobs and security for their employees. The pay of CEOs of these industries has increased fivefold between 1999 and 2002 to up to $45 million per year. Retired generals who become consultants to industry lubricate the system. Thus, everyone is happy. The cycle is mutually reinforcing.

Spinney, an insider who worked in the Pentagon for 30 years, analyzed the Pentagon's behavior, and provided a number of examples. First, there was the proposed spending of $30 billion to replace tanker planes, when in fact a report by Boeing had indicated that the existing planes would be fine for another 40 years. The Pentagon proposed that Boeing produce 100 new B-767s, which it would lease from Boeing. McCain objected to the leasing because leasing would turn out to be $900 million more expensive than buying. The reason leasing was proposed is that it requires less money in the initial years so Congress is more likely to approve the project (Outright Deception 1). The Pentagon's strategy has been to underestimate the cost of weapons systems and ask for more money later (Outright Deception 2). McCain also objected because an analysis of alternatives had not been done. He argued that this was just corporate welfare that was helpful to Boeing. Congressional support of the deal came from congressmen from the states of Washington and Kansas where the planes were to be produced, and from Illinois, where Boeing's headquarters are currently located (Self-deception 4). These congressional representatives received an estimated $2 million in campaign contributions from Boeing. Boeing spent an additional $15 million lobbying federal officials. Finally, by December 2003 the deal was changed to include 20 leased and 80 purchased planes. In 2004, there was no more discussion of this deal, but on June 7, 2005, a 256-page report by the inspector general was reported in the press. The report criticized Pentagon officials and Boeing executives and clearly showed that the deal benefited particular individuals at the expense of the taxpayer.

A second example is the missile defense system that did cost $9 billion in 2004 and $50 billion over the next 6 years. It is supposed to protect the United States from nuclear attacks (Self-deception 5). Expert opinion, reported in a paper published by the Physical Society, is that the system will not work, and even if it does, it will be obsolete by the time it is installed. Spinney also said it would not work. But the White House supports the system because the military–industrial–congressional complex is delighted with it. They use the concept of *spiral development*, which involves deploying the system (in other words you spend the money, so everybody profits, except the taxpayer) and then keep fixing it as you go along, even if it does not work, until some future time when perhaps it may become operational (Self-deception 6). But if it does not work in the end, that is just too bad. By then you are out of office, so you do not get hurt (Self-deception 7)!

A third example was the discussion in 1990 about funding or not funding the F-16 plane. Some congressmen did not want to fund it. As soon as this became evident, General Dynamics, the contractor, went to work. The company sent a letter to all members of Congress with a map indicating how much Pentagon money was spent in their congressional districts. It was implied that this money would "evaporate" if the F-16 was not funded (Self-deception 8). The local press was alerted to describe the negative impacts the district would suffer if the Pentagon money failed to come in (Self-deception 9). A coordinated group of lobbyists pressured Congress and the system was approved.

Spinney's main criticism is that these activities are bad for our national security. We spend a lot on weapons systems (more than most of the other countries in the world combined!) and too little on the kinds of activities that are effective in combating terrorism. For example, to combat terrorism we need many Arabic speakers who can infiltrate terrorist groups. We need anthropologists, psychologists, and other specialists who can analyze the behavior of these groups. Aircraft carriers are not able to do that. But the activities that are needed to fight terrorism are of little interest to the military–industrial–congressional complex. They do not require huge budgets. Instead the Bush Administration is presenting the "Star Wars" system as the way to fight terrorism (Outright Deception 3).

Spinney is a patriot who worries that this system of spending gives Americans the false impression that we have an adequate national defense. In fact, we are not getting enough security for the huge sums that are spent. Many people may lose their lives because we spend our money the wrong way.

Also, although the government is spending huge sums on expensive items, it is not adequately funding the fighting troops. A classic example of not spending enough to help the troops is the case of the M-16 rifles, used in the Vietnam War. These rifles often jammed under combat conditions. There were official reports of "serious and excessive malfunctions." Yet nothing was done because these defective weapons had been purchased in large quantities. Many soldiers were killed because of these malfunctions—a case of criminal negligence.

Too little money for the troops is also reflected in the policies of the Veterans Administration (VA), which provides too little medical support for victims of Gulf War syndrome. The U.S. Army argues this is not a "real" phenomenon (Self-deception 10), but *The Economist* (2003) sees it as a very "real" medical problem. In September 2004 a small budget item was approved by Congress to "study" the problem. The crises that emerged in 2007 in the VA hospitals are another example of insufficient support for the troops.

Spinney is also critical of the Pentagon's accounting system, which consistently fails to balance the books. The General Accounting Office rates the Pentagon as the worst government agency in terms of its accounting procedures. By law, the inspector general has to audit the books of each government department to make sure that the department spends the money the way it was appropriated by Congress. Typically, the Pentagon does not "pass" this audit. The inspector general then waives the requirements because the books cannot be balanced! Paul Wolfowitz, undersecretary of defense in 2003, suggested that about 100 reporting requirements currently in place should be eliminated. Basically, the Pentagon does not know where the money is going, so it is best if the Congress does not know that the Pentagon does not know! Spinney calls it a "moral sewer that is undermining the Constitution."

The belief is that Congress will not appropriate enough if the Pentagon asks for the "real" cost of a weapon. So it asks for less, Congress approves the weapon, and then the Pentagon says that there was a cost overrun (Outright Deception 4). Congress is supposed to have oversight of the Pentagon budget but in fact it has an "overlook" of the budget!

During the 40 years of the Cold War the bureaucracy of the military–industrial–congressional complex has been fine-tuned, so that behaviors that are mutually reinforcing have developed. We identify a threat (first Communism, now terrorism) and then ask for money for the Pentagon. The 2004 budget of $400.1 billion did not cover homeland security or the war in Iraq, and Spinney suggested that a lot of it was unnecessary. The Pentagon, industry, and Congress benefit, but the interest of taxpayers is not protected. Because the taxpayers do not know about the military–industrial–congressional complex, all is well (Self-deception 11).

Spinney used the concept of *cost growth*: When the total Pentagon budget is high, weapons systems cost more than when the budget is low! During the Reagan Administration, the United States spent more on some systems than it did for the same systems during subsequent administrations! Once again, we are spending more because the budget is too high.

In summary, we have here a series of self-deceptions, based on selective use of information. The Pentagon pays attention to "strengthening our national defense" but not to how to do so most economically. Industry pays attention to how to get the largest contracts, not on how to do the job most economically. Congress is supposed to oversee the system, but pays more attention to the benefits of the system for the members' congressional districts than to doing the job most economically. The whole process is political, and has nothing to do with economic efficiency. In the mean time, the deficit is growing!

In 2003, Congress increased the share of the pharmaceutical industry's support for activities of the Food and Drug Administration (FDA). The FDA was created to check on the safety and efficiency of drugs. A November 2003 edition of *Frontline* on NPR indicated that when the FDA was first created it did its job well. But as the number of new drugs created every year increased, the FDA's staff became inadequate. Instead of increasing the FDA's budget, Congress allowed funds from the pharmaceutical industry to be used to expand the staff. This was obviously a conflict of interest. The FDA was supposed to be a watchdog over the industry, but the industry was paying part of its budget.

The result is that a change of culture has occurred. The top FDA officials became inclined to approve a drug even when there were significant indications that it was unsafe and even if it was minimally effective. Top FDA officials structured advisory committee meetings so that industry representatives had 1 hour to present their case while FDA scientists had only a few minutes to provide their criticism. Employees who were critical of the drug were even discouraged from presenting their views. Many left the agency or retired early.

An interview with one of the top FDA administrators was a model of self-deception. He claimed that the culture of the FDA had not changed and that the FDA was doing a good job, even though the NPR program documented several cases where a drug was approved that should not have been. Thousands of Americans became seriously ill or died because the FDA leaned in favor of the industry. In at least one case, the Bayer Co. had evidence for 2 years that a drug was harmful and yet continued to advertise it until many people died, at which point it was withdrawn. The self-deception of the administrators is clear. They have two beliefs: the pharmaceutical industry is funding us so we have a good budget and are doing a marginally good job/we are doing a poor job because we are beholden to the pharmaceutical industry. Clearly, they paid attention to the first belief and ignored the second.

In the United States, the politics of the states east of the Rockies and in the South contrast with the politics of the Northeast, the West, and Great Lakes regions (*The Economist*, 2003). The first group voted for Bush in 2000 and 2004; the second for Gore or Kerry. In the first group, 80% held exceptionally strong old-fashioned values about family and marriage, and stressed patriotism and religion. They vote Republican. Evangelicals tend to lack a college degree, to live in rural areas, and be female and married. As a group they are largely puritanical, and somewhat conformist. People in this group hold the cognitively simple self-deception that unless you are religious you cannot be moral. (Contrary scientific evidence is reviewed in chapter 5.)

The second group has mostly secular-rational values. Secularists tend to be male, college-educated, single, and lean toward the Democrats. In this case, religion is personal, going to church is a social activity and has little to do with original sin. The emphasis is on the internal aspects of religion. The cultural pattern emphasizes tolerance, hedonism, and celebrates multiculturalism; it is found largely in the cities and suburbs and is similar to the culture of Western Europe.

The two groups are different from each other on cultural issues. For instance, attitudes toward abortion and homosexuality distinguish them. For the seculars, abortion is a matter for women to decide; the state should not tell women what to do. There is an overwhelming amount of empirical evidence (Levitt & Dubner, 2005) showing that in America the more abortion the less crime. Also, from the viewpoint of cultural psychology, abortion has to be accepted because women who do not want a child are very poor mothers. Poor mothering may result in poor mental and physical health, and increases the probability that when the child becomes an adult he or she will end up in prison, at a high cost to the taxpayer. Those who support a ban on abortion and also support the death penalty do not realize the contradiction in their position. They wish that the fetus not be killed, but it is okay to kill the criminal who emerged as a result of not allowing an abortion! The cognitively simple self-deception is that they are "saving" a "life."

The definition of "life" is also tricky. The debate on stem cell research has overused that word. When does "life" begin? At the moment the egg is fertilized? That is the position of many anti-abortionists, but the reality is that life begins when an organism is mature enough to be able to live a normal life. This usually happens many months after that. Nature wastes a lot—think of the elimination of thousands of spermatozoa that occurs naturally. The idea of preserving life is a romantic fantasy, a cognitively simple self-deception. The Qu'ran says that life begins 120 days after conception. So, the views of the anti-abortionists are a "local truth" (as defined earlier).

Opposition to homosexuality emerged when humans had to struggle for survival. The ancient Hebrews struggled in a desert environment, where food was scarce and infant mortality high. Because homosexuality does not produce offspring it reduces the chances of the survival of the group. No wonder the religious authorities identified it as a "sin." But the fact remains that it occurs in all cultures (Ford & Beach, 1951). Sociobiologists consider it "normal" in a biological sense, because it is found so commonly among the higher apes (E. Wilson, 1978). Our present condition is very different from the condition of the ancient Hebrews. Now we have done too good a job of surviving as a species. In my own lifetime, we almost quadrupled! We already have 6.4 billion people on earth and we are fast moving toward 8.9 billion (by 2050). This has implications for the adequacy of the available resources and for the environment. From a rational point of view, we should promote homosexuality because it does not increase the population. People who wish to have this lifestyle are doing us a service. Let them do their own thing! If they want to get married, that will not have much of an effect on our society. It will rarely constitute more than 2% or 3% of marriages. The cognitively simple self-deception that it is a "sin" is due to a lack of understanding of why it was defined as a "sin" thousands of years ago.

Racism can be found in some of the beliefs, judgments, and behaviors of a segment of the population of the United States. Thus, policies such as affirmative action are still needed to counteract it. According to my studies (Triandis, Davis, & Takezawa, 1965), this was a very significant issue 60 years ago, and has progressively become less important. I expect that in the next 50 years affirmative action will no longer be needed.

Congress has devised a tax system that is supposed to be fair. But that is a self-deception. Fair tax policies should reflect horizontal equity (those who earn the same amount should pay the same amount) and vertical equity (those who earn more should pay more). Yet this is far from what happens in the United States. In April 2004, *The Washington Post* published the yearly income and tax rates of President Bush and Vice President Dick Chaney. Bush and Chaney paid about the same amount of tax, although Chaney earned 2.3 times the amount that Bush did (i.e., no horizontal equity). I earned one tenth of the amount that Chaney earned, but he paid 12.7% of his income as tax and I paid 18.5% (i.e., no vertical equity).

Human Rights Watch did a study on the Russian army (reported by *Deutsche Welle*, 2003). The group interviewed conscripts and found that many get too little food and what food they do get is often rotten. Also, they receive much hazing from older soldiers. The Russian military regulations specify that there are control mechanisms to ensure that conscripts are not abused. But the mechanisms are not implemented. When Human Rights Watch asked to talk to the Russian Ministry of Defense about this problem they were told that these conditions do not exist because there are adequate mechanisms in place to prevent them. Thus, the conditions continue, they are well known in Russia, and young men of conscription age do everything they can to avoid serving in the army. One would think that the bureaucrats of the Ministry, or higher officials of the Russian government, would be concerned and do something about this, instead of holding the cognitively simple self-deception that everything is just fine.

But this kind of problem seems to exist in the United States also. Reports in the press that the U.S. military do not have the right equipment in Iraq, and that returning wounded soldiers do not receive lifelong support from the VA sound rather similar to the Russian problems. Apparently the VA's budget is inadequate. In some cases lifelong support was given only after the family of a soldier complained to the press and the mass media did a story. Such information suggests the generalization that bureaucracies have a tendency toward self-deception in many cultures.

In 2003, no fewer than 10 members of the Democratic Party declared that they were candidates for the presidential election. It would seem reasonable to assume that half of them did not have the cognitively simple self-deception that they would be chosen to be the standard bearers of the Democratic Party. They probably ran in order to get some national exposure, in anticipation of an ambassadorship or other job in the future. However, the other half probably did have the self-deception that they would be the standard bearers of their party. One can argue that if one did not have such self-deceptions one would not run. It may be necessary to have self-deceptions in order to participate in the political process. In the United States running for president requires having many self-deceptions; yet, it is probably an indication of good mental health.

This chapter reviewed a wide range of cognitively simple self-deceptions by government officials and others running the political processes in this world. Many of these self-deceptions involve inadequate sampling of the available information, with emphasis on sampling what is pleasant and avoiding what is unpleasant. They involve decisions that favor those in power at the expense of those with little power. The same story can be seen when religious authorities make decisions. We now turn to the study of self-deceptions in religion.

5

Fooling Ourselves and Religions

He accepted and absorbed all theories, all creeds, all religions, and believed in none.
—From Robert Ingersoll's eulogy for Walt Whitman, March 30, 1892
(Jacoby, 2004, p. 367)

For most of the 100,000 years that humans have existed on earth they believed that the earth is flat. Even after Eratosthenes (276–194 BCE) measured the size of the globe with considerable accuracy, the view that the earth is flat persisted among ordinary people and even religious authorities who did not accept that the earth is round until the 15th century. Even today there are imams who believe that the earth is flat (Stern, 2003). In summary, external religion is "uncritically accepted cultural knowledge." The majority of humans accept religion the way they got it from their parents, teachers, peers, and religious authorities, without asking many questions about its validity.

Many analysts do not agree with me that external religion is a self-deception. They argue that the essence of religion is that it is a view that is beyond understanding, another dimension that includes mystery, the unknown, and the occult. Of course, that view includes the assumption that natural, everyday ways of analyzing religion are inappropriate. This view verges on the "believe (have faith) and do not research," which was one of the commands I received from the Greek Orthodox Church when I was growing up. With my inclination to research, to explore, to be open to all views, I rejected the faith of my ancestors. In the search for another way of looking at the world I concluded that I could agree only with the Buddha who wanted to see the world without self-deceptions.

This chapter presents evidence that some aspects of religion are cognitively simple self-deceptions. However, spirituality, in my opinion, is not a self-deception and is consistent with good mental health. Emphasis on the first three aspects of religion may lead to violence, if the individual is high in cognitive simplicity (see p. xvi). To sort out the differences between different kinds of religion we need to examine them in some detail, and consider why they develop features that are advantageous and disadvantageous for peace and well-being.

Additionally, we need to consider why religions are more attractive and important in the 21st century than they were in the 19th. My analysis shows that religions reduce perceived uncertainty. The illusion that by praying one controls the way the universe ticks reduces the sense of uncertainty. Furthermore, having a supernatural force that will help in one's endeavors provides an additional illusion of control. It is extremely important for humans to have the sense that they are controlling the environment. When they do not, they become helpless and depressed. Because the world of the 21st century has become more uncertain, with economic insecurity, terrorism, and our ability to see this uncertainty on television worldwide, we are now more concerned with uncertainty, and thus religion is becoming increasingly important. Sister Ortiz (2007), who was tortured in Guatemala, described the extraordinary importance of control in a discussion of the effects of torture. I extracted from her description that the essence of torture is the loss of control. Thus, if religion provides a sense of control it is the zenith of human experience, whereas torture is the nadir of human experience.

DEFINITIONS

Dennett (2006) defined *religion* as a social system "whose participants avow belief in a supernatural agent or agents whose approval is to be sought" (p. 9). Note that this definition only deals with external religions. Thus, for instance original Buddhism and Confucius before 140 BCE, as well as spirituality as discussed in the preface, cannot be categorized either as internal religions (my preference) or as nonreligions. Confucianism became a religion under the emperor Wu-ti (140–87 BCE) when worship of Heaven and Earth and ancestor worship were integrated with the ideas of Confucius (Hodous, 1946). Some humans pray but they do not seek approval. By Dennett's definition, that is not a religion. The "seek approval" clause was included to distinguish religion from black magic.

Although the existence of supernatural beings is one clue that is often used to define religion, another is the existence of the ideas of "sacred" and "profane." The idea of the "sacred" emerged when agriculture became important. Farmers knew that fertility is important in plants, and worshiped the forces that helped the plants grow. These forces became "sacred." Such sacred forces transformed human life also. The Great Mother was such a force and was associated with the sacred and the giving of life. Early humans were faced with innumerable dangers so they needed a sacred, powerful agency that, in exchange for sacrifice and veneration, would protect them. "Sacred" things are mysterious with awesome power and so important to those who hold them that the very act of considering them is offensive (Dennett, 2006). According to Dennett, unless these concepts are present in some form, one cannot speak of a religion.

There are many types of religion. In external religions there are two major types of gods (Dennett, 2006): abstract (non-anthropomorphic) such as Aristotle's (the Unmoved Mover), Spinoza's (God is Nature), and Tillich's (the Ground of All Being). Humans have developed some 100,000 religions, dogmas, and heresies (Wallace, 1966). Their creativity in this domain has been immense. But religions have both integrative (e.g., we are all brothers and sisters) and divisive elements (e.g., I am going to paradise and you are going to hell). Silberman, Higgins, and Dweck (2005) portrayed religion as a double-edged sword that can facilitate both violent and peaceful activism. Integrative religions make life worth living. I have a problem with divisive religions. When I see beliefs like "we are the chosen people" (presumably others were not chosen), "we are created in God's image," "we are at the center of the world," "this land was given to us by God," "those who believe what we believe will go to paradise and those who do not will go to hell," "I can pray and change the course of events," and so on, I see cognitively simple self-deceptions. Silberman et al. (2005) reported a study that indicated that the more traditionally religious individuals were especially likely to predict that the world is likely to become what they wish it to become, and that this future will occur very soon. That fits the definition of self-deception. These religious individuals see the world they wish to see, and the desired world is around the corner.

My major concern with external, divisive religion is that it is often associated with violence (Harris, 2005b) and can be a problem for the planet. Fundamentalism is especially divisive. The opposite of fundamentalism is an "unbiased religiosity" that accepts all religions. That was the position taken by Gandhi and Walt Whitman. I have no objection to religious people who believe whatever they wish to believe, but do not impose their beliefs on others. My objection is to those who wish to convert others to their point of view.

In my opinion, divisive aspects of religion are traceable to at least two factors:

1. Most religions emerged in collectivist cultures, and as we have seen collectivists tend to treat their in-group extremely well and their out-group harshly. It is easy for collectivists to be violent against out-groups.
2. There is struggle for power, but power is not a socially desirable attribute. People learn to disguise their struggle for power by dressing up their actions with religion. Rather than admit that they are struggling for power, they convince themselves that God wants them to act this way. They generate numerous fantasies that help them see themselves in a positive light, when in fact they are just power-hungry.

Furthermore, fundamentalists of all religions do not believe that peace is desirable, because they have a vision that life is a struggle between good (them) and evil (everybody else). In fact, fundamentalists have a negative view of the UN just as they had a poor opinion of the League of Nations. They see world peace as a utopian dream, and some of them believe that St. Peter predicted an atomic holocaust that will not affect the true believers, who would be "raptured up to heaven before the End" (Armstrong, 2000, p. 217). But the unbelievers will suffer the final torture. In short, they see an atomic holocaust as desirable because it will "clean up" the world of sinners!

Integrative religions are good for mental health, and have aspects consistent with modern science (Spilka, Hood, & Gorsuch, 1985). Specifically, genetic studies show that all "humans are brothers and sisters." We share 99.8% of our DNA with those of different races (i.e., our differences are skin deep). Our cultural differences are due to accidents of birth in specific environments requiring different adaptations for survival, or to historical events, or to the imitation of cultural traits generated in neighboring cultures. Christianity, Buddhism, and Islam think that they could be relevant to all humans. Brotherhood is consistent with this vision.

Boyer (1994) provided a general explanation of how religions emerge. One way to summarize his argument is that religions are designed to make sense of the world the way people find it. They reflect the key features of the societies that develop them. Armstrong (2000) calls Islam a militant religion, and even Khomeini thought that it was. One of the doctrines is that if one dies fighting for Allah, the moment his blood is spilled all his sins are wiped out. I am not aware of other religions that so clearly reward fighting. The Qu'ran includes many divisive statements such as "kill the unbelievers." In fact, Harris (2004) quoted five pages of divisive statements from the Qu'ran. Apologists for Islam counter that Harris has quoted the statements "out of context," but it would be difficult to find quite as many divisive statements in the holy books of the other great religions. I suspect that the fact that Islam emerged in cultures of honor (see chapter 3) is an explanation for this feature of Islam. Islam also emerged in a relatively collectivist part of the world (Gregg, 2005) and, as mentioned in chapter 3, collectivist cultures tend toward cognitive simplicity and also see a large distance between the in-group (Muslims of my sect) and the out-group (everybody else). In collectivist cultures, it is acceptable to behave harshly toward members of the out-group. I admit that one can find divisive statements in other "holy" books. My only point is that the density of such statements is larger in the Qu'ran.

But religions also have divisive elements. We live in a world where religious fanatics believe that if they blow themselves up they will go to paradise and feast on milk and honey in the company of 72 virgins. Power-hungry mullahs, who use innocent kids as fodder to promote their political goals, propagate such fantasies. They influence a sexually repressed kid to think of sex with many virgins. One of them said, "I know my life is poor compared to Europe and America, but I have something awaiting me that makes all my suffering worthwhile. Most boys can't stop thinking about the virgins" (Stern, 2003, p. 55). One suicide bomber, whose attack was prevented, had wrapped toilet paper around his genitals to protect them for later use in paradise (Stern, 2003).

We need to consider that some people live in such dreadful circumstances that when they believe that paradise is the "real world" and the present world is just a "temporary" preparation for getting or not getting there, they can be excused for having such abnormal thoughts. For example, some very poor Muslims "escape" reality by thinking that the here-and-now is not "real" but the afterlife is (Stern, 2003). This is a case where extreme poverty becomes bearable by believing in paradise, thus it does not have much relevance for mental health. However, when individuals act out their fantasies by blowing themselves up, or accepting the suicide of their loved ones, there can be some questions about their mental health. Nevertheless, the acting out is not a sufficient clue of their mental health; more information is needed.

Many of the concepts included in religions, such as "paradise," are pure fantasies, wishes rather than reality. Probably no concept has done more harm in the 21st century than "paradise" because it has motivated thousands of terrorist incidents. To have a fiction used as a palliative is fine, but when it is used for terrorism that is when its nature should be revealed. Terrorism is related to conceptions of God. In most conflicts humans would like to have the assistance of a God. Historically, in most intergroup conflicts, a powerful, vengeful God who will destroy one's enemies is a common self-deception, so the terrorists who have a political aim, such as the destruction of the superpower, are likely to see their God on their side.

Spirituality is open to new experiences and is not dogmatic. In contrast, the fundamentalists are closed to new experience and are dogmatic. I am willing to grant that most external religions are benign self-deceptions. Fundamentalist religions, however, often lead to violence and poor mental health. The world needs priests as much as it needs clinical psychologists and social workers. They help people feel that they can control uncertainty. Uncertainty is an extremely negative experience. Bertrand Russell, in a famous quote, said, "What men really want is not knowledge but certainty" (cited in Van den Bos et al., 2006, p. 333). Certainty is an immense gift because life is full of uncertainties (health, job insecurity, wars, terrorism, etc.). A. Cohen, Kennick, and Li (2006) argued that in environments that are uncertain and life is brutal and short, people develop concepts such as soul, afterlife, and the like.

Roccas (2005) found that the more religious persons are especially likely to avoid uncertainty. Some religions promise eternal life. Most religions give people an identity; that is, believers become a part of a community. Religions help people cooperate with those of the same religion, and they allow people to feel a spiritual association with the cosmos. In fact, some religions give meaning to the cosmos. Religions create stability in social systems. The elders of most cultures wish to preserve the status quo, which puts them in a position of greater power than other people. To do so they specify how people should think, feel and behave, but to impose these views it is convenient to evoke the presence of a supernatural being that will punish those who do not conform. Fear of hell, or the equivalent, is an effective way to increase conformity.

HUMANS NEED RELIGION

Religion is a multifaceted phenomenon. Paloutzian and Park (2005), in their *Handbook of the Psychology of Religion and Spirituality*, include chapters with a wide range of theoretical (e.g., evolutionary theory), developmental (e.g., gerontology), and applied (e.g., terrorism) perspectives. Each of these aspects may satisfy a different need. Humans need religion, and religion is good for their physical and mental health. Koenig, McCullough, and Larson (2001) reviewed 473 studies of the relationship between religiosity and health. Of the studies reviewed, 66% reported a statistically significant relationship. Religious people had better health (less substance abuse), lived longer, and received more social support. In general the more religious had better physical and mental health. George, Ellison, and Larson (2002) attempted to find out why. They considered whether the more religious received more social support, had a greater sense of self-efficacy, and/or a greater sense of coherence of the personality. They asked, "Which of these factors is responsible for this link?"

They concluded that each of these factors is relevant and more research is needed.

In any case, religions are useful. Festinger (1983) suggested that gods were invented about 200,000 years ago, at the same time as other basic technology, such as fire, shelter, the wheel, and so on. Gods were the technology that provided the illusion of "controlling" parts of the environment.

Although external gods are self-deceptions, they are immensely useful in creating the illusion that one can control the environment, and in providing meaning for human existence. An example of the way humans construct religion can be found by following the concept of "being in limbo." When Christianity started it was believed that anyone who is not baptized would go to hell. Then, people realized that there was a category, newborn babies, that did not have a chance to be baptized before they died, and would go to hell through no fault of their own. So, they invented the concept of being "in limbo" which is a category of being at the borders of hell and paradise. There is now serious discussion, among theologians, about eliminating the "in limbo" concept and letting the soul of babies go to paradise directly. That feels more "right" in the 21st century. A panel is debating whether "in limbo" should be eliminated (BBC report, 2005), and that is a "serious" issue because it reverses the original 3rd-century concept that baptism is necessary in order to go to paradise.

Humans need an explanation for the creation of the universe, and a force that will give meaning to life. The big bang theory and its consequences are too complex. Rather than deal with a myriad of astronomical, biochemical, paleontological, biological, sociobiological, anthropological, psychological, and sociological findings linking the big bang with current life, humans substitute one simple idea: God. Cognitive simplicity can be satisfying.

RELIGIONS ARE HUMAN-MADE

My studies of religion concluded that God, like most elements of culture (Armstrong, 1993; Herskovits, 1955), is human-made. In fact, humans are a god-generating species that needs external religion; and for most people life without religion is almost impossible.

That external religions are self-deceptions is clear when we do content analyses of the beliefs included in religions. Perhaps the clearest case is provided by Shinto, because it is a folk religion that has evolved less than the universalist religions (Holton, 1946) so it does not include the sophisticated "public relations facets" of the more evolved religions. We see in Shinto beliefs such as "the virtue" of the emperor, that the armies of Japan will always be victorious, Japan is a peerless nation, with a superior race, innately endowed by the gods with unique psychological qualities, there is the conviction of a great national destiny, the duty to spread the glory of Japan throughout the world, and thereby save the world from injustice and wrong, the sacred land of Japan, and so on (Holton, 1946). Of course, the monotheistic religions have similar beliefs such as that humans are made in the "image of God" and "the promised land," but because most of them attempt to be universal, they are not linked explicitly to a particular nation and thus their self-deceptions are less obvious.

Why Religion?

Wallace (1966) identified the following elements as likely to be present in a religion: prayer, music, physical exercise, exhortations, taboos, feasts, sacrifices, a congregation, revelation, symbolism, and belief systems.

Shermer (1999) examined the reasons people give for their belief in God. These include the following:

- I experience God within me.
- Without God there is no morality.
- The Bible says so.
- The universe is God.
- My parents told me so.
- God has a plan for us.
- God is needed to account for good and evil in the world.
- God answers prayers.

When we analyze these beliefs we see that they are mostly cognitively simple self-deceptions. Epicurus (341-270 BCE; 2002) observed that his contemporaries prayed more to hurt their enemies than to advance their own projects. He commented that because most people have enemies (a view that is still current in most of Africa; Adams, 2005), humanity would have perished if the gods answered prayers (Rodis-Lewis, 1975). To examine empirically the issue of whether God answers prayers, we can note the study by Galton (1872). He tested the argument by a certain Dr. Hook that "the Lord interferes with the laws of nature on behalf of those who pray" (p. 125). He reasoned that because the churches offer a prayer every week to grant health and long life to the sovereign, royalty should live longer than other people. He had data from 97 members of royal houses, and found that their average age at the time of death was 64.04. He also had data from 945 members of the clergy whose average age at the time of death was 69.49.

Larger samples included members of the English aristocracy (1,179 cases), which averaged 67.31 and gentry (1,632 cases), which averaged 70.22. Thus, the picture was very clear. Prayers did not influence the longevity of kings and queens. In fact, their age at the time of death was lower than the age of all the other samples examined, which may reflect assassinations and other hazards of their position. In the same publication, an examination of the age of death of the descendents of "righteous peers" found no difference compared with the age of death of "wicked peers." In short, although the researcher admitted that praying "is powerful in ennobling the resolves, and it is found to give serenity during the trials of life and the shadow of approaching death" (p. 135), there is no evidence that it makes a real difference in the life of people, although it provides a self-deception that results in serenity, and well-being. There is empirical evidence that praying reduces blood pressure and has other beneficial physiological consequences (Newberg & Newberg, 2005). The increased serenity, mentioned by Galton, suggests that praying is consistent with good mental health. Thus, again mild self-deceptions are consistent with good mental health.

For centuries, the popes prayed for peace. But the world has always had wars, and these wars have become more lethal in the past 200 years. If prayer had some efficacy surely the prayer of someone considered "holy" should have made some difference!

But prayer can have benefits. Empirical work by Seligman (1975, 2006) suggests that certain actions are good for our mental health. He found that writing down three blessings each evening improves mental health. I assume that many people who pray thank God for their blessings, so they are doing what Seligman instructs people to do.

Speaking of morality, cognitively simple self-deceptions prevail in the United States with respect to abortion and homosexuality. Specifically, there is evidence that in the United States the crime rate decreased soon after abortions became legal. One explanation is that mothers who do not wish to have a child are poor mothers. In fact, there is cross-cultural evidence that mothers of unwanted children have children who are likely to become delinquent or even criminal (David, Dytrych, Matejcek, & Schuller, 1988; Rohner, 2004). The position of the pro-life citizens is a cognitively simple self-deception, because they use only the positive information that being against abortion is theologically approved, but ignore the negative evidence that when abortion was illegal it took place anyway, and many women died each year. It would be ideal to have a society without abortions, but reality is different from the ideal. In any case, in my opinion the right of women to choose to have an abortion trumps other considerations. The reader who disagrees with me about abortion could be correct. To take a position that does not accept the possibility that I may be wrong is dogmatism, and people who are dogmatic are especially likely to be cognitively simple and to have many self-deceptions.

Similarly, the opposition to homosexuality is a cognitively simple self-deception. Homosexuality occurs in all cultures and among the higher apes (Ford & Beach, 1951). The claim, by the president of Iran, that there are no homosexuals in Iran produced a lot of mirth. The objection to homosexuality can be traced to the time, 2,000 years ago, when humans as a species might not have survived if they did not have many children. But now the world is already overpopulated. Homosexuals do us a favor: they do not have children.

French anthropologists Boyer (1994) and Atran (2002, 2007; Atran & Norenzayan, 2004) suggested that religion develops because of the way the human mind works. "Religion ensues from the ordinary workings of the human mind as it deals with emotionally compelling problems of human existence, such as birth, aging, death, unforeseen calamities and love" (Atran, 2002, p. viii)."Human minds appear to be programmed to look for ... agents as the causes of complex and uncertain happenings" (p. 49). In short, our mind is designed to make certain distinctions, such as between the physical and the psychological, and to see an agent or a cause when there is no evidence for such a cause. In experiments, 4-year-olds are shown to be dualists (body and mind are different) and creationists ("Why do lions exist?" "To go to the zoo"; P. Bloom, 2005, p. 112). Thus, gods are "natural hypotheses," reflecting our psychology. Because evaluation (good–bad) is the most important dimension of meaning (Osgood et al., 1975) across cultures, in most cultures there are devils as well as gods.

Dreaming is one of the factors that increase belief in supernatural beings. For example, in the Homeric poems the gods frequently appear in dreams. Concerns about mortality also increase religiosity (Norenzayan & Hansen, 2006). In several experiments priming "death" increased the participants' tendency to indicate that they strongly believed in God, and agreed that they were very religious. Among Christian students, priming their mortality facilitated beliefs even in culturally alien supernatural entities (such as the Buddha, shamanic spirits).

The famous anthropologist Robert Redfield, in the introduction to the classic study by Malinowski (1954), wrote, "Religion is not only people explaining and projecting their dreams; it is not only a sort of spiritual electric—mana—it is not solely to be recognized in social communication—no, religion and magic are ways men must have, being men, to make the world acceptable, manageable, and right" (p. viii).

All fundamentalist religions are divisive. For instance, Moshe Levinger, a Jewish fundamentalist, said that Zionism has been "infected" with the "virus of peace" (cited in Armstrong, 2000, p. 287). One must be extremely militant to see peace as a virus! Christian fundamentalists also feel under attack, worrying about attacks by science, experts, homosexuals, foreign influences, uncertainty. Thus, it is not Islam that is militant, but fundamentalist Islam. However, it is sometimes difficult to distinguish Islam from fundamentalist Islam, because too many Muslims believe that the Qu'ran is the word of God, Islam is the only "true" religion, Allah is intimately involved in human affairs, and Islam is under attack by modernity. Many of these beliefs are self-deceptions.

In their extensive empirical study of modernity, Inkeles and Smith (1974) identified several elements that constitute modernity. Four of these elements are contrary to a large portion of today's Islam, although they were compatible with the Islam of the 7th to the 13th centuries.

1. *Modernity includes openness to new experiences.* The Arab world during the 7th to the 13th centuries was open to new experiences, which leads to cognitive complexity, and absorbed much of the classical scholarship, algebra, and technology from other cultures. But now a large portion of the Arab world is relatively closed to new experiences. One clue is the number of translations into Arabic. In the past 1,000 years there have been as many translations into Arabic as translations into Spanish in 1 year (*The Economist*, 2003). The accumulated total of translated books since the beginning of Islam is about 100,000, and that is about the number of books that are translated into Spanish per year (B. Lewis, 2003). The Arab world currently translates no more than 330 books annually, one fifth of the number that Greece (a country of 11 million) translates (B. Lewis, 2003). In short, these data suggest that there is a closed mind and cognitive simplicity in today's Arab world, in contrast to the Arab world of the 12th century.

2. *In modernity there is a readiness to adopt new behavior patterns, and accept social change.* Most, but not all, of Islam, on the contrary, tends to seek the older behavior patterns. Mohammed is the "model" human and most people should behave the way he did. In fundamentalist Islam the ideal is to copy the lifestyle of the Prophet, even sleep on the same side of the body as he did! It is true that other ultra-orthodox doctrines have similar rules of behavior, for example, for Jews that one should first put on the left and then the right shoe (Margalit, 1991). However, although I have no relevant data, it seems to me that very few Jews follow such rules, whereas a good many Muslims aspire to live like the Prophet.

3. *In modernity there is an orientation toward the present and future, not the past.* Fundamentalist Islam looks at the past, especially the period when the Prophet was alive, and the centuries that followed, when Islam conquered North Africa, southern Spain, and the Balkans as the golden

period. Modern people look at the 21st century (e.g., 2050) as the important focus of their concerns. Thus, modern people are concerned with the overpopulation of the earth, but most Moslems seem to ignore it.

4. *In modernity there is trust in people one does not know.* Most Arab cultures are collectivist (see chapter 3) and collectivism is associated with distrust toward those individuals who are not members of the in-group. The in-group is usually the tribe, and in Islam the in-group usually is "other Muslims of my sect" and secondarily other Muslims. Non-Muslims are usually categorized as out-group. Only the more Western of Muslims are willing to be friends with non-Muslims. The fundamentalists do not even want to shake hands with an "infidel," let alone a nonbeliever.

Thus, there is a definite incompatibility between modernity and a large segment of today's Islam, although there is a good deal of variability, with a large number of Turks, thanks to Atatürk, accepting modernity, yet only a small number of Afghanis do. Muslims readily use the latest devices— fax machines, the Internet, planes, and so on. The use of contemporary devices is a superficial contact with modernity. In my opinion, the essence of modernity is psychological—openness to new experiences, to the future, to behavior change, trust of other people even if one does not know them.

CHILDREARING PATTERNS SHAPE RELIGIONS

Kirkpatrick (2005) outlined a theory of the psychology of religion based on the concept of attachment. Secure attachment occurs when parents are almost always available, supportive, and warm. Insecure attachment occurs when parents are available only some of the time, and are highly critical, negative, cold, or indifferent. He reported American studies that found a correlation between secure attachment and good physical and mental health. Empirical studies have found that people who experienced secure attachment had a close relationship with God, and God was loving and friendly. People who experienced an ambivalent attachment with their parents had a God who did not love; those who feared their parents also had a God who was not loving, as well as unfriendly, and distant. In this publication there was evidence for both the "correspondence hypothesis" that the relationship with the parents corresponds to the relationship with God, and the "compensation hypothesis" that when parents are unavailable and inadequate God fills the vacuum. People living in unstable, stressful environments have highly active attachment systems and are especially likely to find an alternative attachment figure in God. In the modern world with busy parents, secure attachment is a rare commodity; thus health suffers and for some the concept of God may now be less positive than it was in previous time periods.

Lambert, Triandis, and Wolf (1959) found an association between conceptions of deities that are malevolent or benevolent and punitive or nurturing childrearing practices. The researchers studied 62 cultures, on which they had enough information about childrearing and the kinds of gods that were found in the culture. They classified the cultures according to whether the supernatural beings were aggressive or benevolent, and whether the childrearing practices included much or little pain. They found a statistically significant tendency for cultures with aggressive gods to use only punishment and no rewards in their childrearing; whereas cultures with benevolent gods used much nurturance in their childrearing. They then examined a number of theories to explain these findings and concluded that in cultures where children are hurt when they are very young, they become anxious and anticipate punishment. In such cultures, an aggressive god helps the people "make sense" of their circumstances and their world.

As I studied the main religions of the world (Bowker, 2000; Eliade, 1967, 1978, 1982, 1985; Lee, 2003; Smart, 1998), from shamanism—common among hunters and gatherers—which developed about 8,000 years ago, to the classical period (Greece and Rome), to the Zoroastrians, Hindu, Buddhists, Jews, Christians, Muslims, and to the New Age religions, a few facts struck me most vividly.

Humans Are a God-Making Species, Sensitive to Hierarchy

Higher mammals have rudimentary cultures in the sense that they transmit to the next generation techniques about tool making and hunting.

Because hierarchy is in our genes (most primates have hierarchical social structures), religion also helps us make sense of hierarchies. Gods are usually conceived as being in high places, looking down on humans; devils are in low places (Meier, Hauser, Robinson, Friesen, & Schjeldahl, 2007). The linguistic roots of Islam and "submission" are the same. Burkert (1996) saw religions as a system of rank, dependence, subordination, and submission to superiors. Similarly, social exchanges occur in all human communities, and the exchange of sacrifices for gifts from gods makes sense in the same conceptual framework.

Religions Have Many Common Elements

Human biology and evolution press toward competition and selfishness (Dawkins, 1989). Religions press toward cooperation and unselfishness. Also, the essence of the Decalogue, in one form or another, is found in many religions. Broadly speaking, some aspect of "love thy neighbor as thyself" is found in most religions. The Golden Rule may be universal: "Do to others whatever you would have them do to you" (Matthew 7:12); Zoroastrianism: "Do as you would be done by"; Confucius: "What you do not want done to you do not do to others" (Analects 15.23); Mohammed: "None of you is a believer until you love for your neighbor what you love for yourself"; The Buddha: "Do not hurt others with that which hurts yourself," "One should seek for others the happiness one derives for one's self"; The Mahabharata (Hindu): "This is the sum of all duty: do nothing to others. which if it were done to you, would cause you pain"; Sikkhism: "As thou deemest thyself, do deem others"; Hillel (Jewish teacher): "What is hateful to you do not do to others"; Lao-Tse, who initiated Taoism and was a contemporary of Confucius: "I would return good for evil" (*Encyclopedia Britannica*). That seems to go even further than the other statements, and reminds us of the turning the other cheek of Christianity. In short, the great religions have a lot in common. This suggests that the Golden Rule is one of the "truths" as I defined "truth" in this book—the convergence of a belief across diverse cultures.

The common core of world religions is reflected in the Universal Declaration of Human Rights, which was adopted by the UN in 1948. Ishay (2004) indicated that the declaration was the result of the work of a culturally heterogeneous committee. Inputs were provided by Chang, a Confucian philosopher; Malik, a Lebanese philosopher; Cassin, a French Jew who was a distinguished legal scholar; and the work was done under the leadership of Eleanor Roosevelt (United States). Yet, bin Laden denounced the declaration as "against Islam." There is empirical work (C. Sherif et al., 1965) showing that the more extreme an individual's attitudinal position the greater the range of attitudinal positions rejected by this person. Thus, bin Laden's rejection of the declaration speaks about bin Laden's cognitive system rather than about the inconsistency of the declaration and Islam.

Furthermore, Buddhism recommends the attainment of *nirvana* where the fire of desires is extinguished. Taoism recommends swimming with the stream, and argues that if people have no unnecessary desires they will be free. Some Christians glorified the ascetic martyrs who presumably suppressed their desires. One definition of jihad, in original Islam, is "man's struggle against his desires" (epigraph in Feldman, 2003). Thus, more than one worldview recommends the suppression of desires.

Buddhism, Judaism, Christianity, and Islam have also in common the hope that the whole world will be converted to their own point of view. For instance, the self-deception that one's religion will someday become universal was found in Judaism when knowledge of God shall cover the earth as the water covers the sea (Bowker, 1997, p. 5).

Revelations are common. They are self-deceptions consistent with the wishes of the prophet. There is a recurrent theme, in many religions, that the King–Prophet had a direct communication from God, and received

God's instructions on how his people should live. We see this in the case of Hammurabi, who reigned in Babylon between 2067 and 2025 BCE. He received from the sun god Shamash the law code known as the "code of Hammurabi." The same theme is found when Zarathustra (the founder of the religion of the Parsis) had the vision that God instructed him, when Moses received the revelation of the Decalogue from Yaweh on Mt. Sinai. This happened also when Mohammed received the word of Allah in the form of the Qu'ran. This theme appears to be Middle Eastern, but nevertheless sufficiently widespread to be noted as a common element. It even came to America, with Joseph Smith's revelation that started Mormonism.

Humans Make Their Gods in Their Own Image

This view is very old: Xenophanes of Colophon, a thinker of the 6th century BCE, stated that if cows and horses had hands they would paint their gods as cows and horses (*Encyclopedia Britannica*, 1957). Murphy (1975) reviewed much evidence that people make their gods in their own image. Simple observations, also, from traveling around, show that African gods are Black, Asian gods are Asian looking, Hawaiian gods look Polynesian, and of course European gods are White.

External Religions Are Systems of Self-Deception

As a psychologist I am aware that humans have an immense number of "cognitive illusions" (Kahneman & Tversky, 1996). In my opinion, many conceptions of God are illusions. God is in the minds of humans, not "out there." As Farazza (2004) said, God is a wish—for protection, guidance, help, and, through prayer, for the control of uncertainty. What could be more reassuring than to believe that an omnipotent entity will help us win our battles?

Humans make their gods to satisfy their wishes (Freud, 1964). They have delusions such as "we are the chosen people," "prayer can change the course of events," and "we will go to paradise." They feel protected by an omnipotent, eternal God. The German philosopher Ludwig Feuerbach (1804–1872) argued that religion is a projection of the aspirations of humans. That is a good way of summarizing how our wishes can be conceived in this case.

External Religion and Politics Are Closely Linked

Priests and kings are often one and the same. The leader is often considered divine, a descendent from the gods, or at a minimum has a "hotline to the gods." Religious practitioners frequently expound doctrines that increase their power. There are numerous examples where religion is used as a mask for those who exploit. For example, the rebels of northern Uganda started their movement to establish a state that would use the Ten Commandments as the basis of organization. But their movement evolved into a pattern of abduction of children, making the boys soldiers and the girls sex objects for the rebels.

The "holy" books of most religions speak to the human condition in languages that are open to alternative interpretations, thus allowing the powerful to decode them in ways that maximize their power and support the prejudices of "believers." People in power have a vested interest in maintaining the status quo and that can be done best if the masses are threatened with eternal damnation if they do not follow the orders of those in power.

Original Buddhism did not accept supernatural beings. But the people in power found it convenient to argue that they exist because they can control people more easily by having them believe that they exist. The theologian Küng (2005) outlined numerous doctrines of the Catholic Church that in his opinion Christ would object to. Christ would not consider contraception a mortal sin, would accept divorced people, would approve of the ordination of women, would approve of married priests, would love people even if they have had premarital sex, even if they were homosexuals, or if they had used abortion. Mohammed had the greatest respect for women, but the powerful (who, of course, were men) among his followers made women second-class citizens.

Because religion and politics are often linked, it is very important to observe the separation of church and state, as stated in the U.S. Constitution.

Religion and Art Are Closely Linked

Both religion and art can be appreciated even when they are not literally true (Kurtz, 1983). Armstrong (2005) argued that in secular cultures myths were replaced by art. R. Wagner (1954) wrote extensively about the link of religion and art. Humans may be defined by art and religion. Apes have not initiated either, though lower animals when given crayons can produce images that some people see as art. In Thailand I saw a remarkable performance by some elephants that held brushes in their trunks to paint interesting "creations."

The link between art and religion is immense. Leonardo da Vinci saw in the beauty of landscapes "proof" of the existence of God. There is an immense amount of religious art, in museums, churches, temples, and other houses of worship. Architecture that glorifies God can be found on every inhabited continent. A religious service is like a beautiful painting. It is a satisfying fantasy.

Religion has inspired the most wonderful music, paintings, and literature. Listening to Bach's music in his church in Leipzig, Germany, was for me a secular/religious experience. It was secular in the sense that it did not involve supernatural beings. But it was religious because it was spiritual and most emotional; it was a feeling of floating in the universe. Similarly, looking at the ceiling of the Sistine Chapel in Rome one is transported to higher spheres. When the grail theme merges with the communion theme in Wagner's *Parsifal,* I go to heaven. Art is Reality+ and the more it satisfies our needs and conforms to our wishes the more it is a satisfying self-deception. The more uplifting it is, taking us "to heaven," the more it overlaps with religion. Both can provide transcendental experiences. In short, religion is a healthy, life-enhancing "illusion" (Winnicott, 1971) akin to art. Both art and religion are the highest creations of culture.

There is a large discrepancy between the views of originators of religions and subsequent views. The rejection of supernatural gods is widely accepted among scientists and was also the view of the Buddha who understood that all supernatural beings are mere superstitions. Yet, so many of his followers adopted supernatural beings that the Buddha would not recognize evolved Buddhism (Reischauer, 1946). The Buddha tolerated celestial beings because most people need them. The oversimplification of the "master's" teachings is a common phenomenon and applies to most religions, as well as to Adam Smith's free-market economics, Marxism, and to other originators of social movements. Specifically, there is no evidence that the Buddha prayed (Reischauer, 1946), but his followers often pray to him! Contemporary Buddhists often misunderstand his message!

The distortion of the original views of the master can be seen in systematic studies of the "serial reproduction phenomenon" (Bartlett, 1932/1950; Lyons & Kashima, 2003). When a story is told to one person who tells it to another person, who tells it to still another, and so on, the story becomes progressively simpler, more stereotypic, and sharper. As it becomes simpler, it also acquires some of the stereotypic traditional elements of the culture of the storytellers. Thus, because the original pre-Buddhist cultures had celestial beings, as Buddhism evolved it reacquired them. Similarly, the psychology of rumor (Gladwell, 2002) shows that a message becomes simpler as it goes from person to person, some details become more specific but they become assimilated in the cognitive system of the speakers, thus reflecting their culture, expectations, stereotypes, prejudices, and previously available frames of reference.

Ideas found in the original culture are transformed for use in the new one. For example, in polytheism the gods were territorial. In ancient Greece Zeus was on Mount Olympus, Apollo in Delphi, and Poseidon in the sea. After Greece became Christian the Saints maintained these territorial attributes. The God of monotheists is "in heaven" (Mt. Olympus and heaven are mixed up in ancient Greek and Roman writings), while St. Nicholas took the place of Poseidon on the sea. Sea travel can be dangerous and uncertain. People need the self-deception that there is a God who will protect them. Poseidon, St. Nicolas, or Maa Tsu (in Taiwan) have the same function—protecting travelers from the sea. Multiple cultural observers saw sea travel as dangerous and invented an idea that helps them.

There Is a Correlation between Geography and Religion

Most Christians are in Europe and the Americas, most Muslims in Africa and South Asia, most Buddhists in South and East Asia, and so on. This patterning is accounted well by Latané's (1996) theory of dynamic social impact. Through communication among neighbors, beliefs that are geographically scattered eventually become correlated. In short, like all elements of culture, religion spreads through communication, and there is a higher probability that people will hold the views of their neighbors. As religion spreads, cultural knowledge that is widely shared (e.g., stereotypes, beliefs about supernatural beings, spirits) it is especially likely to become part of the belief system (Chiu & Hong, 2006).

IMITATION AND RELIGION

Imitation is an important process in the development of religion. We can see by simple inspection that religions are geographically patterned. People believe what has come to them by tradition, authority, or revelation. If most people they are acquainted with believe in X, they believe in X. Thus, most individuals belong to the religion of their parents and peers and do not question that religion. As with most aspects of culture we like the elements that we happen to find in our environment. Humans are highly adaptive, and can adapt to almost any condition.

Self-efficacy (Bandura, 1989) is essential if a person is going to achieve anything. It includes the idea "I can do this." Many of the activities associated with external religion have specific goals—to mark the transition from one status to another, as in baptism, marriage, and funeral rites; through prayer people ask to be protected from disease, accidents, and other calamities. Praying is especially helpful in providing a sense of control when faced with possible catastrophes. Praying is beneficial because it gives people the illusion of control.

THE DISTRIBUTION OF RELIGIOUS BELIEFS

Religious beliefs are declining in Western Europe (Dogan, 1995). In the United States, many leading scientists belong to the American Humanist Society, which does not recognize supernatural beings. This society takes the position that we are insignificant creatures on a minor planet, in a remote solar system, in one of millions of galaxies (Shermer, 1999). This image is not sufficiently complimentary, so we invent ideas that boost our self-esteem.

The United States is unusual, when compared with the other industrial democracies, because 96% (according to a Gallup poll; see Koenig et al., 2001) of the population believes in God, and substantial groups of people reject the scientific explanations of cosmology. Social psychologist James Jackson attributed the higher percentage of belief in God in the United States relative to Western Europe to the fact that America has a very large number of immigrants from countries with low levels of education. Creationism (or intelligent design—rejection of the theory of evolution) is almost exclusively an American phenomenon, among industrial countries. A 2006 BBC report outlined a study of the acceptance of the theory of evolution in several countries. The American acceptance rate of 40% stands out against the northern European and Japanese rates that exceed 90%. Only Turkey, in that study, had a rate of acceptance as low as that of the United States. Even the Vatican, in 1996, accepted the theory of evolution as a widely accepted "theory of science" (Dawkins, 2003, p. 148). Rejection of the theory of evolution occurs in 45% of U.S. samples but only in 7% of samples in the rest of the industrialized world (Shermer, 1999). Although the United States is high in religiosity, this does not seem to be particularly helpful. It is higher than most industrial countries in the percent of the population that lives in poverty, higher in inequality, and lower in life expectancy (Eckersley, 2004). For instance, its life expectancy is lower than that found in many not especially religious countries. The 2006 *World in Figures*, published by *The Economist*, places the United States 40th in the world in life expectancy (77.9). This is a lower age than Japan (82.8), Hong Kong (82.2), Macau (80.7), France (80), Singapore (79.4), and "atheist" Cuba (78.6).

The self-rated importance of religion is correlated in the United Sates with authoritarianism, ethnocentrism, dogmatism, social distance from minorities, rigidity, intolerance for ambiguity, and prejudice (Shermer, 1999). However, Allport (1950/1967) made a distinction between "immature" and "mature" religious sentiments. He argued that the immature acceptance of religion is unreflective, uncritical, and reflects hostility, anxiety, and prejudice. The mature sentiment is open to experience and is dynamic. The mature is consistent with tolerance. The mature sentiment is consistent with the Hindu Vedas, which states, "Truth is one; men call it by many names." Allport (1950/1967) discussed in detail the relationship between mature and immature religious sentiments and psychopathology. It is only the immature sentiment that claims "God is precisely what I say He is." It is the self-rated importance of religion of the immature that is associated with prejudice and the other psychopathologies. The typical childrearing pattern of this personality configuration is that parents tell their children "do not do that" and when the child asks "why" they reply, "because I say so" (Triandis, 1971). Note that in this case there is no discussion. Some of the verses of the Qu'ran have the same quality of no discussion, no negotiation, and no search for win–win solutions. This is typical of people of low cognitive complexity. Cognitively simple individuals who are extremely religious have been found to be high in black-and-white thinking (Rokeach, 1960), and in prejudice. Most of these studies were done with Christians, but it is likely that similar studies done with members of the other external religions will find the same results. Individuals who are cognitively complex tend to be less prejudiced and show less social distance from minorities than those who are cognitively simple. Consistent with the previous discussion about collectivist and individualist religions, I suggest that perhaps mature religiosity is individualist, whereas immature religiosity is collectivist. Consistent with the argument in chapter 3, collectivism is associated with cultural and also cognitive simplicity, whereas individualism is associated with cultural and cognitive complexity.

There is a corresponding distinction between "subjective religiosity," where praying (an individualistic activity) is an important component, and "socially transmitted religiosity" (which is a collectivist activity). Subjective religiosity is individualist and socially transmitted religiosity is collectivist. In the latter there is an emphasis on ritual and doing what is expected by co-religionists. Hansen and Norenzayan (2006) showed experimentally that the former kind is related to tolerance and the latter to intolerance. For example, members of all religions (Protestants, Catholics, Orthodox Jews, Muslims, Hindus) tested so far, who frequently attend their houses of worship, are more intolerant than members who pray frequently on their own, without attending a house of worship. Among Muslims, those who regularly attend a mosque have a more positive view of martyrdom than those who pray frequently, although of course the two variables are correlated. One can hold one of the variables constant statistically, and see its effect on the other variable. Among Palestinians, for instance, attendance at a mosque predicts willingness for martyrdom, but frequency of prayer does not (Ginges, Hansen, & Norenzayan, in press). In short, it appears that collectivist religions are fundamentalist, and those high on this attribute are willing to become martyrs, whereas individualist religions are high in spirituality, and have an "all humans are brothers and sisters" perspective.

There is much research indicating that a fit between culture and personality is consistent with good mental health (Ward et al., 2001). Thus, cognitive simplicity in a complex culture is likely to reduce mental health. This suggests that Muslims who move to Europe will have difficulties adjusting, and thus it is not too surprising that some of them are willing to blow themselves up.

Among Muslims, those who stress the concept of *ummah* or universal brotherhood appear to be religiously mature. During the pilgrimage to Mecca every man is, at least in theory though sometimes not in practice, equal to all other men. Thus Islam has integrative elements (Ahmed, 2002). However, many mullahs are more interested in power than in religion, and stress the divisive aspects of their religion.

Cognitive complexity (Harvey et al., 1961) is also related to cultural complexity. As discussed earlier, cultures differ in complexity, with hunters and gatherers the most simple, and information societies the most complex. The simplest cultures have animistic beliefs. Everything that moves (e.g., rolling stones, rivers, etc.) has a soul that causes the movement. A step above in complexity is polytheism, as found among the ancient Greeks, Romans, and in parts of the Hindu religion. In Veranassi (Benares), India, one sees temples for specific diseases and those who suffer from the disease are expected to pray in the temple of that disease to get well. But Hinduism also has very complex deities, such as Shiva who appears in different forms both as creator and destroyer. In fact Shiva has more than 1,000 names, showing that he has many qualities (Bowker, 1997). As cultures become more complex their gods become more complex.

Hinduism raises more questions than it answers. Zakaria (2008) presented the Creation Hymn from the *Rig Veda*. I was impressed by two sentences: "Even gods came after creation's day" (I said to myself: They knew that gods are human-made!) and, "Only He, up there, knows maybe, or perhaps, not even He." So, there is the possibility of monotheism, but there is great uncertainty, ambiguity. That kind of thinking probably is linked to cognitive complexity. Compare these sentences with the Book of Genesis, which is certain, cognitively simple!

RELIGIOUS RITUALS ARE DESIRABLE

Evidence exists that religion is linked to good health (Oman & Thoresen, 2005; Pargament, 2002). This link reflects, in part, the fact that many religious people avoid undesirable behaviors, such as the use of drugs. Additionally, religions provide rituals and many rituals are designed to bring about desirable conditions. For example, the rain dance of Native Americans is supposed to bring about rain. Many miracles are associated with rituals. Ritual can be very useful. For example, in cultures with final ceremonies for the dead, people experience fewer symptoms of prolonged grief, such as suicidal behavior, troubled dreams, work-related difficulties, and mental and physical illness (Rosenblatt, Walsh, & Jackson, 1976). But note also that other elements of culture "filter" the way rituals are performed. For example, when a child dies in Egypt people express intense emotional reactions, whereas in Bali they do not. That is because in Egypt, emotional expression is viewed as healthy. In Bali, emotional expression is viewed as "loss of control," and a threat to oneself and others.

Given that rituals are desirable, it seems useful to explore keeping the rituals and rejecting the superstitions (supernatural beings, angels, devils, heaven, hell) found in religious traditions! Most people think that this is impossible, but I think it is possible. I propose later the development of a "religion" without supernatural beings, but with the rituals of each religion. This idea is cognitively complex, and will be rejected by those who are cognitively simple. If we could shed the self-deceptions of religions (celestial beings, afterlife, heaven, hell), and keep the rituals we might have a desirable way for humans to use religion.

RELIGION AND MAGIC

Scholars have had a hard time distinguishing between religion and magic. Styers (2004) wrote a whole book discussing what has been written about this relationship. The antagonism between the two is reflected in the 100,000 witchcraft trials that occurred between 1450 and 1750. Tens of thousands of people were executed for witchcraft. Most scholars of religion see a link between religion and magic.

Ethnographic work reveals that people in many collectivist cultures, especially in Africa, are extraordinarily afraid of supernatural beings and of each other—including family members, friends, and neighbors (Fiske et al., 1998). Anyone may be envious, malicious, or possess the "evil eye." It is assumed that everyone has "enemies" (Adams, 2005). Thus, another person may do "magic" to hurt oneself—make one ill, destroy crops and herds, ruin one's endeavors, and even kill oneself. If a family member transgresses, all members of the family may be punished through magic. As individualism increased in the West, however, belief in magic decreased. Calamities were conceived as due to one's own actions rather than to the actions of others. Nevertheless, magic is still a very important phenomenon in many parts of the world.

Sir James George Frazer (1854–1941) identified the "laws of magic" in *The Golden Bough*, a very thorough examination of magic rituals in many cultures. (This 12-volume study was abridged by T. H. Gaster and published as Frazer, 1968.) In the new version, sections found to be unreliable were eliminated. Because basic human needs are the same around the world we find similarities in the way magic works in most cultures.

Two principles of magic are especially important:

1. Homeopathy (or similarity): like produces like (effect resembles the cause). Examples are as follow: Destroy the image of the enemy. Burn

the effigies of evil people or spirits. Shoot an arrow through the heart of a clay image to produce love. The image of the object is the same as the object. The Christian communion is a ritual with wine representing the blood of Christ. The Muslims sacrifice an animal to remember the sacrifice of Abraham. Frazer offered hundreds of examples of such cases from all over the world. For instance, to produce rain you sprinkle water. Saying the name of the thing (e.g., rain, rain come again) in a spell can produce the effect.

2. Contagion (or the law of contact): once in contact, always in contact. In all mystical religions there is the urge to merge with the deity (contact). Objects act one on the other forever. In the Eucharist, the wine and bread are taken into the body, so the contact is total. Muslims are eager to touch the meteorite called the Ka'ba, which is located in Mecca, and is central to the *hajj*, the visit to Mecca comprising one of the five pillars of Islam. Kissing the hand to obtain a blessing is common in many cultures. In many cultures people do not want their teeth extracted because their enemy can get hold of their teeth (contact) and perform magic that will harm them.

One can also find examples where both principles operate. For instance, you can harm a person if you obtain (contact) some of the person's hair and burn it (similarity). Some psychologists have argued that the refusal of members of some cultures to ask for help from a psychotherapist is based on not wanting to give private information to a stranger. This is similar to not wanting a stranger to get hold of something that belongs to them, like their hair or a tooth. In China a widow claimed that she became pregnant by having intercourse with the clay stature of her husband, and she was widely believed (Lévy-Bruhl, 1910/1966).

Children have been found to prefer to play (contact) with others who are "lucky" (they believe they will become lucky themselves) than with playmates who are unlucky, and prefer groups where people are lucky to the ones that are unlucky (Olson, Banaji, Dweck, & Spelke, 2006). In some primitive tribes, even today (Dennett, 2006; Festinger, 1983) ritual eating of parts of a dead person, or requiring a person who reaches age 80 to commit suicide so that he or she can be eaten, can be explained by magic. Eating means contact with the dead person. Similarity is reflected in the belief that one obtains the same virtues (wisdom, experiences) that the dead person has had. Primitive thought patterns were discussed by Lévy-Bruhl (1923).

Other magical phenomena include taboos, that is, powerful people have mana and should be avoided. Never touch them. To look at such people can cause one to become sick. Their servants must carry them because they must not touch the earth with their feet. Such ideas are obviously functional because they increase the security of the chief.

Frazer also provided a discussion of kings as priests and magicians. Such people are thought to be able to increase fertility, and to be able to get rid of the evil eye. He also provided examples of magical beliefs. Here are some samples: Ravena put his soul in a box and went to war, and was invulnerable in battle. Gilgit put his soul in the snow and could be killed only by fire.

Many ceremonies of modern times derive from activities that were traditional among our ancestors. For example, the Celts were widespread throughout Europe. They were pastoral people who took their cattle to pasture on May 1 and brought it back on October 31. European cultures still observe May 1 and October 31 (Halloween) as holidays. Also related to the latter holiday was the beginning of the year, which in some cultures was on November 1. People went around telling each other that a new year was about to start. Fairies were supposed to come out that night.

Frazer argued that cultures first developed magic, then religion, and finally science. Reading his book I am constantly astonished by the way elements of magic permeate modern external religions. When the control of nature that humans fervently desire is not achieved by religion, then science provides some controls, but the problem is that the laws of science are probabilistic, and several factors combine in complex interactions to determine an event. As we move from magic to religion to science we need more and more cognitive complexity.

The laws of magic operate even among American undergraduates (Rozin, Millman, & Nemeroff, 1986). Specifically, a drink that has been in contact with a disinfected cockroach is rejected, no matter how good it might be (the law of contact). Undergraduates refused to wear a well-laundered shirt that was previously worn by a disliked person (contact). Desirable foods (e.g., delicious fudge) are disgusting when they come in the shape of disgusting objects (such as dog feces), showing the operation of the law of similarity. People are inaccurate in throwing darts at the faces of people they like, but accurate when throwing them to the faces of people they dislike (similarity).

During cultural evolution we build on a previous phenomenon rather than replacing one phenomenon with the next. This is also consistent with studies (G. Jahoda, 1969) that found that African university students used a scientific principle (e.g., lightening is electricity), together with the religious or magical one (i.e., lightning is also made by the god of lightning). This phenomenon of *syncretism* is widely observed in studies of modern belief systems: They contain elements from previous belief systems.

Witchcraft involves the self-deception that one has power, and is able to harm another person by simply wishing it. Where witchcraft is widely used, people tend to believe that most illnesses are the result of someone attacking them with witchcraft. There are superb descriptions of witchcraft in Africa (Boyer, 2001). Locals fear the witches, whereas Westerners do not. The locals explain this by saying that the people from the West have special immunities against witches (Adams, 2005).

Statistical evidence (Nisbett & Cohen, 1996) shows that witchcraft is used especially in those cultures where secular authorities are unable to levy sanctions on criminals and thereby control human behavior. When transgressions in human relations are not investigated and punished by a secular authority, such as the police, a council, or a court of law, members of the culture develop witchcraft, which allows an offended person to punish the perpetrator. A curse is very effective if the person who receives it believes that it is effective. The person who believes that the curse is effective can have the satisfaction of cursing others who believe that the curse is effective.

There is an advantage in knowing that curses are ineffective: Forty years ago a man in India cursed me because I refused to employ him as a guide. He said, "May you die!" My reaction was to just laugh and I am still around. Poets and musicians portraying effective curses, such as in Verdi's *Rigoletto,* do us a disservice because they increase the probability that simple-minded people will expect curses to be effective. Perhaps we should castigate creative artists who increase the probability that simple-minded people will believe in magic. But in the history of art the church paid for a lot of the art that was produced, so there is a tradition linking magic and art.

On the other hand, magic has positive attributes: when people believe that others will use witchcraft if they are harmed, they are less likely to harm others. That is, the fear of witchcraft is a means of maintaining conformity to conventional nonexploitative standards of propriety in interpersonal relations of all kinds—love, friendship, trade, hunting, and so on. Thus, the self-deception that witchcraft exists can reduce harmful behavior.

Belief in sorcery can make people more "virtuous." The African writer Ousmane (1976) illustrates this in a play called *Xala* (impotence). In this play, a successful businessman with two wives and several children was persuaded by the relatives of a young girl to take her as his third wife. As soon as the third marriage was announced there was much conflict between the man and his two families. As a result he became impotent. The impotence was attributed to sorcery. He tried to get rid of the curse by going to the appropriate "healer," but did not succeed. The play ends with the man's business in ruins and all his wives and children abandon him. We see here how belief in sorcery can be used to instruct, control, and regulate people.

Magical phenomena occur when there is a gap between the desirable and reality (Malinowski, 1954). For example, when something goes wrong magic is required to correct the problem. The sea is calm and so the sailor tries to start a breeze. Magic consists of acts of hope. One imagines that the breeze will start, or one expects what one wishes to happen. There is a striking resemblance between the image and the wish (the law of similarity). Magic is founded on "the belief that hope cannot fail, nor desire deceive." The theories of knowledge are dictated by logic, those of magic "by the association of ideas under the influence of desire" (Malinowski, 1954, 2004). In short, magic fits perfectly with our definition of self-deception.

Magic and religion can be placed into the same theoretical framework. Whiting (1994) described "projective–expressive systems" that include magic beliefs, religious dogmas, ritual, ceremonies, art and recreation, games and play, crime rates, and suicide rates. The projective system is the result of the learned (skills, value priorities, conflicts, defenses) and innate (needs, drives, motives, capacities) qualities of individuals. These qualities are the result of childrearing experiences, such as the frequency and intensity of rewards and punishments. The child's learning environment is a consequence of the "maintenance system" that includes the economy, settlement patterns, household type, social structure, law and social control, and division of labor. The maintenance system is the result of the environment (climate, flora, fauna, terrain) and the history of the society (migrations, borrowings, inventions). Thus, the environment and the history of the society result in the religion that is practiced, whose function is to make sense of the environment.

Max Weber (1864–1920) viewed religion as the result of a quest for long life, abundant food and land, averting physical catastrophes, and help in conquering enemies (E. Wilson, 1978). Religion provides identity to an in-group, and sacred rituals that allow us to do something in a strongly emotional situation when we need to be active.

Sociobiology provides one explanation of the emergence of religion (E. Wilson, 1978): In most religions humans are directed to self-sacrifice, which helps many people with very similar genes so that even if the believer dies similar genes survive. There are also mechanisms that ensure helping those who live at the same time and place. For instance, turning down a beggar may result in feeling guilty, and if by chance some misfortune occurs the attribution may be made that not having helped resulted in the misfortune. Thus, religious people tend to help more those who live in the same time and place than do the nonreligious.

Although most religions have magical elements mostly to convince the believers about the validity of the religion, magic is much more specific. Malinowski (1954) found that magic can be focused on the weather, war, coconuts, thunder, medicine, canoe, trading, love, carving charms, fishing, stingray fishing, beauty, or children. Man imagines the outer world in his own image. Primitive and modern religions have very much in common (Malinowski provided a detailed analysis). Most aspects of modern religion can be found in some traditional societies (e.g., even monotheism is found among Australian Aborigines). Myths can account for the extraordinary privileges or duties of certain individuals (i.e., for the great social inequalities) or the severe burdens of rank. They can help people to accept the status quo. Where danger and uncertainty are present magic is likely to be found. Activities that are certain do not require or involve magic. Frazer was correct in calling magic a pseudo-science, because it has many of the functions of organizing activities so as to succeed.

Conformity to the ideology of the group is an important feature of religion and many totalitarian ideologies. For instance, in the Hindu creation myths, those who marry outside the caste go to hell (Yama's kingdom) where they must embrace red-hot human forms. One of Lenin's disciples said that the "true Bolshevik breaks away from his own opinions and honestly agrees with the party" (Malinowski, 1954, p. 115). This is true collectivism, where the individual is totally eclipsed. If each family worked out its own rules of behavior society would disintegrate. Religion and magic integrate a society. Myths can increase self-esteem, by telling about the tribe's special place in the world, and why the tribe has a favored position on earth.

RELIGION AND SOCIAL STRUCTURE

Swanson (1960) provided an elegant demonstration of the relationship between religion and social structure. It links theological beliefs, such as monotheism, polytheism, reincarnation, witchcraft, and so on, to social structure, such as the presence of specialists in communal activities, social classes, debt relationships, and the size of the population. The main thesis is that the character of the gods reflects the character of the social structure. For example, polytheism includes superior and inferior gods, and is found most clearly in those societies that have clear social classes. When there are social classes there is also the belief that if people do not do what is "correct," the supernatural entities will punish them. The function of religion is to make people want to do what they have to do (Swanson, 1960). Thus, in cultures that are hierarchical the gods are hierarchical. For example, the gods of the Mayans consisted of high, middle, and low gods and even had servants.

But belief in high gods is not universal. Whiting (1994) examined 81 hunter–gatherer cultures and only 35% had high gods. Monotheism was found especially in herding cultures. The God in such cultures is always male. Strength is required for survival in such cultures, and thus men have more status than women.

RELIGIOUS DELUSIONS

In 1959, Milton Rokeach (1964) visited the mental hospital in Ypsilanti, Michigan, where there were three patients who thought that they were God or Christ. Patient A was 58 years old and had been in the hospital for 20 years. He said: "I am God." Patient B was 70 years old and had been in the hospital for 17 years. He alternated between believing that he was God or Christ. He also said: "I own this hospital." Patient C was 38 years old and had been in the hospital for 5 years. He thought of himself as the reincarnation of Christ. Rokeach brought them together and observed their conversations over a period of time. Some fragments of the conversations follow: "How can he be Christ, when I am Christ?" "There are people here who are insane," "I know who I am, you do not need to tell me," Patients A and B yelled at each other, whereas C refused to continue the research with Rokeach. Rokeach was especially interested in observing how they resolved the contradiction "I am Christ"/"The other guy says he is Christ." They thought that the other person was not alive, he was just a ghost; or the other person is just "crazy"; or the other person really does not believe that he is Christ but just says that to gain prestige. Some of these Christs thought that they could perform miracles. For example, they "saw" the table raised from the floor (but Rokeach did not).

This is an extreme example of poor mental health. However, all people suffer from some mild delusions. It is common for people to believe that they are better than they really are (see chapter 1) or that they are more honest, or that their "race," nation, or tribe is better than others, and so on. In fact, an epidemiological study by Leighton (1960) included a psychiatric interview of every member of a small community in eastern Canada and concluded that 31% of the population had "symptom patterns and significant impairment" (p. 74). Rapid social change, lack of stable interpersonal relationships, and other factors associated with modernity apparently are responsible for serious impairment of psychological functioning. *The Economist* reported in March 5–11, 2005, that the National Institute of Mental Health estimates that more than 13% of Americans suffer from anxiety disorders, and 9.5% from depressive disorders. Millions more suffer from schizophrenia and bipolar disorders. In short, close to one-third of the population suffer from a diagnosable mental disorder. I took Leighton's course when I was a graduate student, and thought that he was exaggerating the low level of mental health of the population, because he included at that time (1950s) minor disorders, such as being too tense because of overwork. But the mental health status of the population has deteriorated so that 50 years later the National Institute of Mental Health confirms Leighton's numbers.

That modernity in part may be responsible for poor mental health is suggested by studies of immigrants to the United States. The first generation has low rates of poor mental health, the second higher rates, and the third still higher rates similar to the rates of the general population. Of course, there are problems of interpretation. Perhaps new immigrants do not report psychological problems so they can be included in the relevant statistics, or are too poor, or have relatives who do not think of taking them to a mental health facility.

FUNDAMENTALISM

Both Armstrong (2000) and Marty and Appleby (1992) pointed out that fundamentalism (Jewish, Christian, Muslim, Buddhist, Hindu, Sikh, etc.) is a reaction to modernity. Hood et al. (2005), in their *The Psychology of Religious Fundamentalism*, agreed. Modernity provokes fundamentalism. It may be helpful to analyze modern Western culture and discover which of its features result in militant reactions. Maybe we can change some of these characteristics with little loss to ourselves. The first step is to understand why these attributes are offensive to others.

The essence of fundamentalism includes the belief that "my religion is the only one that is valid" and all other religions are invalid or a "sin." Altemeyer and Hunsberger (2005) constructed a 12-item fundamentalism scale (e.g., God has given humanity a complete, unfailing guide to happiness and salvation that must be totally followed) that is answered in a strongly agree–disagree format, and made sense to Christian, Hindu, and Muslim samples. Those receiving a high score on fundamentalism thought that parents want their children to believe what they believe, accepted "creation science," and were enthusiastic in support of proselytizing. By contrast, those who scored low on this scale did not necessarily want their children to believe what they believe, and thought that it is best for them to "search and make up their own minds." Fundamentalists favored a law that would require the teaching of religion in public schools, whereas those scoring low objected to such a law. The fundamentalism scale was highly correlated with a dogmatism scale (sample item: "The things I believe in are so completely true, I could never doubt them"). Fundamentalists did not believe that there could be any event or discovery that could change their mind, whereas those who scored low thought that it was possible that new information could change their mind. Fundamentalists preferred jobs in which their co-workers had the beliefs they had. They rejected homosexuals, were more authoritarian, more right wing, and more conventional. The information base of the fundamentalists was limited; most of their opinions came from authority figures. Altemeyer viewed fundamentalism as the religious manifestation of right-wing authoritarianism, which includes submission to authorities, aggression toward those who disagree with own views, and conventionalism.

Fundamentalism is basically antimodern, antisecular, anti-Communist, and antifeminist. However, in creating an alternative worldview to Western culture it also has some of the attributes of a utopia. Empirical studies show that fundamentalists are more likely to be prejudiced, and to endorse violence toward out-groups, while those with an open mind are more tolerant of others (Silberman, 2005). Violence is often perceived as educating the out-group that is living in "sin," and it is assumed that even fallen enemies will be grateful to have become converted. Fundamentalism has been found correlated with racial/ethnic prejudice, rejection of gays/lesbians, putting women down, anti-communism, rejection of other religions, and authoritarianism (Hunsberger & Jackson, 2005). These results have been replicated across cultures (e.g., Islamic fundamentalists show more prejudice in Shiah–Sunni relationships). Hunsberger and Jackson also mention that fundamentalism is related to cognitive simplicity.

Hood et al. (2005) presented a useful analysis of fundamentalism, which they defined as a meaning system that "relies exclusively upon a sacred text" (p. 6). They argued that fundamentalists consider their text as the standard, and other texts are "good" only if they agree with their text. For example, one of them said, "I have one rule about books. I do not read any book unless it will help me understand the book" (p. 28). The implication is that the book is without error, and in the case of the Qu'ran it is the word of God.

The basic attribute of fundamentalism (Ruthven, 2004) is that the religion's key source is "without error." Thus, the Old and New Testaments or the Qu'ran are said to be literally the word of God and therefore they contain no errors. Yet it is known that these texts were changed over the centuries (Ehrman, 2005). Often that means that fundamentalists take the content of these sources as literally correct. If it says that the world was created in 6 days, it means six 24-hour periods. Among Christian fundamentalists the opposition to the theory of evolution, the authenticity of miracles, the virgin birth of Jesus, his bodily resurrection, his imminent return to judge and rule the world, are not debatable.

Fundamentalists are totally opposed to Higher Criticism, which uses sophisticated methods of textual analysis, and finds evidence that many of the supposedly "sacred" sources have been written by more than one person (Ehrman, 2005; Hood et al., 2005), and errors were made as they were transcribed, because the scribes were tired, hungry, or bored. Most orthodox Muslims are fundamentalists, because they do not doubt that the Qu'ran is the word of God. Yet, the assumption that God is himself the speaker in every passage leads to difficulties (Armstrong, 1993, 2001).

Fundamentalist Muslims believe that the Qu'ran is the word of God. Apparently the language of this work is very beautiful. Armstrong (2006) presented several cases where individuals were converted to Islam by the beauty of the language of the Qu'ran. In short, Mohammed, although probably illiterate, was an extraordinarily talented poet. But the notion that the Qu'ran is the word of God is a self-deception. Mohammed dictated the text to scribes. One interesting incident involved a scribe, by the name of Ibn Abi Sarh (Hood et al., 2005). He was sly; he reasoned that if the dictation was in fact the word of God, if he did not record each word exactly as Mohammed said it somehow God would object. So, he changed a few words here and there. When the dictation said, for instance, "God is all-knowing," he recorded "all-wise." He looked to see if God would react to the alterations. He did not! Thus, Ibn Abi Sarh concluded that Mohammed simply had a fantasy; he rejected Islam and fled to Medina!

My argument has been that all external religions are mere superstitions. It follows that the Qu'ran is not the word of God, because God is a human-made fantasy. In fact many of the "revelations" that Mohammed had, and were included in the Qu'ran, were mere self-deceptions that allowed him to believe what he wished to believe. He was fooling himself! For example, in one incident his followers raided a caravan during a truce. He was embarrassed that his followers did not observe the truce, but the spoils were rich. Then he had a "revelation" that it was all right not to observe the truce, because his enemies had committed acts that were so heinous (Armstrong, 2006). His beloved wife, A'isha, commented that "truly thy Lord makes haste to do thy bidding" (Armstrong, 2006). A'isha understood that it was not God telling Mohammed but Mohammed telling God what to say!

The Qu'ran contains wonderful poetry, consistent with the wishes of most Muslims, but is a fantasy. Yet most believers insist that it is the word of God and it cannot be translated adequately. Note the implication: God speaks Arabic! Such ethnocentrism is universal (Herodotus, 1996; Herskovits, 1955). In any case, the essence of fundamentalism is that the text is the only source of meaning (Hood et al., 2005), and there is no possibility of contradiction to the text.

The majority of religious beliefs are self-deceptions. Content analyses of Homeric poems, for instance, show that most of the time when the gods communicated to humans they told them what they hoped or feared they would hear. Again, motivation trumps cognition. Mohammed was a true believer. He expected God to help him in battle. When he lost the battle of Uhud he was so surprised that he went into a catatonic state, and his followers thought that he had died (Armstrong, 2006). He did not doubt that God was his helper. That is a good example of self-deception and an excellent explanation of why religion is so successful across cultures! To have an all-powerful entity as a helper is extremely reassuring.

Fundamentalism shows cognitive simplicity. A statement such as "there is no God but Allah" is not debatable and is as simple as can be. Fundamentalists are typically poorly educated, dogmatic, and prejudiced. They submit to an authority without questioning it. However, this does not mean that there are no well-educated fundamentalists. For example, Hassan al-Turabi, the head of the fundamentalist National Islamic Front of the Sudan, has studied at the University of London and the Sorbonne, and has a doctorate. But this type of fundamentalist uses religion as a way to get power and is basically the head of a movement for political reform.

The opposite of fundamentalism is my position. I believe that reality can be approximated, with scientific work or when there is convergence among multiple observers from different cultures. There is no reference to a text, and my position requires information from many sources. The essence of fundamentalism is that only information from the one source (the sacred book) is admissible. Furthermore, my viewpoint is constantly changing as new information comes in. The fundamentalist viewpoint does not change.

Hood et al. (2005) argue that fundamentalism is extremely satisfying, and thus the world will have to live with it for a very long time. In fact, cognitive simplicity is very common so that fundamentalism is likely to spread as advocates for it, using the mass media, reach the masses. Young people who are searching for meaning and feel confused by the complexity of the world are likely to become fundamentalists. Hood et al. describe sympathetically Protestant fundamentalism. Pentecostals (who have the delusion that they speak most of the languages of most countries) and struggle with the devil (p. 107), as well as the religions that handle serpents where the faithful believe that they have the supernatural power to control the venomous snakes and thus prove to God that they are true believers, the Amish, and some versions of Islam are presented as examples of fundamentalism.

Fundamentalist Islam has four beliefs: rejection of secular views, opposition to democracy (laws made by people cannot be accepted if they violate the word of God, i.e., Qu'ran), seeking to convert the entire world to Islam, and the prohibition of apostasy from Islam (Hood et al., 2005). It is the duty of every Muslim to kill any apostate because being an apostate is worse than being an infidel (B. Lewis, 2003). Note the cognitive simplicity of this position: one is not to debate, to argue, to reason with the apostate. Killing is a simple act.

Marty and Appleby (1992) presented a somewhat different view. They emphasized the fundamentalist lust for power, and attempts to remake the world. Fundamentalists want society to be run by people who share their own perspectives. They propose radical, cognitively simple solutions to problems. For instance, some Jewish fundamentalists advocate the expulsion of Arabs from Greater Israel, which they define as the covenant that God made with the Jews, so that the State of Israel should extend its borders to the banks of the Euphrates river! Note the correspondence with the October 2005 statement of the president of Iran who advocated that Israel should be wiped out from the face of the earth. The structure of the thinking is the same, only the content is completely different. Similarly, Iranian and Saudi Arabian fundamentalists want to impose their particular version of Islam on their neighbors, and some even want the whole world to adopt their beliefs (Marty & Appleby, 1992).

Many fundamentalist movements start within a religion, in opposition to modern ideas advocated by members of their own religion. They take more extreme positions than even the traditionalists within their religions. Fundamentalists, according to Marty and Appleby, are willing to fight back, to reclaim a place that has been taken away from them, and to convert others to their point of view.

Fundamentalists do not wish to be only rational because they accept dimensions that are "intuitive," such as miracles. They wish to challenge outsiders, even members of their own religion, whom they see as insufficiently "intuitive." They use sharp, cognitively simple distinctions, such as "Us versus Them," "God versus Satan," and "Good versus Evil." Their world is uncomplicated and without conditional statements. At the same time, however, they may use modern means of communication, such as cell phones and cassettes, to influence the masses. Marty and Appleby argued that the use of modern means by fundamentalists may in the end undermine them, because faith becomes a commodity to be bought, conversion can become manipulation, deception may be used, and mechanization may result in a fictitious community instead of a real one.

Fundamentalists are opposed to the "tolerance" of the West—alcohol, nightclubs, violent or sexually explicit TV shows, rock and roll music, and so on. They are very tight (see chapter 3), developing many rules (mostly what one cannot do, what is *haram*, prohibited), and imposing them with large punishments. They are also vertical collectivists (believing that low-status members of the in-group must accept the commands of higher-status members without discussion).

Some writers equate Islam and fundamentalism, because almost all Muslims believe that the Qu'ran is the word of God, Islam means "submission," and in most versions there is no separation of religion and politics. Marty and Appleby view fundamentalism as only one aspect of Islam, not the whole of Islam. There are so many versions of Islam that it is not appropriate to equate it with fundamentalism. There are also many kinds of Islamic fundamentalism, in different countries (B. Lewis, 2003). Some are state-sponsored, promoted by one or another Muslim government for its own purpose; whereas others are genuine popular movements from below. Some are radical, some conservative, some subversive, and some preemptive. Governments in power (e.g., the Saudis), seeking to protect themselves from revolutionary waves, started the conservative and preemptive movements. The Wahhabi sect (the official religion of Saudi Arabia) is one version of Islamic fundamentalism (B. Lewis, 2003). The ones from below, such as the Sufis, are different from the ones that were started by governments.

Some empirical research suggests that fundamentalists are usually rural ignoramuses, countryside "hillbillies" (Ruthven, 2004), out of touch with modern thought. Most of them admit that the only book they ever read was the Bible. They want to ban such classics as Hawthorne's *The Scarlet Letter*, Golding's *Lord of the Flies*, and books by Mark Twain, Joseph

Conrad, and John Steinbeck, because they question faith in God or portray religion negatively.

Fundamentalism is associated with beliefs that make women second-class citizens. Feminism, they claim, is "a disease," the cause of all the world's ills (Armstrong, 2000). Among fundamentalists, there are many examples of distance between men and women, such as separate facilities, different places at parties and in houses of worship, and so on. In some Islamic fundamentalist sects when a wife asks her husband for something she must sit behind a screen. In Hinduism, women were encouraged to burn themselves on the pyre of their dead husbands (the practice known as *sati*, where the woman was supposed to become a member of a sacred class to which the wife of Shiva called Sati also belonged). Husbands never had to burn themselves when their wives died!

In Islam, fundamentalists still hold that the "holy" book allows men to beat their wives, and the stoning of adulterous women (Kepel, 2004). These ideas come from the nomadic cultures of honor that existed in the Arabian Peninsula before the time of Mohammed, and were further formulated after the death of the prophet by misogynous men to satisfy their lust for power. In fact, Mohammed was very kind to women and had great respect for them. His relationship with his first wife, who was very rich and 15 years older than he, was one of mutual respect. But as happens in the case of most religions there is a major modification of the religion as time goes by.

After the Taliban came to power, male opinion resulted in over 90% of Afghan women remaining illiterate compared with 50% of the men. In Kandahar, Afghanistan, female literacy workers were murdered. The Taliban closed 63 schools, depriving more than 100,000 women of their education, and closed the university, sending 10,000 students home, 4,000 of whom were women (Ruthven, 2004). Consistent with their cognitive simplicity the Taliban did not allow women, even those who were physicians, to hold a job because simplicity demands that they have only one role. Women with jobs have many roles, some of which may have inconsistent elements (wife, mother, wage earner, housekeeper, citizen).

Fundamentalists have a poor opinion of experts because they may overturn some cherished belief. They object to modernity, uncertainty, foreign influences (they might challenge their faith), science (it is often inconsistent with faith), and sects that are not perfectly consistent with one's religion (Armstrong, 2000). Thus, basically they are closed to new experiences.

Fundamentalists usually think that they are "better" (morally superior) than other humans. American culture, as seen in chapter 3, is a vertical individualist culture where competition is an important element. The combination of the effects of fundamentalism and culture makes American fundamentalists especially likely to have a favorable opinion of themselves (Whites are better than Blacks, Americans are better than foreigners, etc.). Chapter 1 included a study of high school students who had unrealistically good opinions of themselves. All those views are self-deceptions, but people love their self-deceptions! The trouble is that those who have these self-deceptions are generally not aware that they have them. They think that their assumed "superiority" is "real."

Some fundamentalists insist that people must dress in certain ways, and be very explicit in their public behavior to show that they agree with the in-group. Because the aim of the fundamentalists is to achieve a mythic state of affairs, Western tolerance could very easily destroy the fundamentalist's in-group, since their followers might leave the in-group without punishment. Thus, much violence is directed at members of the in-group who do not conform. In much of Islam, apostasy is punishable by death. The numerous executions that followed the Iranian revolution of 1979 and those carried out by the Taliban in Afghanistan are examples of punishment of those who deviate from the views of the leadership of the religious movement.

Among fundamentalists, the definition of who is "we" is often very narrow. Fundamentalist Hindus, for instance, take the view that Muslims, Sikhs, Christians, and tribal peoples, although they are citizens of India, are not "real Indians." Some Jewish fundamentalists often hold views about the Arabs that are remarkably similar to Hitler's views about the Jews.

Some fundamentalist Christians see themselves in Heaven, whereas other Christians, and "unsaved" members of other religions, will perish miserably. In fact, some consider Catholics as not-Christians, and Episcopalians and Unitarians as atheists; Hindus, Buddhists, and non-Western religions are seen as "Satanic." Jerry Falwell spoke for many American evangelicals after 9/11 when he said, "Mohammed was a terrorist." Fundamentalist Sunnis see the Shiah as not-Muslims; fundamentalist Shiah see the Sunnis as not-Muslims, even "infidels" (Stern, 2003). In short, fundamentalist religions are extremely cognitively simple and divisive.

Fundamentalism is related to cognitively simple political movements, and can be found in all three of the major monotheistic religions. Rabbi Kahane argued that God wants Jews to go to war to create a Jewish state from the Mediterranean to Iraq. Fundamentalist Christians murder physicians who perform abortions. Bin Laden's followers wish to reshape the geopolitical sphere to make the whole world Wahhabi Muslims.

Many fundamentalists want to return to a largely mythical past that they construct according to their wishes. Ideally, everybody would think the same way. That is a simple world. There is a large difference between Muslims who have been exposed to other cultures and tend to have a cognitively complex worldview, and those who have had only limited exposure to the outside world and thus tend to have a simple worldview. The latter can only think within the worldview provided by a narrow definition of Islam. But mere exposure to other cultures is not always sufficient. Egyptian Sayyid Qutb was sent to the United States to study. He felt miserable in New York, and thought that even the pigeons were unhappy (projection!). All the talk, he said, was about money, movie stars, and cars, and American women were most immodest. A church dance struck him as wickedly lascivious. He pronounced the United States a "vast brothel." We need here to consider Qutb's level of adaptation (Helson, 1964), which influenced these reactions. When exposed to a tight culture for years, even a church dance can appear too loose.

In summary, as we review the attributes of fundamentalism, it is clear that they are very similar to the attributes of cognitive simplicity. Fundamentalism is popular around the world because most people are cognitively simple. It is easier to convert others or win elections if one takes a cognitively simple (e.g., sound byte) position. Both educated and uneducated Muslims understand Muslim fundamentalism (Lewis, 2003). Presumably, the factors responsible for the development of cognitive simplicity, such as authoritarian childrearing, must be implicated also in the development of fundamentalism.

But the fact that there are fundamentalists in many countries leads to violence. As Harris (2005b) pointed out, religion is currently the spring of violence all around the world—Palestine (Jews vs. Muslims); the Balkans (Orthodox Serbians vs. Catholic Croats, Orthodox Serbians vs. Bosnian and Albanian Muslims); Northern Ireland (Protestant vs. Catholics); Kashmir (Muslims vs. Hindus); Sudan (Muslims vs. Christians and animists); Nigeria (Muslims vs. Christians); Iran, Iraq, and Pakistan (Shiah vs. Sunni); and so on. Everyday, the press presents violent events traceable to religion.

CONCEPTIONS OF GOD

Armstrong (1993) examined the conceptions of god in *A History of God*. A former nun who was disappointed with monastic life, Armstrong became a scholar. She realized that the doctrines she had accepted without questioning as a child were man-made. Science has disposed of the Creator God, and biblical scholars have shown that Jesus never claimed to be divine. What we know about Jesus comes from many sources besides the gospels, and biblical scholars have examined many more sources than the gospels. Of course, "true believers" only know the Bible.

Armstrong pointed out that people started creating gods at the same time they started creating art. God is the product of creative imagination. She pointed out that the conception of God has been changing over the centuries, and has included both conceptions of God as creator and also simply as the "Unmoved Mover" (of Aristotle) who was eternal, immobile, and spiritual.

That the concept of God has had a different meaning in different times and places is anathema to fundamentalists, who pay no attention to historical scholarship. The Middle Eastern idea of God emerged about 14,000 years ago. In other parts of the world other ideas prevailed, like the *mana* of the tribal chief (in the South Pacific) or the idea among Buddhists that visions and insights are not derived from supernatural forces, but are natural to humanity.

In many conceptions of god, humans had strong links with gods. For example, in the *Iliad* gods constantly appeared in dreams, and interfered in human affairs. Humans and gods have been conceived in some religions as having the same nature, in other religions as having totally different natures. Extraordinary humans were considered to be gods in the Classical World. Even in 2004, when the Greek team won the European football championship, about 100,000 people greeted the team back to Athens, and some shouted, "You are gods!" In some other contemporary religions one finds also that extraordinary humans are worshiped (e.g., in Taoist temples, on Taiwan, I saw statues of Confucius and of some successful generals that the people prayed to). Early gods had limited territorial jurisdictions, and had favorites, such as a particular tribe (e.g., the Japannese in Shinto). Later, gods were everywhere, and showed no particular favoritism.

Paganism was a tolerant religion because there was always room for one more god. Gibbon (1963) pointed out that the Roman Empire provided one of the longest periods in human history when people did not fight each other because of differences in religion. He also provided the much-quoted statement, "The various modes of worship which prevailed in the Roman world were all considered by the people, as equally true; by the philosopher, as equally false; and by the magistrate, as equally useful" (p. 43). By contrast, for monotheists one and only one god can be worshiped. In Islam, one of the five pillars of the religion is that no other gods can be worshiped.

Among the Israelites also there was no tolerance for other gods. They advocated smashing their altars, bringing down and burning their idols. That contrasts with Buddha's serene acceptance of the deities he believed he had outgrown. The monotheists are likely to incite their followers to violence against the nonbelievers, whereas the polytheists tolerated or ignored the nonbelievers. However, a nonbeliever like Socrates, who made a nuisance of himself by asking too many questions, was put to death. Thus, tolerance had definite limits.

In the 16th century, many distinguished theologians, like Martin Luther, believed in witchcraft and saw the Christian life as a battle with Satan. During that period, those whose ideas about God were different from the mainstream were called atheists, even when they had very definite ideas that God existed. For example, Spinoza had a very definite idea about God (God = Nature), and his major book was concerned with ethics. Yet, he was called an atheist. "Atheist" was used as an epithet, for example, it was applied to greedy landlords who raised the rent too high! (Armstrong, 2000). In the 1950s in America the term "Communist" was used more or less in the same way. Each culture has its own ways of insulting, which reveals something important about the culture. For example, northern Italians insult by using a derogatory quality of the person (e.g., *stupido*), whereas southern Italians insult a relation of the person (e.g., "your mother is a prostitute"). The Italian north is relatively individualist, whereas the south is collectivist, which is reflected in the choice of insults.

By the middle of the 18th century in Europe, the idea of god began to be criticized. Religion was seen as a device used by the rich to oppress the poor. The French revolution rejected religion. The intellectuals of the middle of the 19th century admired Marx's statement that "religion is the opium of the people." In 1882, Nietzsche announced the death of God. He proclaimed the birth of the Superman who would replace God; the new enlightened man would declare war upon the feeble.

NEED FOR NEW THINKING ABOUT RELIGION

Because humans need religion it is imperative that we develop a universal religion or worldview that can be contrasted with fundamentalism. As discussed in the beginning of this chapter, religion controls uncertainty. Science also controls uncertainty. Thus, science will be closely linked to this universal worldview. If religion is defined as a belief system that assumes the existence of supernatural beings, then what I am advocating is the development of a worldview, not a religion because it would not include supernatural beings. This worldview would be very similar to original Buddhism or Confucianism before 140 BCE. It would emphasize the Golden Rule and would allow each religion to keep its rituals, music, and traditions, as long as the traditions are not divisive because people feel good when they keep their traditions. It will train people to reduce their desires to a minimum, because much unhappiness stems from too high a level of desires. It will emphasize simple living (reducing desires will result in reduced materialism, overuse of the resources of the earth, and pollution). The deterioration of the environment may stop.

It would teach people to ask before they act, "What would the world be like if everybody did what I intend to do?" (Kant, 1785/1959). Only if they see a good outcome from such action from the point of the well-being of many others should they act that way.

My proposal is that we respect all religions and let them do what they wish inside (symbols, traditions, ritual, music), but not outside (missionaries, advocating interreligious conflict) their purview. However, under some conditions even missionaries can be tolerated if they bring modern medicine to people who otherwise have no access to it. Changing the way of life of a culture requires great care, and can only be justified if it increases subjective well-being, leads to better physical and mental health, to more longevity, and does not destroy the environment.

Unfortunately, in the modern world fundamentalist religion has become intertwined with terrorism, and thus we now turn to an examination of that phenomenon.

6

Fooling Ourselves in Terrorism

The word "terrorism" was introduced in 1795 and was used to denote the intimidation of civilians by their government (Lee, McCauley, Moghaddam, & Worchel, 2004). This is now called *top–down terrorism*. The study of terrorism is popular. There is even a two-volume book called *Encyclopedia of Terrorism*, which has more than 1,000 pages dealing with the topic. Terrorism now may be defined as indiscriminate use of violence against civilian noncombatants in the pursuit of a political aim. Another definition is "the strategic use of terror for the advancement of one's objectives" (Kruglanski & Fishman, 2006, p. 201). In modern terrorism most of the violence is perpetuated by a substate, rather than a state. It can be distinguished from freedom fighting, which involves the overthrow of a regime deemed to be oppressive (Keeley, 2002). Ganor (2005) distinguished terrorism from guerrilla warfare (i.e., a deliberate attack on military personnel to achieve political aims), and from criminal activity, political protest, and revolutionary violence as well. McCauley (2003) defined it more broadly, to include top–down terrorism, such as the liquidation of 42 million people by Stalin, 37 million by Mao, and 20 million by Hitler, as well as from below. I deal here only with "terrorism from below." M. Bloom (2007) provided a good history of terrorism from the ancient Greeks and Romans to the present. McCauley (1991) discussed terrorism and public policy.

The essence of terrorism is the spreading of fear in a significant segment of a population. One may wonder how effective it is. Unfortunately, it is effective. World leaders tend to make pronouncements of the "you are not going to change our way of life" variety in response to terrorist attacks. I am afraid that such pronouncements include self-deception. It would be nice if terrorism made no difference, but in fact it does. Consider the way the life of air travelers has changed all over the world and the restrictions on civil rights. Specific instances include the departure of Spanish troops from Iraq after the Madrid train station bombings, the troop reductions by Britain, Italy, Poland, and others after the London terrorist attacks; and the departure of Arab-country ambassadors after the terrorist execution of the Egyptian ambassador to Iraq in 2005.

However, while recognizing that terrorism can be effective, one needs to consider that terrorism is used by the weak to force the strong to over-react and become self-destructive. When the strong fall into this trap they overplay their hand and hurt themselves. For example, the Bush Adminis-tration played into the hands of the terrorists by elevating their crime into a "war on terrorism." The terrorists love to use the "clash of civilizations" lingo because it glorifies them. They love to see themselves as defending Islam against the "unbelievers." The Iraq war was a colossal error, because it increased the ranks of the terrorists. The provocation by Hezbollah in Lebanon in 2006 resulted in Israel losing international support and being accused of "crimes against humanity."

Many people today associate terrorism with Islam. However, terrorism is practiced by the Right as well as the Left, atheists, Christians, Jews, and Hindus (Richardson, 2006), and even by Buddhists (in Sri Lanka). Nev-ertheless, terrorism is more acceptable in Islam than in other cultures, as argued by Darwish (2006), who is a Muslim opposed to terrorism. She dared to ask, "What gave my people the right to destroy the world in the name of Allah?" (p. 197), and the reaction was to call her an "infidel." In short, according to some imams if you are a "good" Muslim you must favor terrorism.

There is a strong tendency among observers of terrorism to assume that psychopathology is the cause of terrorism. However, most analysts of terrorism do not think that personality attributes are a major factor accounting for terrorist behavior (Kruglanski & Fishman, 2006; McCauley, 2002; Sageman, 2004). In fact Richardson (2006), a Harvard professor, wrote that "there but for the grace of God, go I" (p. vi) because as an undergraduate she almost joined the Irish Revolutionaries. Rather than thinking in terms of personality we should be thinking in terms of the effectiveness of terrorism in the case of people who are weak and are facing formidable military powers (Hafez, 2004). Suicide bombers are the smartest bombs that have ever been devised because they can be accu-rate, devastating, and create fear for a very long time. In the period from 2003 to 2005 posttraumatic stress disorder became an epidemic among the U.S. troops in Iraq, as discussed on NPR's NOW program in May 2005.

Rather than think in terms of psychopathology, one should think in terms of the terrorist as a person estranged from society (Gregg, 2005). When examining the lives of terrorists it is not uncommon to find some sort of trauma, such as the loss of a close relative, loss of personal identity, or an intensive personal humiliation. People who are estranged from society often seek others who are similarly estranged. One of the most important factors in terrorism is the desire to cooperate with others who are similarly estranged (Abrahms, 2008).

Nevertheless, some terrorists have split personalities (Stern, 2003), similar to the case described in the book and the film *The Three Faces of Eve*. Psychiatrists Thigpen and Cleckley (1957) provided an account of a woman who had 22 personalities, and after 20 years of therapy finally developed only 1. Some terrorists have a personality that is very benign when dealing with the in-group and ferocious when dealing with the out-group. As discussed in chapter 3, a large difference in social behavior toward in-group and out-group members occurs in collectivist cultures. Thus, individuals from collectivist cultures are especially likely to develop this kind of split personality. A large study of more than 1,000 Muslims from the Arab countries, Indonesia, and Pakistan found empirical evidence supporting the point that those who tend toward collectivism endorse violence against the West. The study is expected to be published in *Political Psychology* in 2009.

More specifically, in this case, one of their selves is kind to others, and the other self is a morally disengaged killer. It involves the creation of an identity that feels no empathy for the other, and is based on opposition to the other. In a study by Stern (2003), Kerry Noble, former cult leader of the Covenant, Sword and the Arm of the Lord, believed killing Jews, homosexuals, Blacks, and mixed-race couples was "a way of worshipping God" (p. xvi). One is reminded of the 9/11 terrorists who also thought that their act was serving God.

Often, in many conflicts each side has megalomaniac self-deceptions in which someone from "our side," by sacrificing the self, changes the world in a significant way. Such "heroes" become historical personages when one side wins a war and are almost forgotten if their side loses the war. The self-deceptions are reflected also in the names that terrorists choose for themselves, such as "the invincibles," "the army of God," and the like.

"Cognitively simple self-deception" may be a more important way to account for terrorism than "religion." Expert analysts of terrorism, such as Richardson (2006), believe that the major causes are "a disaffected individual, an enabling group (each operation requires a supporting cast of 10 others, p. 107) and a legitimizing ideology" (p. 40). Interviews with incarcerated terrorists indicate that support from the general population and their family is very important in motivating terrorism (J. Post et al., 2003). The disaffected individual may have been humiliated, and the legitimizing ideology may be religious. For example, one martyr-in-waiting said, "The only person [sic] who matters is Allah—and the only question he will ask me is 'How many infidels did you kill?'" (p. 119). The anthropomorphism of this statement is striking! Note also the cognitive simplicity. In any case, Richardson argued that religion is rarely the main cause of terrorism; rather it is a way to legitimize terrorist actions. Other factors, such as territory, nationalism, insults, revenge, economic depravation, desperation, and the like may be as important as religious ideology.

Richardson (2006) used revenge, renown, and reaction as the three major causes of terrorism. In conversations with terrorists, they usually mentioned something the other side had done that required them to revenge the act. For example seeing on TV the way the Americans treated the Iraqis resulted in some cases in wanting to join the terrorist organization. Some mentioned that with their actions they hoped that people would be inspired to write a song in their praise ensuring their immortality. They often have self-deceptions about the reactions their action will elicit. For instance, their action might result in the Islamic world uniting against America. Self-deceptions can also be seen in statements such as "We are confident that no one can harm us if God is with us" (p. 99). Rather than thinking of psychopathology, we should think of terrorism as an effective tool (Kruglanski & Fishman, 2006). In this chapter I focus primarily on the self-deceptions of Islamic terrorists. One of their important self-deceptions is that the West is weak and corrupt and eventually will crumble under pressure. However, we will see that there are several kinds of terrorists, and each kind has a different type of self-deception.

Zimbardo (2004, 2006) made the case that even "good" people can become perpetrators when the situation pressures them toward such actions (see the original study in Haney, Banks, & Zimbardo, 1973). Ordinary people can become torturers (Haritos-Fatourou, 2002). What is required is an acceptable justification, some contractual obligation to do the act, a meaningful role (e.g., "martyr"), altering the semantics (e.g., the victims are "spies), diffusion of responsibility (e.g., God wants me to do this), and making noncompliance costly (e.g., the "martyr" realizes that not carrying out the job implies that he is not a "man"). Some of these conditions involve a self-deception.

Thus, the evaluation of terrorism is complex and we need to understand the psychological, social, economic, and political conditions that have fostered hatred of an "enemy." Religion has a role in modern terrorism, but it is not the most important factor. It helps the recruitment of terrorists ("Join us to help your Muslim brothers who are being attacked by the Americans"). In some cases it convinces the future terrorists that they will be doing "God's work" or "they will destroy the enemies of God" if they participate in terrorism. They are told, "God is pleased by your act."

"God is on our side," "We [al-Qaeda] speak for the poor and oppressed of the world" (Marsella, 2004). These fantasies must be eliminated, but only Muslims can be credible sources of the attitude change that can alter such fantasies. Cognitive restructuring of harmful conduct by religious justifications, sanitizing the language (e.g., the terrorism is defined as a "game plan"), and expedient comparisons (e.g., "The United States attacked us, so we must attack") are among the psychological mechanisms for disengaging moral control (Bandura, 2004).

A number of different mechanisms may be motivating terrorism. One scholar (Rubenstein, 2002) provided a sophisticated analysis supported by extensive citations. Rubenstein argued that "humiliating oppression" is the first factor. Superpowers are militarily successful and groups that are not able to respond in kind feel humiliated and use terrorism as the response. The second factor is that some members of the in-group cooperate with the superpower, and that results in extreme guilt/shame, and further fuels terrorism. The third factor is a sense of purification from the guilt/shame via self-sacrifice. Of course, religious beliefs such as those associated with afterlife, paradise, doing God's work, and the like are also involved.

Consistent with Rubenstein's analysis, Stern (2004) argued that the terrorist process begins with the future terrorist feeling humiliated or feeling second class. A distinction needs to be made between some of the terrorism occurring in the West (e.g., the Ku Klux Klan) and Islamic terrorism. In the case of the former, a group that had the self-deception that its members had high status suddenly realized that they were considered equal to a low-status group. For example, the Ku Klux Klan started with the perceived loss of status when Blacks were made "equal" to them during Reconstruction and again in the 1920s and after 1964. In the case of the neo-Nazis' loss of status, relative to the general population, is overcome by the perceived moral superiority of working to establish a "pure, powerful" new society. Joining a movement also increases the self-deception that members are "strong." This type of terrorist, in America or Europe, often feels "superior" in some way, because they are Christian, White, have the "right" ideology, or are German. When a low-status group becomes equal in status (e.g., Turks get German citizenship) that threatens the Germans' sense of superiority. In many cases, the felt loss of status propels terrorism. In the case of those who kill doctors who perform abortions, the loss of status is overcome with the cognitively simple self-deception that the terrorist is morally superior by preserving the life of babies.

Although my discussion of terrorism focuses on Islamic terrorism, we need to remember that much suicide terrorism takes place in Sri Lanka, among the Tamil Tigers, and there is also nationalist terrorism among the Kurds and in Chechnya and among some groups in Iraq. Pedahzur (2005) described these varieties of terrorism in detail.

At least for some Muslims, the contradiction between believing that they have the only "true" religion and poverty, poor health, and a short life expectancy can be attenuated with the cognitively simple self-deception that God "has asked them" to sacrifice themselves to change the world. For 1,100 years there has been a confrontation between the West and Islam. When the Muslims expanded into Africa and Europe in the eighth century, they saw as their goal the conversion to Islam of the whole world (B. Lewis, 1990). In the south of Spain, by the 11th century, they created a wonderful society, with philosophers who introduced the ancient Greeks to the West, who brought mathematics from India, who had universities, and hospitals where physicians were accredited. For example, Averroes (1126–1198) was a famous commentator on the work of Aristotle who mastered theology, jurisprudence, mathematics, medicine, and philosophy. However, the counterattack of the West in the 15th century was an effort to overwhelm the Muslims and put an end to Islam (B. Lewis, 1990). In the 19th century, the West was more successful than the Muslims and that has humiliated Islam. Even today, bin Laden hopes for victory to establish Islam as the religion of the whole world. Thus, this confrontation is part of the history of today's terrorism.

Humiliation is a broad term and includes feelings associated with revenge. Certainly, revenge is at times a motive for terrorism when another person or a group has killed a person's relatives. Reciprocity is a human universal (Gouldner, 1960). Sometimes retaliation is made explicit, as happens in the Israeli–Palestinian confrontation, when the Israelis have killed a Palestinian and the terrorist organization "justified" the terrorism with reference to that event.

Cognitively simple people have only one or at most a few identities. When the one identity is threatened the reaction is more violent than happens when the person has multiple identities and one of them is threatened. Research shows that when an identity is threatened, individuals experience strong hostility toward the threatening agency. Among Muslims, the identity of being Muslim is likely to be very strong. Modernity and globalization include the view that all religions are equally valid, which is offensive to many Muslims because they believe that they are the *only* religion that does what God wants done. They assert that the Qu'ran is the word of God, and no other religion reflects God's commands as does Islam. Additionally, globalization tends to use English as the common language, but because the Qu'ran is in Arabic, God speaks Arabic, and the use of an "inferior" language, instead of God's language, is also offensive. Thus, among some Muslims, modernity and globalization can generate hostility toward countries that are modern or strongly associated with globalization.

Fundamentalist religions are opposed to modernity. Modernity emphasizes a secular perspective, which makes it, in the views of fundamentalists, the "enemy of God." Fundamentalism is a perspective that is cognitively simple, and is attracted to other cognitively simple perspectives such as Nazism and communism. Thus, in the 1930s the Middle East easily allied itself with Hitler. The Baath parties were copies of Fascist regimes. When Nasser came to power in Egypt he attempted to modernize the country, and allied himself with the Communists. Soon, the Communists were dominating that region, and the United States supported Israel as a counterweight to the Communist influence. The struggle between modernity and theocracy became especially clear in 1979 during the Iranian revolution against the shah.

The colonial powers and later the United States supported regimes that were not democratic, but were theocratic, such as Saudi Arabia, so as to keep the oil flowing smoothly. The Saudi regimes financed Wahhabi Islam, which is compatible with Sunni but incompatible with Shiah Islam. Funds were given to *madrassahs* that taught an anti-Western, antimodern ideology. This ideology was especially useful when the *jihadists* fought the Soviet Union in Afghanistan. In short, al-Qaeda's ideology has a considerable anticolonial, antimodern, and theocratic basis. In any case, once the al-Qaeda terrorists are trained, they are urged to take action on their own. "Use your own money; do not wait for instructions from the top." Their dispersion makes anti-terrorist measures difficult.

Modernity is associated with cultures that are complex, loose, and individualist. Fundamentalism has cultures that are relatively simple, tight, and collectivist. Understanding the roots of Islamic terrorism is impossible without understanding this contrast and the history of the cultures of that region.

In some of Islam there is a link between Islam and violence as a result of strong influences by cultures of honor (Nisbett & Cohen, 1996), which are more militant than other cultures, and because Islam is tight. Tightness results in a high probability that humans will break some rule or norm. That is only human. Breaking rules results in Muslims feeling guilty, and believing "I am not as good a Muslim as I should be." Then, they look for a way to become "good" Muslims. The recruiters of terrorists convince simple-minded people to blow themselves up in order to become really good Muslims. Moreover, the "package" of rewards promised to martyrs (see later discussion) is extensive, and includes the elimination of all previous sins, thus the fact that one broke some rules is no longer relevant if one becomes a martyr.

Not only killing oneself but also killing others can be seen as being a "good Muslim." Remember that in the Netherlands, Mohammed Bouyen, who killed Theo van Gogh, the producer of a film critical of Islam, said in court: "I acted in the name of my religion." In short, by killing he saw himself as a good Muslim.

Another effect of tightness is that it may make some young Muslims more fundamentalist than their parents. The mechanism is a bit complicated. The first point is that in all cultures young men resent those in authority. In 19th-century Vienna, Freud developed the argument that there is an "Oedipus complex" that includes hostility toward the father. Among the Trobrianders, a matrilinear society of the South Pacific, Malinowski found that hostility was directed toward the mother's brother, who was the person in authority in that culture. When those in authority are authoritarian, the son is especially likely to resent authority. As a result, he is likely to try to become ideologically different from the source of authority. Becoming very much more or very much less tight than the father can accomplish this. But because Islam is tight, revolting against the father by becoming loose implies not being "a good Muslim." Thus, to revolt against the father the son has to become much more (tight) fundamentalist than the father. Additionally, if the son has no job prospects and hates the world and himself, becoming a suicide bomber looks very attractive.

The instructional manual of al-Qaeda indicates that terrorism is conceived as reflecting "the mind of God" and the terrorists believe that what they are doing is "for Allah" (Juergensmayer, 2000). This is a superb diffusion of responsibility. Religious terrorism is symbolic and designed to make a political point and/or recruit other "servants of God." The megalomaniac element in self-deception is very common among terrorists. Some say that they are blowing things up in order to "protect" God! The cognitive confusion between a God that is supposed to be omnipotent and simultaneously in need of protection does not seem to bother such terrorists. Cognitively simple people do not pay attention to contradiction (Rokeach, 1960).

These terrorists often see modernity and the secular state as atheist and tyrannical, leaving mystic yearnings unanswered, thus they feel justified to commit acts that will change the state. They also tend to be cognitively simple, not realizing that the consequences of their acts work against their religion. Certainly, the terrorism of 9/11 in America, then in Bali, Madrid, and London has reduced the esteem that people worldwide have for Islam. These acts incited Harris (2004) to write a book advocating the elimination of all religious faiths. In short, the cognitively simple information processing ignores an important factor: There is worldwide condemnation of Islam.

Pape (2005) made a major distinction between ordinary and suicide terrorists. Ordinary terrorists are not especially well organized, whereas suicide terrorists have a strategic agenda and are especially effective in achieving their goals (suicide terrorism involved only 3% of the more than 4,000 incidents that occurred between 1980 and 2003, but killed about 9,000 people, whereas ordinary terrorism killed on the average one person per incident). Pape made a good case that suicide terrorism pays from the point of view of the terrorist organization.

Suicide terrorism, according to Pape, has three principal causes: (a) a strategic plan by a terrorist organization designed to reach a particular political goal, (b) social support for terrorism by a significant segment of a population, and (c) an individual ideology or religious orientation that makes the future terrorist susceptible to pressures by the terrorist organization to commit suicide. Pape examined the 315 suicide terrorist attacks that occurred between 1980 and 2003. About 50% were associated with Muslim fundamentalism, and 25% were perpetuated by the Tamil Tigers, a secular Marxist–Leninist Hindu-background group in Sri Lanka. The political goal of the terrorist organization is typically the "liberation" of their homeland from some out-group (United States, France, Israel, Sri Lanka, Turkey, Russia, India). Pape presented extensive data showing a correlation between the occupation of land by an out-group and the frequency of suicide terrorism and showed that, on the whole, suicide terrorism, over a more than 20-year period, achieved its political goals. Suicide terrorism is most frequent when there is a difference in religion or ideology between in- and out-group. This is because it is easier to relabel the suicide that would otherwise be taboo, as "martyrdom." Most of these suicides take place out of a sense of duty to the community or for a noble cause, such as "freedom." To "die for one's country (or religion, or ethnic group)" is universally seen as legitimate. This usually involves some occupier of one's homeland. For instance, the more Jewish settlers there are in the West Bank and Gaza, the greater the number of suicide operations.

Pape argued that when suicide terrorism is seen as a war for national liberation, it makes the so-called war on terrorism by the Bush Administration misguided. If 9/11 was due to the presence of U.S. troops in bin Laden's homeland that is a very different view of that event than the argument of the Bush Administration. Pape estimated that the occupation of Arab countries by the United States has generated 10 to 20 times more al-Qaeda suicide attacks than Islamic fundamentalism by itself.

Muslim terrorism needs to be examined in a broader historical context. Muslim intellectuals have a long historical perspective. They are still smarting over the crusades, long forgotten by the Europeans. They feel upset by the defeat and dismembering of the Ottoman Empire in 1918, which they saw as a continuation of the Caliphate (i.e., the linking of the ruler and God) and its replacement by Turkey, a secular state under the leadership of Mustafa Kemal Pasha, also called Atatürk. The dismembered empire was divided by the colonial powers into artificial states that were governed by individuals who were often seen as agents of the colonial powers.

Especially important in terrorism are self-deceptions such as "I act for the sake of God" and "there is an afterlife that martyrs will go to after they blow themselves up." Both themes are found in Atta's (the leader of the 9/11 attacks) "last will." The "will" can be found at http://abcnews.go.com/sections/us/DailyNews/WTC_atta_will.hrmal. Here are a few sentences from it: "God prepared an everlasting paradise for the martyrs..."; "God said: "Obey God and his Prophet..."; "God will provide a cover for us. ... Increase your mention of God's name ... present to God your sacrifices and obedience ... God said ... you will enter paradise. ... " It is difficult to overestimate the role of obedience in human affairs and by extrapolation in terrorism (Milgram, 1974).

Shared commitment to an ideology and group solidarity with others who have similar beliefs seem to be more important factors in terrorism (McCauley, 2002) than does personality. Abrahms (2008) emphasized the need for estranged people to work with others who are estranged as a motive for terrorism. Roy (2004) stressed the *esprit de corps* that can be found in al-Qaeda. Intensive identification with an in-group that favors terrorism is most important. The fact that 95% of Saudi Arabians view al-Qaeda favorably is a major failure of the Bush Administration. The presence of a public that supports the terrorism, in the form of bystanders who applaud terrorist acts, is an important factor making terrorism more probable. Also, a weakening of self-regulation mechanisms, the lack of focus on the detrimental effects of terrorism, such as the killing of children (a typical cognitive mechanism in self-deception) and the ability to dehumanize or blame the victims are important factors. Sanitized language, such as calling terrorism a "game" or the terrorist gang a "team," or the victims "spies" or "infidels" also increase the probability of terrorism. Terrorism may also be caused by competition among terrorist organizations for the attention of the public or for resources to be obtained from people predisposed to support the terrorism (M. Bloom, 2007).

The term *unbelief* is widely used by Muslims, especially fundamentalists, to include the West, especially the United States, Russia, and Israel. But sometimes it is used even to characterize a Muslim sect that is different from the sect of the speaker. Thus, Shiah fundamentalists sometimes call the Sunnis "infidels," and vice versa. The essence of fundamentalism is that there is a very narrow definition of who are "us" and a very wide definition of who is "them." The Qu'ran has many statements urging killing those who do not believe. Thus, this volume is a perfect example of "unbelief" that justifies my getting killed by the fanatics.

Redefining the status of the victims is common. For instance, bin Laden argued that all Americans pay taxes, taxes enable the United States to attack Muslims, therefore all Americans are guilty and should be killed. Note the cognitive simplicity: No consideration is given to that fact that many Americans would rather not pay taxes! Once the ideology states that "America has declared war on Allah" (Caracci, 2002, p. 73), it follows that one must attack it. Similarly, Hamas has argued that all Israelis served at some point during their life in the armed forces, thus they are military personnel, not civilians. Rationalizations are common in human affairs. Comparison with greater evils also helps bin Laden. America killed many people when it used the atomic bomb, therefore killing 3,000 people during the 9/11 attacks is "nothing serious." Note that the kind of logic used by terrorists often starts with the conclusion, and then assembles arguments supportive of the conclusion. This is called *associative thinking* and has been found in many cultures, including the pronouncements of the some of the leaders of the USSR (Glenn, 1981). Terrorism has greater probability of occurring when the terrorist sees a large difference between self and the victims. The difference may be based on religion, social class, ethnicity, language, ideology, values, and so on.

Hating everything, including life, naturally makes suicide bombings more probable. The contradiction between the belief that one has the ONLY "true" religion on the one hand and poverty, disease, underdevelopment, and bad government on the other hand must be grating Muslims either consciously or unconsciously. Some support bin Laden as a way to resolve this contradiction. We see here how self-deceptions and wishful fantasies undermine life itself. In short, here is a possible explanation of the events of July 7, 2005, in London. Why did these four young men want to kill their fellow citizens? Was it that they felt discriminated against, lived in poor neighborhoods, were aroused by revulsion by the events in Iraq, and hated the British? Generalized hatred can result in hating everything, including oneself. Thus a suicide mission is understandable.

This analysis of terrorism is consistent with the views of Jessica Stern (2004), who has interviewed terrorists of most fundamentalist religions, from America and the Middle East to Indonesia. She stated that terrorism begins with the future terrorists feeling humiliated. They are enraged because they feel that they are second class. By taking the identity of "martyrs," with God on their side, makes them feel strong and superior. The invasion of Iraq was also a colossal mistake because it humiliated Arabs all over the world because it was militarily successful in a brief time period. In just a few weeks the regime collapsed. Humiliation is one of the causes of Islamic terrorism. We need to recall that in the period from the 7th to the 11th centuries, Islam was glorious, both militarily and as a society with medicine, science, and art that were superior to the West. The decline of Islam relative to the West is humiliating.

The 1991 coalition occupied a Muslim country and that has been the main cause of recent al-Qaeda terrorism (Pape, 2005). Some Arabs started a new calendar, "the age of al-Qaeda" according to which 2005 is Year 4. Insurgents receive moral support from many Arabs all over the world. If we are to win the so-called war on terrorism we must reject the self-deception that we are "winning" that war. Instead, we must work to stop the humiliations that we impart around the world. Research by

Shteynberg (2005) showed that people in collectivist cultures, are more likely to want revenge against a humiliation than people in the West.

To win the so-called war on terrorism hearts and minds need to be changed. To do that, we need to put ourselves in the shoes of the local population. They see Americans as occupiers. They explain to each other that we are there (a) to wipe out Islam (that view goes back 1,000 years to the Crusades, and was reinforced by the invasion of Iraq), and (b) to get the oil. The only way to invalidate these views is to get completely out of Iraq. If we are out, obviously we are not interested in either wiping out Islam or in the oil. We should be very explicit that we are leaving because we respect Islam and we can do without the oil. As long as we stay there the local population will have its own self-deceptions, supporting its hostile views. For example, they circulate rumors that Americans are raping Iraqi women; as such rumors fit the needs of the population they are believed. It is one more example of how motivation trumps cognition. There is little evidence of rapes, but the rumor feeds the needs of the population, so they transmit it again and again. Of course, al-Qaeda will claim a victory after we leave. We need to point out that the United States went in to Iraq to eliminate Saddam Hussein and we achieved that. After accomplishing that we determined that our presence was causing too much tension, so we left. It is not possible to win all the hearts and minds. The local people will have their self-deceptions no matter what we do. But some will accept our arguments, and that is the best that can be achieved.

TRANSLATIONS OF AL-QAEDA WRITINGS

Ibrahim (2007) published translations of the writings of the leaders of al-Qaeda, bin Laden and Ayman al-Zawahiri. A few quotes that seem useful because they provide information about the motivation and way of thinking of some terrorists are presented here. They also provide good examples of cognitively simple self-deceptions.

Motivation

slay the idolaters whenever you find them. (p. 11)

Al-Qaeda was especially upset with a declaration by Saudi intellectuals titled *How We Can Coexist*. It was too conciliatory, and "prostrated to the West." They wrote a 40-page critique in which they included all kinds of inaccuracies (e.g., Hindus burn women along with their husbands, something that was stopped many years ago; they stated that the West does not practice any religion, suggesting that they have the cognitively simple belief than only Islam is a religion), they included exaggerations of

Muslim suffering, claimed that only their own views have any validity, they objected to the statement that "there is no compulsion in religion," which they characterized as a distortion of the truth (actually the statement is in the Qu'ran, but the Qu'ran has many contradictory statements, and its early parts are quite reasonable, whereas the last part is much more negative, so that one can sample the negative part and claim that the early part is false). They tell the Saudi intellectuals that they have no right to speak for all Muslims (only al-Qaeda can do that) and they are upset by the effort of the Saudis to bring Christianity and Islam closer to each other. They state that the West is correct in thinking of Islam as the religion of jihad. They claim that the Saudi declaration "destroys religion," ignores the "fundamentals" of Islam, is apostasy from religion, and "pulverizes Muslims." They object to moderation. They claim that according to the West's definition of terrorism, Mohammed was a terrorist and because he is a model for the behavior of all Muslims they should act that way also. They associate jihad with glory, honor, and truth.

Al-Qaeda defines the in-group as Muslims and the out-group as non-Muslims and stresses the need to fight the out-group, which is characteristic of collectivist cultures (see chap. 3). A clash between Muslims and non-Muslims is inevitable. They believe it is acceptable to deceive non-Muslims. They see loyalty to the in-group and enmity to the out-group as totally appropriate. They claim that Allah forbids friendships with the infidels: "Befriending believers and battling infidels are critical pillars of a Muslim's faith" (p. 111).

Cognitive Simplicity

All Muslims are obliged to overthrow any leader who does not govern according to *shariah* law. Islam and democracy are totally incompatible.

al-Qaeda actions can be summarized as "an eye for an eye." (p. 6)

fight them until … all religion belongs to Allah. (p. 13)

Every American man is an enemy. (p. 281)

Self-Deceptions

The West will convert to Islam. (p. xxix)

Allah loves those who commit suicide for religion. (p. 150)

The infidels will not stop until they destroy the believers. (paraphrased from p. 79)

[Note: It is typical of attackers to claim that they are defending themselves.]

May Allah place the London bombers in Paradise. (p. 183)

The writing of al-Qaeda is highly ethnocentric, which is an aspect of self-deception because they condemn any norm that is different from Islamic norms (e.g., the charging of interest, the drinking of alcohol, using women to serve passengers on airplanes).

AIDS is an American invention. (p. 204)

The White House creates wars in order to enrich American corporations. (paraphrased from p. 207)

The murder of Sheik Ahmad Yassin "terrified the whole world." (p. 234)

This is a good example of the "False Consensus Effect." (Kruger & Clement, 1994)

In summary, we see here people who process information poorly, are cognitively simple, and employ numerous self-deceptions, aiming to impose an Islamic theocracy on the whole world. Such psychological states are probably very difficult to change, thus making any kind of discussion with them fruitless. It is unclear if most terrorists share this ideology, but I guess that many do.

A TYPOLOGY OF TERRORISTS

There are several types of terrorists. The motivation and self-deceptions of an individual terrorist are likely to be *a mixture* of the motivations and self-deceptions of the various types. We now turn to a detailed discussion of eight types of terrorists, and their self-deceptions.

Type I Terrorists: Middle-Class Ideologists

Most terrorists are male. However. there are also some female terrorists. In this section I use he, rather than he or she, to make the reading a bit easier.

Type I is a middle-class ideologist who is out to change the world. He is likely to have some sort of megalomania, believing that he can really do so. Sometimes a protest takes place, such as opposition to the presence of atomic weapons in Germany as in the case of the Baader-Meinhof gang, or opposition to the Vietnam War as in the case of the Weathermen. When the protest does not have an effect, terrorist acts follow to make the public notice the views of the protester.

Also very important in the case of Type I Muslim terrorists is the belief that hurting the West is favored by a large number of Muslims. The more outrageous the terrorism, the more likely it is that young men will join the ranks of al-Qaeda (Kepel, 2004). Thus, bin Laden is not only "talking" to the West but also to Muslims worldwide, whom he wants to recruit in a grandiose global jihad to make the whole world Muslim. He aspires to become the Caliph (leader) of Islam (B. Lewis, 2003). He expected the masses to rise up against their governments as a result of the 9/11 attacks.

Although megalomania and self-deceptions are important and many people have self-deceptions, an additional factor is needed. Abrahms (2008) convincingly argued that estranged people seek others who also are estranged and are happy to cooperate with them. He stated that 80% of al-Qaeda members are cultural outcasts living at the margins of society. If the others are terrorists, they also become terrorists. In this case, terrorism can be seen as "value-expressive," that is, it gives the terrorists the chance to tell the world what it is that the gang of estranged people hate.

Type I terrorists are middle or upper class and "modern." They are familiar with technology, the Internet, and if they marry are likely to marry a woman of their own choice rather than someone specified by their parents. In fact, these terrorists are usually cut off from their parents, as can be seen from the observation that the families of the 9/11 perpetrators were surprised that their offsprings were involved in the event and claimed there must have been a case of mistaken identity (Roy, 2004).

One subtype of Type I terrorist comes from the Arab countries (Egypt, Saudi Arabia), whereas the other consists of Muslims raised in the West, who experienced racism, loneliness, prejudice, and discrimination and were converted to fundamentalism by fanatical mullahs in the West.

The first subtype does not come from the poorer Muslim countries, such as Somalia (Sageman, 2004). Sageman obtained data on 394 terrorists available in the public domain. Of these, 75% came from upper- and middle-class families, and from the more wealthy Arab countries. Far from being immature teenagers, their average age was 26, 75% had professional training, and many went to secular schools. His analysis suggests that at some point these individuals were disappointed, even humiliated, in their secular life. Something dramatic happened, as when Atta (the leader of 9/11) went to Saudi Arabia on a hajj and returned committed to do something "for the glory of God," or Tamil Tiger Dhanu (the woman who killed Rajiv Gandhi) was gang raped by soldiers. These individuals found and joined comrades who had similar difficulties, were intensely religious, and hated outsiders. In short, most had friends in the jihad or a strong ideology and simply joined them.

This type of terrorist does not fit well in his society. He might not be able to get the kind of job he considers ideal. He shifts from secular to religious values. Instead of career advancement and material wealth, he focuses on self-purification or an inner struggle for the sake of God (greater jihad). Thus, authentic Islamic spirituality (mythos) replaced professional life (logos). The shift was from the material to the spiritual, from a short- to a long-term vision, from individual concerns to communitarian sacrifice.

Divisive Muslim mullahs suspend normal morality when dealing with the out-group. Dr. Abdel Rahman, famous for his participation in the 1993 attack on the World Trade Center, stated, "Taking gold from a Christian is not theft" (Wright, 1985, p. 183).

We must not confuse the perpetrators of the 9/11 events with the overwhelming majority of Muslims. Their relationship to Muslims is the same as the relationship of the Khmer Rouge or Mao's Cultural Revolution to communism. They have something in common, but they are a fringe group. Lewis (2003) stated that from the point of view of orthodox Islam, the attacks were a blasphemy because the perpetrators claimed to be doing them in the name of God, his Prophet, and His scriptures. Orthodox Islam does not allow the killing of innocent people. Thus, the attackers were theological outcasts.

We must think of terrorism as an edifice. It has several bases on which the edifice is built. Most fundamental is the realization that a large segment of humanity (about 800 million according to UN estimates) is starving for lack of food. When people see children starving they become very angry. Furthermore, many of these starving people (especially in Africa) are fellow Muslims, sick (with AIDS, etc.), without clean water, and in many cases refugees (according to the BBC, 80% of all current refugees are Muslim) who are displaced by ethnic conflict and civil wars.

Thus, here we have a powerful contradiction in the minds of the potential terrorists. They may well say to themselves, "We live according to the word of God (i.e., the Qu'ran), and yet we suffer. There must be a devil that is creating this condition." Who is that devil? Obviously it is modernity and the West, especially the United States.

The link between the West and Satan is explicit in the manual for the 9/11 attack, found in the luggage of terrorist Mohammed Atta (Mneimneh & Makiya, 2002). It states that those who admire Western civilization are followers of Satan. The belief that Satan exists is widely found among monotheists, so this can be a powerful argument against adopting Western views.

Terrorists of this subtype, then, are intellectuals in undesirable social environments who are inclined toward action. It is notable that social change is incremental rather than all or nothing. Most revolutions do not accomplish their most radical agendas. Specifically, the French, Russian, and Chinese revolutions that tried to change the nature of humans did not succeed. After some years, the French went back to their aristocratic behaviors, although admittedly without the role of the church and without the substance of exploitative estates that existed prior to 1789. By 1990, the Russian revolution had failed and religion became important once more. By 1975, the Chinese revolution shifted to "it is good to be rich."

The conclusion from this argument is clear: As long as superpowers occupy lands, have policies that increase socioeconomic inequalities, and support aspects of colonialism perpetuated by the International Monetary Fund (Stiglitz, 2002), discrimination, injustices, and domination of societies by a small elite, there will be revolutions and terrorism.

Upper middle-class people in some parts of the world sometimes read history selectively to promote their ideology. They hold self-deceptions that glorify their in-group and fuel violence. A good example is provided by Jewish terrorism. The chief of the Israeli Security Service considers the Jewish radical right groups as having a lot in common with Hamas (Stern, 2003). They read the history of Israel selectively, so that they view the land from the Mediterranean to the Euphrates as "belonging" to Israel. They have the self-deception that "it was given to them by God" thousands of years ago. The settlements are a way to start taking it over, although UN resolutions and international law are inconsistent with these actions. At this time about 200,000 settlers are located on Palestinian land, twice their number as at the time of the Oslo Agreement of 1993. There is a correlation between the number of settlers and the number of terrorist incidents (Pape, 2005).

Additionally, the Jewish extremists would like to blow up the Haram al Sharif or Dome of the Rock. This is an exquisitely beautiful building built between 688 and 691, and is the place where, according to Muslim self-deception, Mohammed rose to heaven and a handprint of the angel Gabriel is embedded in the stone. As an admirer of art and architecture I visited this building many times in between 1984 and 1986. I would consider its destruction a sacrilege similar to the destruction of the Buddhist statues by the Taliban in Afghanistan. Yet the local Jewish extremists consider that the building is "temporary" and that it should be destroyed in order to build the Third Jewish Temple, on the site that was traditionally the location of the earlier Temples. They see the land as "sacred" and as the only place where the temple can be built. Thus, their thinking is simple, narrow, and uses magic (the law or contiguity).

King Solomon erected the First Jewish Temple around 1,000 BCE. It was destroyed by the Babylonians in 586 BCE but was rebuilt as the Second Temple. The Romans in 70 CE, in turn, destroyed it. The current extremists want to build the Third Temple on the very spot where the Dome of the Rock is located.

The self-deceivers of all three monotheistic religions believe that "they know" that the Messiah will come and reign from that small peak. The Jewish Temple, according to one of the extremists, is like a "telephone link to God." It is "just as the navel is found at the center of a human being, so the land of Israel is found at the center of the world, Jerusalem is at the center of the land of Israel, and the Temple is at the center of Jerusalem, the Holy of Holies is at the center of the Temple, the Ark is at the center of the Holy of Holies, and the Foundation Stone is in front of the Ark, which is the point of Foundation of the world" (Stern, 2003, p. 89). This is the triumph of self-deceptive ethnocentrism. Ethnocentrism is linked to prejudice and war. The Messiah fantasy is dangerous for our species, since some fanatics favor an atomic war to speed up the coming of the Messiah!

Placing this type of terrorism in an even broader framework, we note that humans sometimes place violence in a grandiose framework of saving their religion, their ideology, their language, or some other in-group attribute.

Grandiose frameworks that link violence with religion can be found in many religions: the Hindu tales of the Ramayana and Mahabharata were accounts of wars in which gods and kings fought. Similarly, the Buddhist Dipavamsa and Mahavasma provided accounts of the glorious battles of their kings. The Old Testament contained many wars. Later, the Crusades and the wars of religion provided Christian examples. The link of violence and religion may well go back to the times when humans were hunters, killing animals and each other. They had to give meaning to what they were doing and inventing religions helped in doing that. Humans have a tendency to inflate perceptually their selves. When others challenge their image that they are at the center of the world or God's chosen people they become violent. Because their fantasies are not based on evidence there is nothing to discuss; fighting is the only thing they can do.

A subtype of Type I terrorist comes from immigrant communities in the West and is a neo-fundamentalist reacting to Westernization, and responding to loneliness, racism, prejudice, and discrimination (Roy, 2004). The worldview of this subtype is cut off from the original cultures and attempts to build a universal religious identity that is neither Western nor linked to the original cultures. Modernization includes a shift from collectivism to individualism (see chapter 3). Western Muslims often stress the importance of the self (individualism), which is often antithetical to their original cultures. The result is that some Muslims in the West pay more attention to individual than to cultural-religious issues. This infuriates Muslim religious leaders in the West who are losing control of the masses, thus they become especially fundamentalist. They manage to convince some of these young men, to become "born-again" fanatical Muslims. Conversion to fundamentalism takes place both in mosques and in jails, since many of these young men do not fit well into Western culture and are in jail. Western governments need to develop programs of cross-cultural training (Triandis, 1994) to help such young people adjust to their new culture. But most of the governments use a "sink-or-swim" approach, and the sad truth is that these young people are unable to swim.

In any case, the self-deception of Type I terrorists is that through martyrdom they will change the world in favor of Islam, and go to paradise. To modify this type it will be useful to have respected Muslims argue that (a) martyrdom is unlikely to change the world, and (b) it is incompatible with Islamic orthodoxy to kill innocent people. According to a paper presented by a psychologist at the Asian Psychological Association meetings in Bali, Indonesia, in 2006, such arguments can be 90% effective in rehabilitating terrorists. I am not convinced, but let us encourage more research along these lines.

Type II Terrorists: The Desperately Poor

Type II terrorists are very poor and live in an extremely unsatisfactory environment. Among 20- to 30-year-old Palestinians, for instance, unemployment is close to 80%. They have no prospect for a job or marriage. For many of these young people, death is better than life. This is especially so when martyrdom promises a wonderful afterlife. Deprivation (of food, clothing, money) combined with exposure to authoritarian parenting, and a limited range of choices increase the probability that an individual will become a terrorist (Freeney, 2002). Pape's (2005) data suggest that this type of terrorist constitutes about 10% of the suicide incidents.

"Rather than causing terrorism, poverty and inequality are risk factors that increase the likelihood of terrorism" (Richardson, 2006, p. 57). In some countries, living conditions are extremely unsatisfactory. This is the breeding ground for Type II terrorism. In chapter 1, I summarized some of the determinants of subjective well-being. Many of the factors that lead to subjective well-being are lacking in many countries, which increases the probability of terrorism.

However, most poor people will not become terrorists. Only very few, especially when inspired by some elements of Islam, will turn to violence. Some of the elements that may be relevant are discussed here.

A detailed profile of Iran, Kuwait, Bahrain, Saudi Arabia, Egypt, and the North African countries (Wright, 1985) shows that some of these countries do not provide basic services to their citizens, such as a free primary school education, medical care, and old-age pensions. Under such circumstances it is easy for recruiters to convince sexually repressed young men to become "martyrs."

The inadequacies of the governments of these countries suggest that some of their citizens may become terrorists. In a more general sense there is resentment and envy (Piven, 2002) in the countries that have a low standard of living, generally found in the "South," against the wealthy countries found in the "North." Terrorists of this type are expressing the envy of the South for the wealth of the North. Some men are eager to join al-Qaeda, and other terrorist organizations because that increases their status and provides resources. Terrorist organizations have links also to other radical, revolutionary, often Marxist, organizations. It is an ideology that fights the inequality of some humans having yachts while others live on $1 per day.

The "martyr" is likely to point out that we all die, so one might as well die "for the sake of God" (Hafez, 2004, p. 7). The self-deceptions are embedded in the Qu'ran where in chapter 2, verse 154 it states that "And call not those who are slain in the way of Allah 'dead.' Nay they are living only ye perceive not." The mission is often described as a "test" or a challenge to prove one's courage and manhood. The advantages of "martyrdom," according to the Prophet, include

1. Remission of one's sins at the moment the martyr's blood is shed.
2. Immediate admission into heaven, so martyrs do not suffer the "punishments of the tomb." (Note that this assumes that dead people are aware of their tomb!)
3. The privilege of accompanying prophets, saints, and righteous believers in heaven.
4. Marriage to heavenly maidens.
5. The right to intercede with God on behalf of seventy relatives.
6. Protection against the pain of death.
7. Entry into the highest gardens of heaven (Hafez, 2004; Ibrahim, 2007).

The "Gardens wherein flow rivers" (Qu'ran, chapter 3, verse 195) is likely to be especially appealing to people living in the desert. The manipulation of the believers with these promises is likely to be effective because death is made to seem so easy and the rewards so many. Humans probably did not develop the self-deception that there is an "afterlife" until agriculture developed, when they saw that plants go through different phases. Unfortunately, it is now a lethal fantasy that fuels terrorism and could result in the end of our species if the terrorists get hold of atomic weapons.

In Palestine, many parents are worried that their children will become martyrs, and seek help from Palestinian mental health workers. However, there are also parents who state that they are joyful that their children have become martyrs. In one case, a man had three wives and 25 children. One can see that, in that context, a loss of one child in return for the SR 20,000 ($5,333) that Hamas gives to each family, to which Saddam Hussein used to add $10,000 to $25,000, makes the sacrifice more tolerable.

Hamas is definitely aware that poverty, humiliation, deprivation, and hopelessness make martyrdom and paradise more appealing. When Israel was formed in 1948, 600,000 Palestinians were evacuated. Now, with the lack of family planning, they have become 4.5 million. The population explosion guarantees poverty. Hamas tells its followers that all Israelis serve in the army so they are not civilians but military, and thus killing them is acceptable. Furthermore, the pattern of attacks on economic targets by al-Qaeda, in the United States (9/11), Turkey, and Saudi Arabia, suggests a plan. The plan may be to make the world as poor as possible and thus increase the flow of martyrs. In fact, the plan is partially successful. The 9/11 terrorism attacks did cost about $80 billion and pushed 11 million people in the developing world into poverty (Annan, 2004). It has resulted in the bankruptcy of several American airlines, and United Airlines abandoned its pension system.

The link between religion and power is seen in the way innocent children are sometimes used to attain the political goals of the mullahs. For example, during the war between Iran and Iraq, young Iranian volunteers ran over minefields to clear the way for the Iranian ground assault. The martyrs-to-be wore white headbands to signify that they embraced death; they shouted *Shaheed* (martyr) repeatedly, and they literally blew themselves into "heaven" (Wright, 1985, p. 37). Islam is not just a religion. It is a complete way of life, combining politics, religion, and culture and is enveloped in fantasy.

Many martyrs are recruited from very poor families. One of the leaders of terrorists groups in Pakistan estimated that 85% of the operatives come from poor families and only 3% from rich families. Many of these families have a dozen or more sons, and it is noble to "sacrifice one to God." One mother stated that she was proud to have a son who was a martyr, but she sobbed as she said it. The father was also proud; his status and that of his village increased when his son became a martyr (Stern, 2003).

Whereas the operatives come from the poor classes, the bosses use jihad to improve their financial status. The operatives have complete faith in their bosses, but the bosses "preach about proper behavior for Muslims, but don't abide by the rules themselves" (Stern, 2003, p. 214).

Hamas exploits the poverty of Palestinians. However, at the same time it provides social services not provided by the Palestinian Authority (PA), and thus is often seen positively, whereas the PA is considered corrupt. Early Christian martyrs also received social services and rewards (Stern, 2003). Hamas uses videotapes taken of suicide bombers to publicize their commitment to sacrifice for the good of the community. Social pressure to participate in terrorism is strong, and people are threatened with ostracism if they do not participate.

Interviews with the leaders of Hamas (Stern, 2003) indicated that they saw their role as one of organizing and coordinating, not participating directly in the bombings. In short, their image is that of political activists. An aspect of organizing is to collect money from charitable organizations to fund the bombings. Government money is laundered when given to such organizations, so that there is no direct link between a government and terrorism (Stern, 2003).

Playing with words is often used to justify the bombings. For instance, Islam forbids suicide. But the terrorist leaders argue that the bombings are not suicide but martyrdom, something entirely different! We are reminded here of Orwell's (1968) discussion on playing with words among Western politicians.

Hamas has created glamour for the bombings that result in martyrdom. As a result, in the streets of Gaza, children play a game, called *shuhada*, which includes the mock funeral of a suicide bomber.

The leadership of Hamas accepts that some aspects of Western culture are desirable (Stern, 2003). They accept technological advances, democracy, elections, the information revolution, and the industrial revolution. Other aspects are rejected. They object especially to dancing, drinking, the mixing of sexes, and seductive behavior. Let us not forget that some Christians went through this phase in the Middle Ages, and some contemporary Christians agree with Hamas.

In many countries of the Middle East, divisive fundamentalist clerics work on young men without jobs or prospects, and insist that all good Muslims have the obligation of jihad (Stern, 2003). If they do not participate they will be punished in the "afterlife." The atmosphere of al-Qaeda camps is one of extreme coercion to participate in killings. Even torture was used in some cases on those who did not embrace the violent code.

But most of the members of al-Qaeda are happy to participate, because for once they feel strong. They have status, glamour, prestige, friendship, and money. Murdering the "enemies" is "doing good." Life becomes clear and simple. Good and evil are in stark relief. They aim to damage the enemy's economy and provoke the enemy to overreact, thus showing his ruthlessness and weakness.

Atran (2003) argued that terrorists are not poor, and presented data consistent with this argument. However, it all depends on sampling. If one samples Type I terrorists the argument is sound. But that does not mean that Type II terrorists are uncommon.

The self-deception of this type of terrorist is that through martyrdom he will go to paradise. Improving the conditions of life in failed states can help combat this type of terrorism. Their societies need jobs, schools, and medical facilities. These states need a massive program similar to a Marshall Plan that brings funds from the developed to the developing world as needed. The EU has a mechanism for doing this within Europe. It needs to be done more broadly. At the same time, population controls policies, and policies that allow transparency in the way the funds are spent are essential, otherwise the transfer of funds will be useless or support terrorism.

The simplicity of fighting evil and doing God's work, as found in Type II terrorists, is even more pronounced in the case of Type III terrorists, who are even simpler thinkers.

Type III Terrorists: The Extremely Cognitively Simple

Type III terrorists think simply (see the discussion on cognitively simple vs. complex worldviews in chap. 3). These individuals are confused by social change that is too rapid and complex; thus they seek a simpler life. Globalization has unanticipated consequences, such as dislocation and psychological dysfunction, making the individual unable to cope with the new economy (Stevens, 2002). The cognitive simplicity associated with fundamentalism is an important element in this way of thinking. Blind conformity to a leader is an aspect of this way of thinking. Among the cognitively simple are individuals who try different religions and finally pick one that makes sense to them, such as John Walker Lindh who picked Islam (Roy, 2004). It is likely that the overwhelming majority of terrorists are cognitively simpler than their peers. But of course, most people are cognitively simple. The additional factor needed is that they feel estranged from society and by joining the gang of terrorists they find "soul mates."

The oil-rich countries of the Middle East have experienced enormous social change in the past 50 years. Some individuals who were perfectly happy in their tents found themselves in palaces, with scores of servants expecting orders. They were thrust from a simple to a complex world. Fundamentalism is a simple way of thinking and does help such individuals find their bearings.

As discussed in the previous chapter fundamentalism is related to dogmatism and authoritarianism. There is a body of research that measures these personality attributes (Adorno et al., 1950; Altemeyer, 1996; Rokeach, 1960). It has found that true believers (i.e., the ones who believe that everything in the Bible came from God and see no contradictions in religious dogmas) are dogmatic. Dogmatism and authoritarianism are highly correlated.

A simple way of thinking, found among some Muslims, can be seen in statements such as "Democracy is a great sin against God, and an oppression for the people" and "Eliminate the French in Morocco, and kill all those who speak French in public." To understand the "logic" behind these statements one needs to remember that, for divisive fundamentalist Muslims, government must come from God, not from humans. Democracy is government by the people for the people, and thus does not come from God, and therefore it is a sin. We see here how the self-deception that there is a God in "heaven" undermines democracy in Islamic cultures. Western influences oppose Islam, and speaking French indicates persons who are influenced by the West, and thus such persons should be killed. Note the cognitive simplicity: "I disagree therefore I kill. If I can kill all those who disagree with me, there will be a perfectly simple world!"

When the world is confusing, some people seek a simpler world. Under those circumstances cognitively simple people crave to link with terrorists gangs that provide discipline, and few options. The strictness of the militant religious groups and the clarity they offer about self and others are part of their appeal. Religion provides many "no-nos," thus making the world simpler.

Fundamentalist versions exist in most religions and are found in many parts of the world. They predispose people to think simply, ideologically, and associatively—an idea that is associated to a religious "truth," or assumed "truth," is true no matter what the evidence (Glenn, 1981). Dogmatic thinking is black and white, and is typical of fundamentalists (Rokeach, 1960). This type of thinking often develops when children are told without explanation that a particular norm must be observed (e.g., with a statement such as "It is so stated by the Bible, Qu'ran, or whatever other authority"). This is very different from cultures where different points of view are expected, valued, and debated, or in East Asian cultures that use dialectical thinking (Nisbett, 2003), where contradictory points of view can be both true and false under different circumstances.

The simple type of thinking also develops in *madrassah* schools, such as the ones found in Pakistan. Approximately 40,000 men are trained each year in practical skills required for war. In such schools, one learns very little else besides the discipline and advantages of jihad. One young man said that in the evening "we read books and hear lectures about atrocities against Muslims around the world" (Stern, 2003, p. 124). One of the important aims of these schools is to convert Pakistan to a theocracy. Funds come from Saudi Arabia and other oil-rich countries. *Madrassah* are schools that do not charge tuition and provide the students with room and board. The curriculum consists almost completely of religious studies. In fact, one of the principals rejected mathematics and physics, as having nothing to do with the training of "good people." "We teach them for God, not for a job" (Stern, 2003, p. 230). Pakistan does not provide free schooling, so the *madrassah* have a competitive advantage. A large *madrassah* had 2,800 students from all over Asia, including Afghanistan, Uzbekistan, Tajikistan, southern Russia, and Turkey. The ideology is not only anti-American; it is also anti-Shiah, the denomination of Islam found in Iran and in 60% of Iraq.

The Pakistani government wants to broaden the curriculum of these schools to include some science and computers. But the schools are resisting: "Why should we expand our curriculum? It was designed 1,200 years ago in Iraq and is far superior to the curriculum of the secular schools"

(Stern, 2003, pp. 227–228). The respondent mentioned that they had computers in the school but that the students downloaded pornography and one of them (horror of horrors!) even corresponded with women! In short, computers can be seen as evil!

The contrast between God's instructions about how to live (i.e., the Qu'ran) and the conditions of suffering of the people one loves corresponds to the God–devil contrast found in all monotheistic religions. It includes many more such contrasts such as believer–nonbeliever, good–evil, and so on. Dichotomous thinking reflects a simple mind.

Polytheistic religions lacked strong contrasts between good and evil because different gods did different things. Polytheism is often associated with tolerance for different religions (Gibbon, 1963). Similarly, research shows that cognitively complex thinking is associated with tolerance for minorities. Polytheism also has the advantage that one can pray to one god, and if there is no effect, one can switch gods and pray to another one (Festinger, 1983). Because there are many gods, one can keep doing this for a whole life, and never get discouraged!

In Islam, virtuous action requires acting to do God's will (to carry out God's intention), rather than according to one's own intention (e.g., for revenge, or hatred). In short, the terrorists who carried out the 9/11 attacks may well have seen the contradiction between living according to God's instruction and the suffering of believers, as an indication that God wanted them to correct this contradiction. The manual for a raid, explicitly makes the connection between the 9/11 events and the work of God. "The sense throughout is that the would-be martyr is engaged in his action solely to please God" (Mneimneh & Makiya, 2002).

The Taliban is an example of simple-minded Muslim fundamentalism. There are, however, other cognitively more complex Islamic movements. The so-called Islamists can be distinguished from the divisive fundamentalists, because they try to reconcile Islam and modern life. The Grand Ayatollah Yusef Saanei of Iran, for instance, interprets the Qu'ran as giving equal rights to men and women. He also rejects discrimination because of race or ethnicity. He even stated that abortion is permitted in the case of extreme poverty or overpopulation.

We see the terrorists as evil; but they see themselves as good. In fact they are totally convinced of their goodness. The purification of the world is a kind of bliss. This bliss is offered to those who join the terrorists. The fact that this type of terrorist can experience bliss is a very important point. "The powerful yearning for bliss cannot be denied if we are to fight terror in the name of God, the gravest danger we face today" (Stern, 2003, p. xxix).

Cognitively simple terrorists can also be found among Jews (the kind who attacked Muslims praying in a mosque) and Christians (the kind who blow up abortion clinics). An interview with one of the Christian religious fundamentalists found a desire to turn America into a Christian state with laws that are in accordance with the Old Testament. A Christian group called itself "The Army of God." This sentence translates into Arabic as "Hezbollah" (the Muslim terrorist group in the Lebanon)! Some Christian extremists hold views that are parallel to Jewish and Muslim fanatics. Here is one exchange: "Do you believe that America needs a civil war?" The answer is "Yes" and furthermore there are several self-deceptions, such as "most people that I know ... agree with me on this." "The major part of America thinks there should be civil war." "People are fed up with affirmative action, immigration" "People feel attacked. Everybody I know feels attacked" (Stern, 2003, p. 166).

In the United States, the Christian "Army of God" argues that killing abortion providers is justifiable homicide. Like American politicians, the Army of God plays with words. "Do you support violence against doctors and abortion clinics?" elicited this answer: "I support defensive action. If an unborn person were being murdered right here it would be our duty to defend him" (Stern, 2003).

The desire to "purify" the world turns activists into murderers. In 1994, Paul Hill, a former Presbyterian minister, shot and killed a doctor in Florida. He argued that the "abortionist's knife is the cutting edge of Satan's current attack" (Stern, 2003, p. 167). "The present abortion laws ... are unjust in the eyes of God" (p. 167). Again we see a megalomaniac self-deception: He knows what God sees! "One must obey God rather than men," he stated, the exact same argument used by the Muslim Brotherhood (see chapter 5). The Army of God supports the use of chemical and biological weapons. Hill was asked if he thinks of himself as a martyr and he replied "yes"(p. 170). He stated that he goes through the same life events that Jesus went through. Again we see the megalomania that is often found among all kinds of cognitively simple self-deceivers, and among patients in mental hospitals who believe that they are God (see chapter 5).

After individuals join a terrorist gang they are desensitized so they can kill. Desensitivity training requires learning to see the enemy as less than human. In the United States, cult leaders usually create their own religion, picking elements from existing ones. The cult leaders often take more than one wife. They develop an ideology that claims that America is a "sacred land" and it is time to take the land "back from God's enemies." Selective interpretation of religious texts is often used to justify violence.

An extensive interview with an Indonesian Muslim terrorist leader, whose followers have been sent to Chechnya, Bosnia, Kashmir, and Afghanistan, provides some more information about the way the cognitively simple mind works (Stern, 2003). He was a man with an elementary school education who studied Islam for years in most of the countries of the Middle East. He argued that Muslim sects that are different from his own, such as the Wahhabis and Shiah, are not "real" Muslims. This sharp black-and-white thinking is typical of cognitively simple individuals.

According to this Indonesian terrorist leader, globalization is a crusade to destroy the family. He sees a clash of civilizations between Islam and the West, and argues that because Islamic thought is far more "modern and scientific" than the system adopted by the West, Islam is bound to win (Stern, 2003). Some self-deceptions are so pleasant!

In cognitively simple cultures conformity is widespread. A 12-year-old student at a *madrassah* was asked how he feels about the Shiah. He said that they are infidels. How does he feel about America? "Down with America." The interviewer asked him why he felt that way and he answered, "Everyone says that." When asked if he knew why that was so, he answered "no" (Stern, 2003, p. 230).

On the other hand, complex thinking characterizes revisionist Muslims. They pick the 11th century as the ideal period because it was when Islam led the world, with the exception of China, in the arts and sciences. From AD 800 to 1,500, Arabic was the language of science, as English is today. Islamic medicine was sophisticated, featuring competency tests for doctors, drug-purity regulations, and hospitals staffed with nurses and interns. Arabs created the first universities, before Bologna, Oxford, Paris, and Salamanca. The decline started with the Crusades, which divided the centers of science in the Islamic world. Then the Ottomans took over most of the Islamic world, and they were more interested in conquest than in science. Finally, the colonial powers weakened Arab societies even further, so that today the Arab unemployment rate is among the highest in the developing world, the Arab brain drain is enormous, with a quarter of the graduates in the sciences leaving the Arab countries, one in four Arab adults can neither read nor write, education consists of teaching local interpretations of the Qu'ran rather than mathematics and physics. There are only 19 computers per 1,000 persons instead of the world average of 78.3.

The change from the emphasis on science to the self-deceptions associated with religion has been accompanied by a shift from complex to simpler thinking. In *The Age of Sacred Terror*, published in 2002, Daniel Benjamin and Steven Simon observed that the world has become more religious in recent years than it was in the 18th and 19th centuries. Even Zionism started by being secular and later became associated with religion. They noted the emergence of new religions, such as Shoko Asahara in Japan, and the greater religiosity of Americans in the 21st century as compared with the time of the American Revolution. At the time of the revolution, only 5% of Americans were regular churchgoers (S. Jacoby, 2004). An amazing 35% of Americans today indicate that they are thinking about the end of the world when they see the news on CNN. This shift toward religion may be another indication of escape from complexity. Religion does provide simple truths. Oklahoma terrorist Timothy McVeigh's favorite reading was the *Turner Diaries*. It is a world that explains complexity by using simple "truths." The 9/11 events have increased insecurity and uncertainty, and as a result have made people more cognitively simple, and more religious. There is considerable empirical evidence that when people feel uncertain they gain certainty by adhering to traditional behavior patterns, and they become more politically conservative, less tolerant of diversity, and less open to new experiences (Van den Bos et al., 2006).

Note the conversion of about 100,000 Europeans and many African Americans to Islam, the shift from the Catholic Church to Evangelical churches in Latin America, the loss of membership in mainstream churches in the United States while the Evangelical faiths are flourishing. In all these cases there is a shift toward cognitive simplicity. Rather than the complicated theology of some versions of Christianity (e.g., does the Holy Ghost derive from God only, or from both God and Christ?), the shift is toward a simpler faith. Islam, with its five pillars of faith, is simpler than many other religions. It appeals to the cognitively simple across the world. Research on cognitive complexity found that only about 10% of college samples are really complex. Complexity is related to education, so that most of the general population is cognitively simple. These observations suggest that, unfortunately, in the future there will be even more terrorists of this type.

The self-deception of this type of terrorist is that his world will become much better if complexity is destroyed. This type of terrorist can be countered by making people cognitively complex. Unfortunately, this is a very time-consuming activity. It requires exposure to situations of debate, where different points of view are examined. Educational programs that expose children to more than one point of view, and adult programs that permit discussion of different points of view are needed. Seeing that a solution can be good in one circumstance and bad in another would be helpful.

Type IV Terrorists: Social Failures

Type IV terrorists are social failures who are looking for a "cause" that will give meaning to their lives. Finding other social failures with whom they can work is an important factor in terrorism (Abrahms, 2008). This type may also be found in 10% of the total number of terrorists incidents.

In a competitive society some people are bound to fail. The experience of intense deprivation while others are materially successful can cause an individual to turn to terrorism. In the United States, neo-Nazi groups have this background. Successful groups, such as the Jews in Germany, the Armenians in Turkey, the Chinese in Indonesia, or the Tutsis in Rwanda, may become the targets of terrorism.

Additionally, marginal people seek a "cause" to acquire status. When they live in a secular society, with separation of church and state, they feel that religion is disvalued because it does not have a central place in regulating life. When there is no religion, they believe, there is insecurity, chaos. Terrorism can give religion public recognition.

Kerry Noble was a Christian fundamentalist terrorist in the 1980s. He was convicted of murder, of firebombing a synagogue and a church that accepted homosexuals, and many other crimes. By 1998 when he was interviewed by Stern (2003) he was a former minister, a penitent neo-Nazi, a regretful bigamist, and a repentant terrorist. Noble was a failure in high school, volunteered for the military but was not accepted because of a previous illness, and eventually was called to the ministry. This occurred after smoking marijuana, when he found himself "standing before God," who gave him the gift of teaching and pastoring. During his terrorist period he wanted to replace the "Zionist occupied government of the U.S." with a Christian one and stop "humanism" and "materialism." He felt that he had a personal relationship with God. He said he had heard God's voice and thought that he could persuade the Messiah to return more quickly by killing people. This thought pattern is consistent with the grandiose notions found among many psychopaths who think they can make the Messiah do their bidding.

Thus, he was first a failure, but after joining a group of religious fanatics he took part in plotting assassinations of federal officials, politicians, and Jews; he was also planning the sabotaging of gas pipelines and electric grids, and the bombing of federal buildings, like the one that was bombed later in Oklahoma. Such people often have grandiose self-deceptions. For instance, the leader of Noble's group of fanatics thought of himself as the "founding father of the second American Revolution" (Stern, 2003, p. 27).

One "cause" that attracts some social failures is protecting the rights of their co-religionists. Since "true faith" is attacked it is proper to kill innocents, and in their view this is religiously permissible. Fear of a godless universe, of chaos, loose rules, and humiliation, requires extreme action.

The self-deception of these terrorists is that they will become social successes through terrorism. "I will be in the news, on TV" has been mentioned in some cases. The way to approach this type requires clinical work. Seeing the difference between being famous and infamous can be helpful.

Type V Terrorists: The Power Hungry

Type V terrorists focus on power. Greed for money, land, or goods leads to behaviors that are also found in the mafia. In many cases, becoming a terrorist means that the poor young man suddenly has money, power, and prestige. Former addicts and petty thieves who find in Islam an escape from their impoverished life (Roy, 2004) as well as members of minorities (Blacks, Latinos, etc.) who find in Islam a rebuke of racism, also belong to this category. There is no information concerning the number of this type, but this type may be predominant in about 10% of the terrorists.

The motivation of the Type V terrorists is based on greed and desire for political power, land, and money. A main activity of some Pakistani militants is attacking the Indians in Kashmir, although they also attacked the Indian parliament in December 2001. Because the Kashmir dispute is about 50 years old, by now the leaders of the terrorist organization have become much more concerned with financial and political goals than with Kashmir (Stern, 2003). Some Indians in Kashmir are also corrupt, selling arms, information, food, and so on, to the Pakistani terrorists (Stern, 2003). In short, for both sides, the conflict has become a business.

In many cases, the terrorists reported that God spoke to them directly. But how did they know that it was God and not the Devil? This is the problem with fantasies. They are typical self-deceptions, where wish fulfillment is operating. Obviously, thinking that God speaks to you is more agreeable than believing the Devil is speaking to you.

Some terrorist organizations become simply criminal gangs, switching from grievances to greed. Crime can be justified as a means to the greater good. Thus, robbing a bank (e.g., the 2004 case in Northern Ireland) is seen, in the context of "purifying" the society, as a means to a good end.

A few former terrorists see through the fraud and become disappointed with the organization. Specifically, they started by thinking that the organization served a religious cause and later realized that it was a business. One of them (Stern, 2003), for instance, realized that jihad was used to enrich the leaders. The manager of the terrorist group received a salary that had the buying power of about $100,000 per year. The emir used to live very simply, but later acquired big cars, and lived in a palace. The former terrorist realized that he was being used. He wanted to write a book to expose the fraud, but his friends told him that he would be assassinated.

Al-Qaeda has complex business links to other organizations (Stern, 2003). It uses international relief agencies as a cover for espionage, proselytizing, coup planning, and transferring weapons. Charitable organizations also provide a cover for money laundering. A fraction of the funds end up in al-Qaeda's coffers. But the problem is that al-Qaeda also provides, in Muslim countries, legitimate charitable assistance to the poor, the sick, and so on. It is a kind of terrorist United Way (Stern, 2003).

Muslim charities collect money from affluent businessmen; they solicit in houses of worship, hold auctions, fundraising dinners, and press conferences. The terrorist organization has agents whose job it is to collect funds. They are paid cash bonuses for successful fundraising in different countries, such as Saudi Arabia. Money comes also from foundations that help the families of martyrs and from regional governments.

In addition, they engage in criminal activities, like smuggling, drug traf-ficking, but they do also run legitimate businesses (just like the mafia!), and they get help from some governments. They make alliances with terrorist organizations all over the world, so that they can get material help from them. Some of the organizations that have been linked to them are neo-Nazi, White supremacist organizations in different parts of the West.

Because al-Qaeda sees globalization as a means of subjugating Muslims, it strongly opposes it and has links with some organizations that are op-posed to the World Trade Organization (Stern, 2003). Basically, this is the struggle between a world order that represents the elite financial inter-ests of the world on the one hand and on the other the various national, regional, ethnic, cultural, religious, linguistic, and economic groups who wish to remain independent of the international order.

Barber (1995) argued, with some justification in my opinion, that both globalization and the emphasis on preserving indigenous cultures un-dermine democracies. Certainly, democracy suffers when corporations rather than parliaments make the major economic decisions. The case can be made that the New World Order loses its appeal among pop-ulations made vulnerable by perceived humiliation, and violations of human rights, perceived economic deprivation, confused identities, and poor governance (Stern, 2003). But also the preservation of indigenous cultures often is inconsistent with democratic processes. Democracies too often insist on the assimilation of indigenous cultures to the mainstream culture. For example, a French law that does not allow students to wear religious symbols is designed to avoid the fragmentation of France. Frag-mentation results in ineffective political action and disillusionment about democracy.

This type of terrorist is like most criminals. His self-deception is that crime will pay and he is not going to be arrested. There are short-term advantages to this terrorism; one does get power and resources but the consequences can be prison or death. Countering this type of terrorism re-quires clinical interventions that increase the development of self-control, learning to avoid immediate gratification, and acquiring a long-time per-spective.

Type VI Terrorists: Nationalists

In many parts of the world terrorism takes the form of communal conflict and Type VI occurs where there is communal conflict. One community revenges the real or assumed misdeeds of the other. This is a situational response to the actions of the other community, so that this type of terrorism may best be conceived not as a personality type but as a result of conformist social pressures. Communal conflict usually involves fundamentalist simple thinking mixed with ethnic pride and/or nationalism. The conflict in Israel–Palestine, Chechnya, Kashmir, Sri Lanka, Indonesia, the Philippines, and elsewhere is due to nationalism supported by religion. In Sri Lanka 60,000 people from the Buddhist and non-Buddhist (Tamils, Muslims) communities lost their lives in a conflict that has lasted for two decades.

In Indonesia, the Suharto government moved Muslims from crowded Java to Maluku. This changed the demographic balance, and created the impression among the Christians of that island that they were being squeezed out by the Muslims. Communal conflict developed, with riots, burning of houses, and other forms of ethnic cleansing. In some cases the Indonesian military helped the Muslims against the Christians. Many of the groups that became linked to al-Qaeda were created by the military in support of their political aims. Both sides in the conflict proclaimed their ability to provide protection to co-religionists for a fee. In short, there is an aspect of the mafia in the case of some of these terrorist groups.

Indonesian Islam is "traditional," and has incorporated elements from the religions that existed in those islands at earlier times. So, there are some elements from Hinduism, Buddhism, and animism mixed with Islam (Stern, 2003). Nevertheless, Indonesian Islam is sympathetic to the struggle of other Muslims.

Communal conflict is also found in Kashmir. After the Russians left Afghanistan the jihadists were out of work and causing trouble. Sending them to Kashmir was a way to employ them. This is an important point because it suggests that once people have been trained in jihad they need to be kept busy. If the civilized world is to avoid attacks it needs to provide constructive employment to these fighters!

Basque terrorists also fall in this category. If the Basques were to become independent their leaders would profit, but the majority of the population would only experience psychic benefits, and their economic status would probably not change much.

The self-deception of this group is that fighting other groups can be better than negotiations, discussion, and mutual accommodation. Countering this type of terrorism requires training in conflict resolution techniques. There are professional groups that provide this kind of training, but it is expensive.

Type VII Terrorists: Lone Wolves

Type VII is found in cultures of honor (see chapter 3), where people learn to be fierce. Sometimes these terrorists act as lone wolves, avenging some offense or injustice. The original cultures from Arabia to northwest China were nomadic, and thus their goods (cattle, camels) could be stolen more easily than in agricultural cultures. Nisbett and Cohen (1996) showed that such cultures emphasize honor (see chapter 3 for details). Men are trained to be fierce and warlike so that their enemies will not steal their easily movable goods. In such cultures also, lone-wolf terrorists are likely to emerge. People who are socialized to be fierce can easily kill when they have a grievance.

The lone-wolf type of terrorist is not organized into a group. Mir Aimal Kansi, who killed two CIA agents in 1993, was a Type VII terrorist. Lone wolves often create their own ideology that combines personal vendettas with religious and political grievances. Kansi was against American policies that he deemed "un-Islamic." He supported bin Laden because he stands up for all Muslims. He argued that non-Muslims deny the last prophet and do not surrender to God. They are rebellious people who work against Islamic countries. His killings were the result of revenge, and when asked if he thought about the relatives of the people he killed he said, "When I think about the family members of the victims it troubles me. But when I think of the damage the U.S. government has caused Muslims, it's much worse than what I did" (Stern, 2003, p. 176). Here again, we find selective perception. Kansi believed in a clash of civilizations, and that Islam would win because it is a superior culture. One of his arguments was that the population of the West used to be one fourth of the world and now it is one sixth, a clear "decline." On the other hand, the Muslim population has doubled. But this argument is clearly a self-deception because it focuses on the size of the population and ignores the fact that as the population of Muslim countries increased their GNP per capita decreased, their health and subjective well-being declined.

The glorification of one's own culture is a common self-deception found in all cultures. Herodotus (1966) identified this ethnocentrism some 2,500 years ago after he visited 30 cultures around Greece. Anthropologists (e.g., Herskovits, 1955) who study different cultures have repeatedly found ethnocentrism. The widely held self-deception, as stated by a member of a Florida School Board when discussing courses on diversity, is that we have the best culture in every way, compared with all other cultures and with all periods of human history.

To counter this type of terrorist requires the experience of law-and-order over a long period of time, so that the need to be fierce can become less pronounced. The self-deception of the Type VII terrorist is that terrorism can provide long-term well-being.

Type VIII Terrorists: The Ad Hoc Terrorist

Type VIII is a sleeper terrorist. This terrorist happens to have the right citizenship or language skills and is asked by the terrorist organization to "stand by" until the moment when his skills or qualities can be used. A number of these terrorists were involved in the blowing up of the American embassies in East Africa, because they had the right citizenship. The al-Qaeda personnel set up the operation and then left East Africa so they would not be caught. The self-deception of this type of terrorist is that he will have a great career as a martyr. However, often his services are not used and he is neglected by the organization.

HOW CAN WE SUCCESSFULLY BATTLE TERRORISM?

Going back to the motives discussed in the previous sections, it is clear that as long as there are major inequities in the world there will be at least one ingredient present that can fuel terrorism. However, the essential ingredient may be that people who are estranged from society are likely to become terrorists. They join groups of "soul mates." Thus, the strategy for combating terrorism has to include the development of double agents who can create doubt in the minds of terrorists that their fellow terrorists can be trusted. If they are not sure that they are dealing with true soul mates, the group is likely to disintegrate. The Italian government dismantled the Brigantisti of the 1980s by commuting prison terms in exchange for actionable intelligence, and by infiltrating the Red Brigades (Abrahms, 2008). They bred distrust within the groups. It is also worth experimenting with changing the minds of prisoners by arguing that they are being taken advantage of by the organizers of the terrorist groups, and one does not go to heaven but to nowhere, by blowing oneself up.

The Economist (July 19–25 2008, p. 17) suggests that we should highlight the views of jihandist who have renounced violence, publicize stories about jihadists attrocities against Muslims, enlist Muslim religious leaders to denounce jihadists as heretics, back Islamic movements that emphasize policies inconsistent with jihad, discredit and neutralize jihadist ideologies, play up personal and doctrinal disputes among jihadists. In sum, the idea is to create doubts in the minds of jihadists.

Another important way to deal with terrorism is to refuse to be terrorized! If we are not terrorized then we have defeated terrorism (Zakaria, 2008). Of course, that is easier said than done. However, when people are in a battle they face the probability of death. They usually stop thinking about that probability and go on fighting. If we use the perspective that occasionally some acts of terrorism will occur and we should continue to live our lives in an ordinary way, no matter what happens, we might defeat the terrorists. Again, a Buddhist perspective about not being too attached to anything can be helpful.

Thus far we examined defects in human information processing and their implications for politics, religion, and terrorism. We now need to examine if there is something we can do to overcome these defects, and increase the chances that we can move toward a world that maximizes health, longevity, and well-being for most humans.

7

What Can We Do?

This chapter discusses what we can do to make ourselves and others more cognitively complex, with fewer large self-deceptions. It suggests that there are some major problems facing the world and the United States that remain unsolved because people have cognitively simple self-deceptions. Finally, the chapter examines a number of practical things we can do both as citizens and as responsible individuals in this imperfect world to move toward the ideal of good health, high subjective well-being, and longevity for as many humans as possible without deterioration of the environment.

Most governments in the world pursue policies that do not meet the criteria of good health, longevity, and preservation of the environment. It is time for citizens to demand that their governments take these goals seriously. Governments use cognitively simple self-deceptions to pursue goals that they consider important—more economic development, territorial integrity, power for the current government, and the like. My point is that when these goals undermine the really important goal of the well-being of the population, they are not valid. Take, for example, Kashmir. *The Economist* (2006) reported that 80% of the 5 million people in the valley of Kashmir are physically and mentally unhealthy because of the conflict between Pakistan and India. Of 510 people interviewed, 10% had lost an immediate member of their family; 13% had witnessed a rape. People feel so unsafe that they prefer staying in the hospital to going home. Mental illness is widespread, with 33% of the respondents suffering from "psychological distress." The mental health of the children is undermined and an entire generation is growing up that has not lived one day without fear. The same horrible conditions apply in the Sudan, Chad,

Chechnya, Iraq, and many other parts of the world. The point is simple: should geopolitical goals have more priority than human goals? What is the morality that justifies the conflict in various parts of the world? I am not taking sides. Probably in most cases both sides of the conflict are guilty. I am just raising the question of goal priorities and the failure of policies that do not consider human well-being as the top priority.

HOW TO DECREASE COGNITIVELY SIMPLE SELF-DECEPTIONS

To increase cognitive complexity, education is the long-term method. A mindset that looks at both the pros and the cons of each issue, that requires multiple sources of evidence in support of a particular position, an emphasis on moderation (nothing in excess), the experience of debating, of arguing and an openness to new experiences are all likely to be helpful. Unfortunately, in most of the world humans do not have an opportunity to increase their cognitive complexity, and I admit that these policies are expensive and long-term. Religions also are generally opposed to too much questioning, too much looking at the other side of an issue. Thus, in general, the more dogmatic the education, the more cognitive simplicity there is.

More cognitive simplicity results when situations include time pressure, are stressful, or result in information overload, and when humans are tired or under the influence of alcohol. If most decisions require careful evaluation of many factors, cognitive simplicity is likely to reduce the quality of the decisions. If we keep that in mind, we need to stop and ask ourselves, "Am I in a situation that is likely to lead to cognitive simplicity? If so, let me take some time off, relax (e.g., breathe deeply), before making the decision."

Self-deception can decrease if people become self-critical (i.e., if they ask themselves, "Is the way I see the world due to a self-deception?"). An "internal conversation" (Archer, 2003) can decrease self-deception. Furthermore, as people reduce their needs, their self-deceptions should decrease. Unfortunately, we live in societies where the advertising industry spends billions to increase our needs. We must realize that we are being manipulated. More needs do not result in more subjective well-being. On the contrary, fewer needs set us free. Thus, it is desirable when we make a judgment to ask ourselves, "Are my needs, wishes, or hopes involved in this decision?" If the needs, wishes, and hopes are intense there is a high probability that we are having a self-deception.

Another helpful hint is that self-control and self-regulation are important virtues, and people who develop these skills are likely to have fewer self-deceptions. They might develop a program of cutting down on their needs one by one until they reach nirvana, which is a condition where one is totally free. Then one is able to help others, and that will result in high subjective well-being.

The problem is that we have a need for self-deceptions. Can we become convinced that reducing self-deceptions is desirable? Because self-deceptions are pleasant it is difficult to reduce them. Furthermore, minor self-deceptions are desirable. It is only the major self-deceptions that must be avoided. The nothing in excess principle must be used to decide what to do. In any case, mature living (Levine, 2007) and happiness require a Buddhist viewpoint that stresses being in contact with reality, but allows some minor self-deceptions. Unfortunately, it is easier to tell people "do" or "do not do" than to say under Conditions "X & Y do" but under Condition "Z do not do." The conditional acceptance of self-deception is a real problem because only cognitively complex people can use the correct perspective.

Most religions, especially Islam, foster a tight culture. Deviation from the orthodox views is punished. Then it is difficult to develop cognitive complexity or avoid self-deceptions. Furthermore, the processes described here to avoid simple self-deceptions are difficult to institute in the case of Islam because this religion emphasizes blind obedience to Allah, and does not encourage criticism of widely accepted views, self-examination, exploration of multiple points of view, and the like. However, education that requires the examination of different points of view, in domains such as technology, is likely to be nonthreatening to religion, and thus acceptable, and may start the processes outlined here.

People should be taught to examine systematically whether all relevant factors have been considered when making a decision. Are the factors supported by multiple data sets, so that they are unlikely to be mere self-deceptions? Humans are basically intellectually lazy, and are likely to ignore factors that complicate decision making. Thus, they need to force themselves to look for factors that do not first come to mind. Then they need to overcome self-deceptions by asking if a particular judgment is a self-deception. Is this perception of the world excessively pleasant? They should learn to ask, "Did we select only positive factors? Did we give negative factors enough weight?" As humans develop the habit of questioning their views and decisions, suspecting that they might be self-deceptions, they will become more realistic and accurate in seeing the world. Furthermore, it is important to learn how children acquire self-deceptions (Feldman & Custrini, 1988) and control such tendencies.

Tavris and Aronson (2007) recommended that people pay attention to cognitive dissonance. If individuals become aware that they are in a state of dissonance they might be able to avoid some foolish decisions. If a dissonant idea is encountered, it might be helpful to ask, "Could this be a good idea?"

PROBLEMS THAT WE CURRENTLY FACE THAT MIGHT BE SOLVED WITH MORE COGNITIVE COMPLEXITY AND LESS SELF-DECEPTION

The Environment

Global warming is a phenomenon that is bound to produce self-deceptions. The topic is very complex, and one can always sample information that is consistent with one's motivation and ignore information that is inconsistent with it.

There is now much evidence that we pollute the environment to the point where we have changed the climate (Flannery, 2006; Kolbert, 2006; Linden, 2006). Climatologists have stated that the probability is 95 out of 100 that the floods in Western Europe and the excessive heat in Southern Europe, in summer 2007, were caused by global warming. We can see local environmental damage with the death of the Aral Sea, the burning rainforests of Indonesia, the collapse of the Canadian cod fishery, the melting of the glaciers that supply Andean cities with water, the dust bowl forming in northwestern China, and the depletion of the U.S. Great Plains aquifer (L. Brown, 2003). There were an unprecedented number of hurricanes in 2005, which most experts attribute to the warmer-than-usual seawater in the Atlantic Ocean. Global warming increases the variability of the climate, so that both extreme heat and extreme cold are likely to be observed.

Al Gore's *An Inconvenient Truth* presents convincing evidence with pictures showing the way things were both 30 years ago and now, confirming the melting of glaciers. This is a serious matter. For example, 40% of the water used by China and India comes from the glaciers of the Himalayas, which are gradually disappearing. Thus, 20% of humanity will eventually have insufficient water. What will they drink?

Climate change causes floods in one place and droughts next door, it may change the gulf stream (which also happened several thousand years ago and resulted in an 1,000-year ice age in Europe), it may melt Greenland's ice and/or parts of the Antarctic, which may result in the sea level rising. Apparently we do not know how much it will rise, it might be 30 inches or as much as 20 feet. As climate changes there will be more tropical diseases in the most populous areas of the globe.

Some scientists, financed by the oil industry, are skeptical about the phenomenon of global warming, but the scientific evidence is overwhelming. Of 928 scientific articles published in the past 10 years, not one disputed that the phenomenon is real (Gore, 2007). Yet half the articles in the popular press argued that the phenomenon may not be "real." The problem is with the way the news is presented. The professional ethics of journalists require the presentation of both sides of an argument. Yet the public does not understand that the two sides are not equally valid. The science side represents a minimum of 5,000 years of graduate work, and probably an equal amount of data gathering and analysis. The other side is a self-deception, based on the needs of the person who expresses an opinion. That person usually has no scientific training. Thus, one side is based on 10,000 years of scientific study, and the other side on zero scientific work. Yet the press presents the two sides as being equally valid!

Here is again a case where motivation trumps cognition! Most oil companies do not want the phenomenon to occur, so they have the self-deception that it does not occur, and because they finance, advertise in, or in some cases even own the media, they inspire articles that claim that there is "no real problem." Gore showed that there is much that we can do to reverse global warming, but most of us have the self-deception that "all is well," and there is no need to change our lifestyle. He presented a number of specific steps we can take but most critics focus on a cognitively simple argument such as "the price of heating houses will increase."

Demand for water has tripled in the past 40 years and in some places it has outstripped the sustainable supply. Water tables are falling and wells are going dry. Rivers are also being drained dry. Illness due to dirty water or bad sanitation results in "close to half the population in the developing world suffering from one or more diseases associated with inadequate provision of water and sanitation services" (*The Economist*, 2004, p. 75). One of the best predictors of long life is access to clean water and sanitation. More than 50% of humanity does not have these basic resources.

As I see it, we humans may not be able to deal with this threat because it is a very complex phenomenon, and with our inclination toward cognitively simple self-deceptions we are likely to believe that "something will work out in the future." The phenomenon is complex enough that meteorologists with powerful computers have trouble tracking it. Is it likely that the general public will comprehend this threat? Nevertheless, I am a bit optimistic because of the Australian elections of 2007. For the first time in the history of the world a government change can be traced largely to the different positions on the environment between two political parties (Conservatives and Labor, and Labor won the election). Young people, who are one-third of the Australian electorate, voted primarily on the basis of that issue (NPR Report, 2007).

The threat to the environment is related to many topics, such as the population explosion, high levels of consumption resulting in the overuse of resources, the production of huge quantities of garbage, rivers that contain untreated human sewage, and so on. An NPR program (*Inside China*, 2007) documented how physical health, longevity, and well-being have been undermined by the pollution of the Chinese environment.

Population Explosion

Many of our problems stem from overpopulation. The world is already full (Korten, 1995). I have seen the problem with my own eyes. When I was young the world had less than 2 billion people; it now has 6.5 billion and is moving toward 9. I believe that 2 billion was much better than 6, from the point of view of comfort, and preservation of the environment. I have seen crowding, pollution, and extreme competition where once people used to be comfortable living in pristine environments. When I visited China in 1988 I had trouble taking a picture of the Forbidden City from the hill behind it because of the pollution. We cannot stop global warming if we do not stop the population explosion, because *each week* there is a new set of 80,000 people on earth who will want a decent standard of living that will increase global warming. If people are to have a decent life we must stop the population explosion.

> Environmental impact on the environment = population × affluence × technology
>
> —Ehrlich (2000)

In short, multiply the population by the level of consumption and the technology that requires resources and you get the impact of these factors on the environment.

Overpopulation results in competition for scarce resources. As the economies of China, India, and the rest of the less-developed world improve, the competition for resources increasingly will become more significant. The earth does not have enough resources for everyone to reach the Western standard of living. We need creative, multidimensional, realistic solutions. If we do not succeed we might become a failed species!

Turnbull (1972) described a tribe in Africa called the Ik who were displaced from their hunting grounds by a national park. The Ik had few resources, relative to the number of its members. The competition for these resources was so great that parents ate while their children starved; they took food from one child to give to another, deciding thus that some would live and others would die of hunger. It was a horrible society, which was the victim of competition for scarce resources. Unless we control the population of the earth, at the rate we are going, in another century, much of the earth might be such a society! We already have some societies that approach this condition. In West Africa one of every four children is malnourished, has a poor immune system, and is likely to die. That region has pockets that already have high levels of disease, crime, scarcity of resources, refugee migrations, collapse of nation-states, empowerment of private armies, and international drug cartels (Korten, 1995).

In Rwanda, the population density was so extreme that many people consciously decided that they had to kill as many other people as possible to reduce the density. The result was a genocide in 1994 (Diamond, 2005). Cynical politicians encouraged one tribe to kill the other. It is imperative that the countries of the developed world help the countries with excessive population increases to stop their population explosion, and increase the social services that these states provide to their people—more free education, especially for women, more health services, more social security, and more old-age pensions. Educating women will reduce the number of children each of them has, and the population explosion in general.

The population explosion is linked to the environment. At the present rate of change of the world, we are going to run out of resources. We are going to create environmental catastrophes that will eventually reduce our numbers through pollution and disease. If this happens and/or if we become like the Ik, we will have been a failed species. Diamond (2005) showed that civilizations often collapse when the physical environment is abused. For example, deforestation brought about the end of the Easter Islanders. Transporting and erecting their extraordinary statues required huge amounts of wood. As the population grew, more trees were cut down. No big logs were left to build canoes, so they lost their chance to fish, then they ate all the birds, and finally they killed one another.

Given the human tendency toward self-deception, most of us say, "New technologies will be developed that will make up for the depleted resources," "We might go to the moon or other planets to get resources," and so on. Most of these ideas are pipe dreams. The reality is that we are already in trouble and unwilling to face it.

Too many of us think of survival as a goal. That is not enough. Decent survival for *all* humans is what we need to look for. We see on TV appalling pictures of misery and drought in Africa and conflicts over land in the Amazon basin. We are far from achieving decent survival for all. We need to test our actions and our institutions against this standard: do they increase the chances of the decent survival of all members of the human race? The evidence is already clear: about 25% of humans do not have a decent life. Inequality in lifestyle is linked to violence, and misery for all, terrorism and the like.

Overpopulation and poverty are interrelated. Global poverty could be reduced if $330 billion per year, which is 1% of the global income (currently at $33 trillion per year), were directed to the goal of increasing the GNP per capita of the poorest countries. Former French President Chirac suggested that a 1% internationl tax be distributed for education and other similar projects in the poor parts of the world. It could reduce half the poverty of the world by 2010. Jeffrey Sacks and 250 experts have provided a blueprint to the UN for how this can be done successfully (*The Economist*, 2005). The world spends about $900 billion each year on armaments. If 33% of these funds were directed to education in failed states, so that the *madrassah* schools in the Muslim world could have competition from secular schools, we would be much safer.

Of course, every corner of the world is not overpopulated. In fact, the birthrates in parts of the world (Italy, Germany, Russia, Japan) are too low. In general, the wealthy countries are not growing as fast as the poor ones. If this trend continues, there may not be enough resources for the wealthy to help the poor get out of poverty. Low population growth stresses the pension systems, and is especially problematic in Japan where 20% of the population is over age 65 (*The Economist*, 2007). Longevity is 82 and people retire early because those with much tenure in an organization are too conservative and the system favors early retirement, to allow the young to bring new blood into the organization. Clearly, in such cases there is a need for social change, such as valuing the young more, allowing women to participate in the labor force in larger numbers and the like.

Overconsumption

Overconsumption and environmental destruction are correlated (Boivie, 2003). As mentioned already, if all humans had a Western standard of living the world would need five times the present resources of the earth. American corporations "manufacture desires for material goods" (York, 2004, p. 79) by spending twice as much on advertising and in influencing the politicians to adopt their goals as the United States spends on education. Buying is used to reduce unhappiness, but overconsumption is unhealthy (Kasser, 2002), reduces the quality of the environment, and is likely to exhaust natural resources.

Inequality and Overconsumption

Increased inequality is somewhat related to overconsumption, because where there is inequality people consume, in part, to establish their status in the society. Inequality is undesirable (it fosters crime, intergroup conflict, etc.), yet present world conditions leave much to be desired. In the United States, the states with high inequality of income have the highest homicide rates per 100,000 ($r = .72$).

Since the 1970s, the United States has been experiencing a steady increase in inequality. The pay of CEOs is now on average 400 times that of the ordinary employees in their corporations. In 1970, top corporation executives earned 39 times the pay of average workers (Hébert, 2003). So, on this index, at least, we are moving in the wrong direction. In the United States, the top 20% of the income distribution is now nine times greater than the income of the bottom 20%. Only 40 years ago it was six times as much. In Sweden it is three times as much. In 1968 the mean household income of the top 20% was $81,883 in 2002 it was $143,743, an increase of

75%; but the bottom 20% numbers were $7,419 and $9,990, an increase of only 35% (Associated Press, 2004). We have become a society of greed.

In many Western countries politics has become synonymous with corruption (Walker, 2002). Of course, in non-Western countries the situation is even worse (Li, Triandis, & Yu, 2006). Additionally, too many corporations have adopted a philosophy of greed, resulting in Enron-type corruption.

The appalling rates of violence in American schools are, in part, due to the high competitiveness of the society (Aronson, 2004). The children want to stand out, to be the best. When they do not succeed, when they are not popular, they become angry. Anger increases cognitive simplicity and sometimes turns to violence, especially when guns are easily available. The unpleasant harassment and bullying that occurs in schools is part of the same malady. It is an indication of too much emphasis on one-upmanship. The cheating among athletes, as reported by Sen. George Mitchell concerning baseball, is also due to excessive competition. The wisdom of "nothing in excess" is confirmed again.

Summary on Population and Environment

By considering only GNP per capita, we ignore well-being as a criterion for evaluating social change. We must use multiple criteria, and mental health is certainly an important one. A multidimensional index was developed for Australia (Eckersley, 2004), but it needs to be developed for the rest of the world

Overpopulation, overconsumption, environmental degradation, urban decay, and inequality, are key problems to be solved if we are to move toward the ideal of good health and high well-being for all. Yet most existing religions can be faulted for not providing suggested solutions to such problems. They accept the world the way it is. We need to rethink what we are doing and think of activism, government policy changes, and even suggest modest steps that anyone can take to improve the lot of humans on this planet. Religions have done a good job of fretting about poverty, poor infrastructure, crime, and international conflict, but they have not addressed the more fundamental problems of overpopulation, overconsumption, and environmental degradation.

The sad conclusion is that we have created a world that supports our illusions while we are harming other people. Such illusions often reduce our mental health. We need to assess our world critically, and change it in very many ways to control the self-deceptions that decrease our mental health.

Democracy on the Decline

In the United States, we have the self-deception that we live in an exemplary democracy. The sad fact is that our present democracy has become seriously distorted, especially since the 1990s. It is now approximating a plutocracy of some large corporations that lobby Washington to pass the laws they want, even when ordinary people want something else. No fewer than 36,000 lobbyists, of one type or another, 14,000 actually registered (see *The Public I*, 2005) are working in Washington. How many lobbyists did the Founding Fathers visualize?

Gore (2007) documented the decline of American democracy in considerable detail. One of his important points is that democracy requires information to move from both the electorate to the leaders and vice versa. The current pattern is one of information flow from the politicians to the electorate (mostly via television) and there is little flow of information in the other direction. As a result, people are not interested in the political process. The inability to influence the political process results in apathy and inattention to what is happening, and is a failure of democracy. For example, when asked to name a Supreme Court justice some mentioned George W. Bush and others Arnold Schwarzenegger! Only 11% knew that William Rehnquist was the chief justice at the time of this poll (Gore, 2007).

Obama (2006) correctly identified the need for nonpartisan voting districts, same-day registration, and elections held on the weekend as a way to increase participation in the democratic process. The more the electorate is paying attention the more integrity is rewarded. Free television and radio (see later discussion) would reduce the need for millions of dollars to win an election, which increases the influence of special interests. A number of rules in the House and Senate need to be changed to increase transparency and encourage more probing reporting. Frank (2004) described the distortions of democracy in detail.

Derber (2004) argued that America had "corporate regimes" during the Gilded Age of robber barons, which ended with the trust-busting presidency of Teddy Roosevelt; the Harding and Hoover era, which was overthrown by F. D. Roosevelt; recent years also result in corporate regimes of the "born-again robber barons" of the Bush Administration. He predicted this regime will be overthrown because of its abuse of the economy (corporate welfare), the degradation of the environment, and its imperialistic foreign policy (shaping the global corporate order under the political and military direction of the United States). He presented solid evidence of the profit motive being the only criterion of public policy, and the abuse of the public good so that the friends of the administration can realize maximum profits. This book runs parallel with Korten (1995, 2001), who argued that big corporations are ruling and ruining the world, not just America. The corporations employ 170,000 public relations specialists to disseminate their message, while the public is aware of what is going on through the services of only 40,000 news reporters. Two factors seem to have been the major culprits in the distortion of democracy: television and globalization through free trade.

Democracy also has a problem: we live in a world that is very complex, yet most of us are cognitively simple. When students are tested, only about one third of the students score high in complexity. When the majority of the electorate is cognitively simple, the leaders are forced to be cognitively simple also. During the South Carolina presidential debate of 2007, when candidates were asked how they would respond to another terror strike, they mentioned attack, retaliate, and pulverize somebody. This was a cognitively simple eye-for-an-eye response. Only Barak Obama answered in a complex way (make sure the emergency response is effective, ensure that intelligence is good, figure out who was responsible, then move with allies to dismantle the network of terrorists). His response was correct (Zakaria, 2008), but the other candidates attacked him for not having the fortitude to be president. Then, realizing that the public expected a simple answer he mentioned retaliation as well.

Television

Television is the major source of news for the majority of voters in the West. The average child aged 2 to 5 watches 4 hours and the average adult 4.5 hours of television per day (Gore, 2007). Research shows that as people spend more time watching TV they interact with each other less, and their brains change in subtle ways, so they process information differently (Gore, 2007). They are less likely to debate public policy, and thus to become motivated to participate in public life by voting. Excessive TV viewing results in people valuing the exotic; the unusual, the mysterious, and science fiction becomes confused with "reality." This may well increase tendencies toward self-deception. Furthermore, in a world where we accomplish a lot by pressing the keys of our computers, we tend to look for simple, quick solutions. This may well increase cognitive simplicity. Then the scientific attitude may be deemed too complex and may be rejected.

We see troubling trends that confirm these hypotheses. There is more superstition, more reliance on astrology, the paranormal, exorcism, reincarnation, levitation, psychic healing, cults, UFOs, and on magical solutions now than in the past 100 years (Kurtz, 1983). In the United States, 1,250 out of 1,500 newspapers have astrology columns, essentially helping people to fool themselves. What makes a buck is good even if it is foolish or unconstitutional. Furthermore, too much of the general public spends its time dreaming of getting on TV. We have become a society where the greatest accomplishment is to appear on TV rather than to produce useful products or ideas.

Commercial television has to make a profit. In mid-20th century, the news was a loss leader, but in the 1980s, according to R. Weston of the Television Foundation, the networks determined that they could make money with "attractive" news programs. "Attractive" means using a tabloid content—more sex, gossip, and violence. One of the best-established facts in social psychology is that viewing violence increases violence. No fewer than 1,142 studies have found this to be true, and 528 studies found that people act antisocially after viewing violent behavior (Richards et al., 2003). But the producers of TV programs ignore this evidence because it does not suit them. That is a clear case of "motivation trumps cognition," which is the general phenomenon in self-deception.

Moreover, to make money one has to keep the viewers watching. With viewers having access to many channels, the average viewer watches a news program for 7 minutes, and then switches to another channel. Research has shown that 40% of the viewers say that they are liberal, 40% that they are conservative, and 20% that they are independent. But, those who are conservative tend to stay with one channel longer than those who are liberal. A switch in viewing time from 7 to 11 minutes is enormously more profitable for the TV companies! Thus, it pays to increase the conservative point of view in the news because the station makes more money. In short, a Republican rather than a Democratic bias is more profitable, and the journalism ethics of presenting each point of view fairly and accurately, as verified by at least two sources, is no longer used as widely as it used to be.

Also, television networks are owned by major corporations, which control who gets appointed to select what will be presented and to comment on the news. The networks even control what is advertised. A 2006 advertisement by MoveOn.org was rejected by CBS on flimsy grounds (Gore, 2007). The networks provide very little analysis. In America, only NPR does a good job of analyzing the news, but its viewers are few relative to the millions who watch the commercial networks. Finally, because corporations can spend money on advertisements, they can ensure that they get their way. Politics has become a war of ads rather than a rational debate of the issues.

Candidates can no longer get elected to a political office without advertising on radio and television. The enormous cost of such advertising makes the influence of people with money much greater than it should be in a democracy. Presidential elections in the United States are now "giant auctions" (*The Public I*, 2004). We are increasingly becoming a plutocracy, where only the rich can get elected. A publication of the Center for Public Integrity, which employs several investigative reporters concerned with the public good, titled *The Buying of the Presidency* (2004), revealed that in 2004, George W. Bush received about $500,000 per day in political contributions. Most of the recently successful politicians have received large sums from Wall Street firms, and thus these firms are not regulated too strictly, which undoubtedly means they are able to make more money and perhaps not pay as much attention to the public good.

Beschloss (2007) argued that great presidents are characterized by "courage" (i.e., they are willing to take the chance that they might lose an election if they do something unpopular that they believe is good for the country). "I'd rather be right than be president" was the way Lincoln said it. The problem is that such people are unlikely to get elected in the 21st century. In 1956, Sen. John F. Kennedy put it this way: Politics has become so expensive, "so mechanized, and so dominated by professional politicians and public relations men . . . that any unpopular or unorthodox course arouses a storm of protests" (p. 31). In short, the cost of politics is undermining democracy, and is bad for the country. Yet, the advertisers are making so much money in this political system that they are unwilling to see it change. The essence of the acts of "courage" in Beschloss' analysis, as a historian, is that the presidents had a broad, complex vision that the public could not have.

Television converts political discussions into exchanges of cognitively simple sound bites. Two-minute ads attacked a judge's decision that took 500 pages to explain, and the ad told the viewer not to vote for that judge! Some corporations use advertising to eliminate judges who might not favor them. It is clear that politics on TV results in cognitively simple voting.

In my opinion, the mass media are not paying their fair share for using the public airwaves. During a political contest they should be required to give 10% of prime time free to those political parties that have obtained support from more than 10% of the registered voters. The arguments against this suggestion are self-deceptions. I was told that it is not possible for the industry to absorb these costs, because running television systems is so expensive. It seems to me that if all TV systems are required to give this free time there will not be any at a competitive disadvantage. They can charge other advertisers more. Political debate is a public good, while advertising beer or detergent only benefits certain segments of the public.

Until approximately 1980, the role of the U.S. government was to control the corporations, and avoid abuses, such as the large-scale movement of jobs abroad. However, after about 1980, corporate welfare became the focus of government. It is not coincidental that the need for funds for political TV advertising became especially acute about that time. Political advertising on television started around 1950, but it took some time before it became the dominant way of campaigning.

Television is also a negative factor because all over the world people see the glamorous, unrealistic lifestyle that is presented as "normal" in the West. Too many people from developing countries want to come to the West, and take terrible risks to get here. Many die on the way. In many parts of the world, where the unemployment rates are very high, young people are ready to blow themselves up and become martyrs (see chapter 6) rather than stay where they are.

Globalization

Globalization and free trade are also distorting democracy because most of the major economic decisions have shifted from parliaments and governments to the board rooms of major corporations. Jobs move from the rich countries to the poor ones. But many of the countries of the developing world exploit labor, lack labor standards, and do not protect the environment. Although this increases the profits of the multi-nationals it decreases the well-being of some segments of the population. To be for or against globalization reflects cognitive simplicity. In fact, the picture is complex. The more educated both cross-nationally and within nation, do better economically. The masses do less well. It seems to me that globalization should move toward large markets, such as the EU, North American Free Trade Agreement, and Central American Free Trade Agreement, cautiously, only after the relevant countries have developed high standards for the protection of workers and the environment.

Globalization probably has the net effect of deteriorating the physical environment, because the less developed economies do not invest in the environment. As the less developed become like the most developed they also consume and pollute like the most developed, and that is detrimental for the environment. Overconsumption, deterioration of the environment, and exhaustion of natural resources are intercorrelated.

To fix the problems of globalization requires the cooperation of most of the countries of the world. During the period from 1945 to 1970, the United States was the leader in developing international institutions, and it should do so again. In recent years, however, the United States has withdrawn from internationalism by not accepting the International Court of Justice, and failing to sign international agreements such as the Kyoto protocol. As a result, the world is much more anarchic and dangerous now. The "neo-cons" of the Bush Administration stressed the exceptionalism of the United States at Davos and made a bad impression (*International Harold Tribune*, 2004), even among America's friends. This is the kind of behavior that is making our enemies even more determined to hurt us. We are losing the so-called war on terrorism because of the self-deceptions of the Bush Administration.

The Gender Gap

The position of women in the world is unequal and needs change. Kavita Randas, on the NPR NOW Program in April 2004, presented Indian data showing that when women are educated their children are healthier. For every year of a mother's education there was a corresponding reduction in the probability that her children would get sick. Educated women have their children later, reducing the population explosion. Educated women in South Asia and Africa are battling HIV infections and prostitution much more effectively than less well-educated women.

Communitarian Values

The Communitarian Platform spells out details about the kinds of society that is most desirable. It includes certain values. Here, I cite one paragraph from the Internet (http://www.gwu.edu/~ccps/platformtext .html):

> Our response is straightforward: We ought to teach those values Americans share, for example, that the dignity of all persons ought to be respected, that tolerance is a virtue and discrimination abhorrent, that peaceful resolution of conflicts is superior to violence, that generally truth-telling is morally superior to lying, that democratic government is morally superior to totalitarianism and authoritarianism, that one ought to give a day's work for a day's pay, that saving for one's own and one's country's future is better than squandering one's income and relying on others to attend to one's future needs.

No Luxuries

We seek unnecessary luxuries "to make a statement," while one third of humanity goes to bed with an empty stomach. I think this is immoral. Furthermore, standing out from the crowd and being "better" than others results in envy. In *Mein Kampf*, Hitler mentions how much he disliked the Jews of Vienna, where he grew up in impoverished circumstances. They flaunted their wealth, and wore clothes that made them "stick out." How much future violence might be avoided if people do not "stick out" unnecessarily?

Unfortunately, most of what we do in the West does not meet the test of a good society. Chapter 1 listed the factors that result in high subjective well-being. A review of these factors shows that we do not do what is required for optimal subjective well-being. To repeat: in the developed world we consume resources at a rate that is unrealistic, even immoral, and dooms the environment. We operate on simple principles, like Marxism, the free market, or religion. But the world is much too complex for such simple principles to deal with it effectively. The cognitively simple self-deceptions reflected in these principles are that we can solve most problems if we just have more Marxism, or more free markets, or more religion. Muslim fundamentalists do not see their religion as holding them back from improving their economic conditions. Some have the self-deception that if they return to the 7th century (i.e., have more of the original religion) they can live better in the 21st century.

Buddha had a very wise principle: Reduce your needs and your desires. Modern science supports Buddha. Money is only good to the extent that it maintains good health (Stewart, on the views of Spinoza, 2006). The more people stress financial success, the more dissatisfied they are with both work and family life (Nettle, 2005). Even rich people are less happy if they have materialist values when compared with rich people for whom money is unimportant. Materialists have poor relationships with people, because they treat them as objects to be manipulated. Kasser (2002) went even further and argued that "materialistic values harm those around us . . . (and) damage the health of the planet" (p. 87). They interfere with marriage, parenting, and community bonds; furthermore, overconsumption "driven by materialistic desires threatens the ecosystem" (p. 92).

The problem is that the economic system we have constructed requires materialism and overconsumption. If people stopped buying, the system would collapse. We need extensive research to think through how we can have simultaneously prosperity, good health, and subjective well-being. Economists focus on income, but income is not equivalent to health, or to subjective well-being in a world that has limited resources and a deteriorating environment. We need to develop an economy of limited resources, whose success will be judged by the health and well-being of the population. The development of this economy is, of course, the job of economists, but the criteria I have been advocating (health, well-being, longevity, protecting the environment) rather than increases in the GNP should be the criteria for success.

The data tell us that wanting too many goods is bad for us (Kasser, 2002). Extensive empirical work by Kasser and his associates shows that people with materialistic values are less happy than people who are not too interested in "things." Empirical studies summarized in Kasser (2002) suggest that the desire to be rich has been found to provide statistically significant increases in a person's violations of the rights of others; hostile, defiant, disobedient behavior, hyperactivity, overconsumption of alcohol, marijuana, poor interpersonal relationships, paranoia, excessive attention-seeking, mood swings, being intentionally inefficient, excessive need to be taken care by others, avoidance of social interaction, and excessive desire for control at the expense of flexibility and openness.

Depression and anxiety, physical problems such as frequent headaches, personality disorders, narcissism, and antisocial behavior have been found to be associated with too much concern for materialism, fame, and a good appearance (e.g., being beautiful). Insecurity and unfulfilled needs result in materialistic values, and these values prevent people from satisfying their basic needs and achieving an optimally meaningful, high-quality life. Economic insecurity makes people more materialistic. What is important in life are human connections, empathy, generosity, and low stress. Strong bonds and intimacy with family and friends, as well as with communities and helping others result in high-quality life. Failure to have this kind of life results in overconsumption that uses the resources of the earth in an unsustainable way, and damages the environment. Global warming is a consequence of overconsumption.

Kasser is not indicting wealth itself, only the desire for it, which is a cognitively simple self-deception. The evidence suggests that adults who focus on money, image, and fame are lower in vitality and higher in depression, and experience more physical symptoms of stress, such as backaches and sore muscles. Reading Mozart's biography (Gay, 1999), I was impressed with his strong desire for fame and fortune, and his strong depression at the end of his life. At age 35 he wanted to be as famous as he was at age 10. He was still productive, having just composed the *Magic Flute*, one of the best operas ever composed, yet he was depressed! I had the sense that had he avoided this depression he might have lived another 20 years, instead of dying at age 35. The world would have been so much richer if he had lived longer, and he might have been happier if he had not been so obsessed with fame and fortune.

This view was also part of the wisdom of Lao-Tse as early as the 6th century BCE. He put it this way: "The stronger the attachments the greater the cost, the more that is hoarded, the deeper the loss" (Wing, 1986, passage 44). There is a vicious circle: the quest for money results in an inner sense of social and spiritual emptiness; then advertisers tell us that we will fill the emptiness by buying their products, which requires money, so we quest for more money (Korten, 1995). Eckersley (2007) argued that the Western cultural pattern that emphasizes materialism and individualism is undermining the health of the population. The luxury industry is the cancer of the society. If the society had fewer luxuries, there would be less temptation for politicians to get money and golfing vacations in Scotland from lobbyists, and the environment would not deteriorate as much. Read the newspapers with an eye on how often crime, violence, destruction, and unhappiness are traceable to money! I see these connections often.

However, some people take antimaterialism to an extreme and try to live without any possessions. Here the nothing in excess principle must be used. We need some income to be comfortable and healthy. It is also unnecessary to eliminate all desires. In fact, it is acceptable to have goals and desires that will improve the lot of others. People need to experience self-actualization. Goals and desires such as the elimination of wars, inequality, famines, and poor physical and mental health, the preservation of the environment and population control are necessary. We should select those politicians who can deliver them, and vote out of office those who do not work for them.

The world is divided in many ways—by education, religion, economics, philosophy, aesthetic preferences, social relationships, and politics. Each cleavage can be a barrier toward the goal of a better life for all. We need to become aware that politicians and religious leaders often take advantage of these cleavages to increase their power. They also use the prejudices of the populations they rule to improve their power. Thus, segments of the world are condemned to wars, terrorism, disease, and death, because those who rule have a narrow perspective and cannot see how damaging their policies and behaviors often are. A major problem is that policies are created to meet only one criterion—maximize profit, get elected, reduce pollution. We need to develop policies that maximize several criteria simultaneously, such as economic development with population control, with the preservation of the environment, and with increases in health, well-being, and longevity.

We need to convince those who create public policies that the cleavages mentioned earlier are unhealthy for the world, and any policy that increases inequality or differences, is bad for the health of the planet. Public policy often uses just the criterion of high income. That is not desirable. Human health and well-being should be the criteria.

In addition to the cleavages just mentioned, there are other divisive aspects of the world—criminal gangs, drug pushers, producers of unhealthy products (e.g., cigarettes), the exploiters of workers, the pushers of prostitution, and so on. It is discouraging to contemplate these divisions, where making more money is the common denominator. This is why I advocate that luxuries should be considered immoral. People who have too luxurious a lifestyle should be considered suspect. I later list specific organizations that work toward the goal of health and well-being for all. I propose that societies should develop norms that provide much financial support to such organizations.

I am guessing that in the West more than half the population consists of passive consumers and uncritical thinkers. This has bad consequences for political life; and is detrimental for democracy. Specifically, people fail to vote, and they do not spend time on and are not analytic about public affairs. Politicians have fixed the voting districts in America so that 98% of the Members of Congress are reelected (*The Economist*, 2005). That has the effect of making congressmen feel independent of the voters. Thus, congressmen pay attention to the party much more than to the voters, because the party can run a competitor against them in the primaries. These changes have resulted in much greater party discipline, which means that congressmen vote according to what they are told by the party rather than according to what they think is best for the country. Too many members of the electorate as well as congressmen vote on the basis of one simple criterion, rather than on the basis of multiple criteria. As discussed above, democracy has been undermined also by the need to raise money for political campaigns.

The Future of Religion

The secular perspective of humanist philosophy, presented in this book, needs to be supplemented with some consideration of religion. In my opinion, original Buddhism (Bhikkhu, 1956; Levine, 2007) provides the most realistic guidance toward the good life. However, the spiritual aspects of the other great religions can also achieve the same goal.

We need to institute discussions among the religious leaders of the world, so they can identify the shared, constructive, integrative elements of their religions. Most people do not have the scientific training and philosophical bend necessary to live with the perspectives of humanism (Lamont, 1997). But religious leaders who are open minded, and have some scientific training, should be able to develop a universal religion that supplements humanism and is acceptable to most people. The criterion for the development of a new worldview is to maximize well-being and mental health while preserving the environment.

Hans Küng, of the Foundation for Global Ethics, has identified numerous points of agreement among the great religions concerning what is ethical behavior. In addition to some version of the Golden Rule, which I mentioned already as being universal, there are many other points of agreement, such as reverence for life; no violence, deception, greed, stealing, exploitation, or humiliation of others. Respect and fairness when dealing with others are central points in most religions. Although the ethical codes are similar, differences occur in dogma and ritual. We need to pay attention to the fact that religious authorities have to keep their jobs and one of the ways to do this is to find differences from other religions.

My view is that because traditional behaviors and ritual are psychologically soothing they should be preserved. People feel comfortable when they behave in traditional ways. Such behaviors can take place without reference to superstitions, such as to supernatural beings. Care should be taken, however, not to let the ritual become too similar to an obsessive-compulsive disorder (Dulaney & Fiske, 1994). In short, traditions and ritual can be "too much of a good thing" and again "nothing in excess" is recommended.

People should not try to convince others to use their ritual. Individuals can hold whatever dogma they wish (after all, all dogmas are equally invalid), as long as they do not impose it on others. People can believe whatever makes them feel good, as long as it is not divisive and they do not impose their views on others. In short, there can be a diversity of private beliefs, but there should not be evidence of this diversity in public

life. We need a world in which people realize that although external religions are self-deceptions, they are needed by most humans and may be
good for their mental health. The rituals of different religions are needed
because most people need them to mark major transitions, such as birth,
marriage, and death with proper ceremonies. In an ideal world, there will
be "ritual tourism" where people will take part in the rituals of others and
will be fascinated by the different ways in which other people mark major
transitions. They will not want to impose their traditions on others, but
will appreciate differences in traditions.

I enjoy immensely the masses composed by Bach, Beethoven, Verdi,
and many others. Handel's *Messiah* is a masterpiece. Much of the music
of Wagner has elements that take me to heaven. Wagner's *Parsifal*, for instance, is essentially a religious opera. It is my favorite opera. It involves
monks who believe that they have the chalice from which Christ drank
when on the cross. With the logic of magic (see the discussion of magic in
chapter 5), anything touched by Christ is sacred, miraculous. When I see
in the last scene of the opera the monks bowing to the chalice I empathize
with them, and for a moment I feel the mystery of the ritual. I find this
a greatly moving scene. One does not need to believe in supernatural beings in order to be moved by Wagner's art. In short, I think it is possible
to have the rituals of a religion without supernaturals.

Similarly, the houses of worship around the world are filled with price-
less art treasures, and one can admire them without reference to supernaturals. I felt moved by the complexity of Hindu art as seen in New Delhi,
Calcutta, and around Bhubaneshwar in Orissa, the serenity of Christian
art of Ravenna, Rome, and Paris, the colors of Islamic art in Istanbul,
Jerusalem, and Isfahan (Iran), the richness of Buddhist art of Chiang Mai
(Thailand), Bangkok, and Nara (Japan), and above all by the majestic scale
of Angkor Wat (Cambodia). One can admire Machu Picchiu (Peru) without reference to the beliefs of the Incas.

I expect that many people will need the rituals of their religions, in order
to feel good. But do they really need to have also the superstitions of their
religion?

We need to take into account that globalization threatens the identity of
members of cultural groups, and religions provide people with an identity. Thus, no wonder religions are popular. To the extent that they are
integrative, they are benign self-deceptions and we must welcome them.
But we need to suppress them if they are divisive. This raises important
issues about freedom of speech that require discussion. In Spain, for instance, the government is considering the monitoring of the sermons of
the imams. It makes sense. If the imam advocates brotherhood and peace
he should be welcomed. But it is an entirely different sermon if he advocates terrorism. When we realize that sermons are often cognitively simple
self-deceptions, it is a matter of "public health" to control them. Should a

democratic government censor a sermon? Can it afford not to do so? In Turkey, religion is monitored and the sermons of religious authorities are "controlled." Granted, this raises questions about civil rights, but when divisive sermons result in violence, the state is justified to protect itself. Such controls of free speech also occur in Western Europe and the United States when speech incites violence.

Each religion might exist as it does now, as long as its leaders reject fundamentalist perspectives (my "truth" is the only "truth"), and link with the other religions in order to identify common goals that will improve the lot of most humans. Ritual, especially the singing and dancing associated with many religions, needs to be preserved, even if we accept that celestial beings, heaven, hell, afterlife, and the like do not exist. Even prayer can be accepted as a benign self-deception because people need it. There are analogous rituals in modern life. When we touch wood or say "Gesundheit" after someone sneezes, we do not really believe that we are changing the course of events. But it is polite or satisfying. Similarly, to sing hymns can be satisfying even if they are sung for our own pleasure rather than to influence some deity. People feel good when they do the customary, and when a ritual is customary it can be used.

Thus, when we view external religions as systems of self-deception that are good for our mental health, we can accept them for what they are—helpful to give us a sense of identity, of fellowship, and the illusion of control over the environment. Additionally, the internal aspects of religion are useful in providing us with a meaning of life and in helping us to have a spiritual sense of unity with the cosmos.

Religiosity is increasing all over the world. Experts tell us that three new religions start every day! This is understandable, because the world has become more unpredictable and television makes this unpredictability more salient than it used to be. When a tsunami, a major earthquake, and several hurricanes occur frequently, it is understandable that people feel insecure. There is also fear of terrorism, of unemployment, of the possibility of nuclear war. Global warming has increased climate variability and the unpredictability of the climate. People have unrealistic aspirations about lifestyles that they will never attain. Religions give people a sense of control over uncertainty, so naturally people flock to them.

We should definitely teach the core of our religions to our children. They should learn the universal norms that are shared by most religions: treat others with respect; do not do to others what you would not have them do to you; test each of your actions to see if the world would be better if everybody were to do that. The goal of increasing the well-being of as many people as possible is concrete. We can test each personal action and public policy against it. Public opinion polling can be used as the criterion to test the effectiveness of each policy: each reform can be considered as an experiment. Experiments sometimes work out and sometimes do not. We learn from the failures as well as the successes.

One of the virtues we must teach our children is self-control, because it gives a person a chance to think about the consequences of action. Self-control is the master virtue (Geyer & Baumeister, 2005). One of the widely accepted theories of criminality uses self-control as the central concept. Criminals are low in self-control, focus on immediate gratification, and have a short time perspective (Gottfredson & Hirschi, 1990). To test an action against the "Would the world be better off if everybody did this?" criterion requires time.

Intelligence and self-control are unrelated, so that extremely intelligent people sometimes do stupid things because they lack self-control. A classic example was President Clinton's relationship with Monica Lewinsky. Clinton, according to Greenspan (2007), was one of the most intelligent presidents, but he lacked self-control. (Incidentally, he probably should not have answered the question about his sexual relationships; instead he should have said, "That is an improper question." Lying was unnecessary.)

Another consideration is the relationship of means to ends. The two are so closely related that rarely does a good end justify a bad means. Children should also learn by seeing adults acting in the correct manner: be helpful, loyal, forgiving, honest, responsible, and a true friend. This should go together with emphases on achievement, reliability, responsibility, self-control, and persistence. They should also learn that being superior to others is not a value. Being broadminded, favoring social justice and equality; seeking a world of beauty, unity with nature, wisdom, and protecting the environment should be the important values.

Many of our norms and traditions are designed to support the existing power structure. That is especially clear in the case of most institutionalized religions where the clergy has developed norms that help it stay in power. As we strip norms of their supernatural legitimacy, they can be changed. A world with only the religious leaders who emphasize the integrative aspects of religion will be a safer world.

One benefit of such a program is that the lifestyle of the West, which scandalizes religious people in Asia and the Middle East, will change. There are many activities that take place in the West that 50 years ago were simply not done because they were in "bad taste." As our culture has become looser, public sexual behavior, violence, and extreme hedonism have become acceptable in ways that were not acceptable 50 years ago. We need to take into account that such activities really scandalize people in other cultures, especially in tight cultures (e.g., Muslims and others) just as much as we are scandalized by the Muslim treatment of women (e.g., denial of education, stoning of women who committed adultery, and female circumcision).

We need to develop a dialogue around the world among the cultures of the world. What does scandalize you the most? We can then ask ourselves, Can we change that? It is a self-deception that if we change aspects of our culture we will be less happy. Happiness is quite robust, and people have been found to be happy even when their material conditions or health deteriorated.

Each of us has hundreds of identities. Some of them are inconsistent, and we learn to see ourselves as different people under different circumstances. My Indian friend who said that he was a "meat-eating vegetarian" had it right. He normally was a vegetarian. But when others ate meat he ate meat. The Buddhist wisdom of not giving too much emphasis on any desire or quality is something for us to keep in mind. We need not preserve every aspect of our cultures.

As globalization takes over many of us will not survive unless we change. We need to develop new survival skills, and one of the most important is the skill to get along with people from other cultures. We need to train our children to be culturally intelligent (Earley & Ang, 2003), that is, to be able to get along well with the members of most cultures. The realization that systems of self-deception are at the base of many of our lifestyles, norms, and values should liberate us to change our cultures so as to offend as few people as possible in other cultures.

If creating conditions where everyone on earth has a decent standard of living is the ultimate goal, we have a very great deal to do. Most of our institutions are not aiming at that. Only some nongovernmental organizations have this goal. Furthermore, the economic arrangements of the world at this time are rigged to favor the rich countries at the expense of the poor (Stiglitz, 2002). We have much work to do to change institutions such as the World Bank and the International Monetary Fund, so that they will aim more effectively at the reduction of abject poverty in the less developed world.

SOME PRACTICAL THINGS TO DO TO ACHIEVE THE ADVOCATED PURPOSE OF LIFE

Korten (1995) suggested a number of concrete steps that might be taken to move toward a better world. For example, we might pressure governments to introduce taxes for international movements of money, luxury consumption, upper-class incomes, and inheritances. We might support grassroots political movements, born of concern for public accountability, social justice, and environmental sustainability. We might control the tax exemptions of corporations related to lobbying; we might increase emphasis on public education and public charities. We should eliminate political advertising on television, total campaign expenditures should be limited, and political campaign costs should be covered by public funds and small individual tax-deductible contributions. We can commit ourselves to live by the values of simplicity, love, peace, and reverence for life.

Amitai Etzioni (2004) provided a number of suggestions that are reasonably practical. He took a "nothing in excess" position with respect to our cultures. The West is much too individualistic (freedom to do one's own thing, no matter what its effect on others) and should become more concerned with community and social controls in favor of the public; the East is much too high in social controls and should increase the emphasis on individual freedoms, human rights, and the freedom of exploration. In short, the West has an excess of autonomy and a deficit of community; the East has an excess of social control and a deficit of autonomy.

Etzioni argued that if we are to create a society that is safe, healthy, free, and caring for others, where all can live in dignity, the rich will have to sacrifice, the way West Germany did to integrate East Germany. We will need to accept international humanitarian laws, such as the International Court of Justice. States will have to act as coalitions, where each member has veto power.

He favored support of what he terms *soft* religions, rather than secular perspectives, on the assumption that true believers cannot give up their faith altogether. I would translate "soft religions" into the "integrative aspects of religion." He discussed schools that include both secular and religious topics, as opposed to the *madrassahs* that are advocating the divisive aspects of Islam. He examined how the world can deal with international organized crime, trafficking in people, environmental degradation, and the spread of infectious diseases, piracy, and cyber crime. He proposed the formation of transnational communitarian bodies (TCBs) that would include leaders who bond with each other for the purpose of accomplishing specific tasks, such as dealing with environmental degradation, torture in prisons, and so on. Amnesty International, Greenpeace, and the International Committee of the Red Cross are examples of such TCBs. He proposes mechanisms for the improvement of the economies of less developed countries. For example, as countries receive help to develop, once they reach a certain level, such as $10,000 per capita per year, they will start repaying into a revolving fund that will help other countries. He proposes changes in the structure of the UN, and the development of a Global Security Authority to combat crime and terrorism worldwide.

Some of these changes will require much time. But we can also act immediately to improve the lot of as many humans as possible around the world. Specifically, I suggest that we can analyze every one of our actions, and those of the political leaders we elect, to check if it is consistent with the goal of improving the lot of humans around the world. If we do that, we will see that many of our actions are inconsistent, and detrimental. Specifically, U.S. foreign policy has increasingly included a component of world domination. We are perceived in many countries as a terrorist state, especially after the attack on Iraq. My criterion of consistency across multiple observers from different cultures rejects the American self-perceptions that we are a peaceful nation. It is true that most Americans think that we are peaceful, but when the rest of the world thinks that we are domineering and aggressive, I must conclude that our self-perception is a self-deception.

In the past, authors such as Plato in his *Republic*, Sir Thomas More in *Utopia*, Francis Bacon in *New Atlantis*, Thomas Campanella in *The City of the Sun*, and James Harrington in *Oceana* attempted to state the characteristics of the ideal commonwealth. These utopias were Western. However, in the East also Confucius described the "great community": a society without crime, selfishness, war, and social divisions. It is a society where the basic material needs are sated with something left over to spare, but contains no ambition for higher levels of consumption. It advocates "voluntary simplicity," a way of life that is less object-rich. The current Chinese government is supporting this lifestyle because if China developed the American lifestyle it would require enormous resources that are simply not available.

An examination of these works shows some common attributes. First, the values are collectivist or communitarian. For instance, Plato viewed a commonwealth designed to make the average person happy even if many individuals are unhappy. More argued that man should dispense with his own advantages for the good of others. Campanella stated that what is good for society, not what is good for individuals, is most important.

Second, the "nothing in excess" principle is behind most of these utopias. Plato advocated moderation in desires, and stressed justice, temperance, courage, and wisdom, and rejected both wealth and poverty. The ordinary "goods" of beauty, wealth, strength, rank, and good connections within the state are said to be corrupting. More advocates modest clothing, rejected jewels, and was anti-hedonist. Campanella wanted neither wealth nor poverty.

Third, the authors do not escape the confines of their times. For example, both More and Plato did not question slavery (neither does the Bible!), although the latter disapproves of Hellenes making slaves of other Hellenes through war. Any position that we may develop today will also reflect the 21st century, and will be flawed for the long run.

High rates of consumption go against the nothing in excess principle and are not compatible with a good environment. Yet we have developed a lifestyle that is resource hungry. We are generating huge amounts of garbage; in short, we are not using our resources well. We are caught in a vicious circle of emphasis on "more luxuries than the Jones'" and our economic system depends far too much on high rates of consumption. If people stopped buying the system would collapse. "Voluntary simplicity," as advocated by Confucius, is anathema to advertisers, yet makes perfect sense in the 21st century.

There are some steps that individuals can take to counter some of the undesirable trends just discussed. We can support organizations financially, and even join some of the ones that move us toward the purpose of life advocated above. Some help the poor, the sick, the persecuted and the oppressed, such as Amnesty International, Doctors without Borders, Habitat for Humanity, Human Rights Watch, the Red Cross, and Save the Children Federation. Some work for greater equality, such as United for a Fair Economy. There are organizations that work to solve the population explosion problem, such as Population Communication International, and Population Connection (previously, Zero Population Growth). There are organizations that work to increase peace in the world, such as the United Nations Association of the USA (UNA-USA), The Carter Center, and the National Peace Foundation. There are organizations that support research to cure diseases, such as the Alzheimer's Association, American Cancer Society, American Diabetes Association, the Arthritis Foundation, American Heart Association, and many others. There are organizations that work to protect the environment, such as Earthjustice, Environmental Defense, National Wildlife Federation, and Physicians for Social Responsibility. If we distributed 10% (a tithe) of our annual income among such organizations, we would be moving toward the purpose of life advocated above. Most churches expect a 10% donation. Because I advocate a secular philosophy, I propose that we increase our giving to organizations such as the ones just mentioned.

IN SUMMARY

Given what we learned in this volume, we can summarize the substance of the argument this way: We humans are chance creatures of evolution on an insignificant little planet, in a corner of the universe. It is good for our mental health if we see ourselves with modesty (we are not too important), and if we follow Buddha's insight by minimizing our desires. If we see our condition realistically, without self-deceptions, we can ask, What is the purpose of life? A purpose of life is to make life on this planet as good as it can be for as many people as possible, while preserving the environment. That means we must strive to maximize good health, for all humans. Health is "a state of complete physical, mental, and social well-being" (World Health Organization, 1948). Additionally, we should try, ideally, to provide the conditions of a good education, and self-actualization (individuals can become what they are capable of becoming), for all humans. In essence, we must make sure that the well-being of as many people as possible is as high as possible. Of course, the world includes criminals, sadists, and other undesirables. Part of the task is to "control," rehabilitate, or neutralize them. There is far too much violence in the world, and we need to use rational methods to reduce it (Marsella, 2005).

This goal is enormous, and thinking that we can reach it is itself a self-deception, because it is unlikely that we can. But let us think of the wisdom of Nkusi, a 12-year-old Black South African boy who had AIDS acquired from his mother, and who died 1 year after he said this: "Do what you can, with what you got, in the time you have, and in the place you are." As I argued many times in this book, we need a goal that is greater than ourselves, even if it is unrealistic, even if it is a self-deception.

This goal can be used as a standard to criticize cultural practices that reduce well-being. For example, Western culture is too materialistic and there is much we can do to change that. I for one stopped paying attention to most messages I identify as "advertisements." I refuse to be manipulated. We can also pay attention to cultural patterns that hurt people. For example, in some cultures widows are defined as "evil women" because there is the mistaken assumption that they "caused" their husband's death (Tseng, 2001, p. 178). As a result, they are rejected by their family, which leads to depression and other forms of poor mental health. In India, there are 31 million widows who have only three options: If the family permits it, to marry the younger brother of their dead husband, remain on the margin of the family for the rest of their lives, or commit suicide. *Water*, a film that documents this condition, suggests that they live "in hell." Their life is regulated by beliefs about pollution and other nonsense, which were developed by men in power to maximize their advantages. Such cultural beliefs are dysfunctional, and people should be told that they are just reflecting ignorance.

A sound explanation of what is a "cause" and how it can be determined with careful double blind studies may induce people to stop believing such nonsense. Numerous examples of dysfunctional beliefs have been listed (Tseng, 2001), such as the belief that the "soul" can be lost, that spirits can possess a person, that some event is due to the breaching of a taboo, and that sorcery was involved in some misfortune. In general, the more ignorant the people, the more likely they are to have dysfunctional beliefs. Scientific education is necessary to reduce the occurrence of such beliefs. Dysfunctional beliefs cannot be eliminated unless they are replaced with scientifically valid beliefs. Of course, this requires much more education than is available in most contemporary cultures.

However, such bizarre beliefs are not only found in the less developed part of the world. Even in supposedly "enlightened" America not long ago, and sometimes even today, there is anti-Semitism, exclusion/rejection of African Americans and homosexuals, rejection of interracial marriage, and many other prejudices. I am not advocating interracial marriage because the data indicate that the more similar the cultures of those who marry the more stable are the marriages. But there are situations when individuals will choose such a marriage, and there should not be a belief that necessarily this is socially undesirable.

There has been a major cultural change in the United States during the past 50 years. The values of the Puritan settlers of the country emphasized community, self-control, temperate living, and devotion to spiritual life. Now the culture emphasizes commercialism, acquisitions, and self-indulgence. It is a change from moderate tightness and collectivism to extreme looseness and individualism. The change is not for the better!

We know enough (Kazarian & Evans, 2001) about what makes people healthy and happy (Wallis, 2005, special issue of *Time Magazine*, 2005) to use it as a standard for the whole world. Physical health is not culture-specific. If we can reduce the incidence of heart disease, cancer, diabetes, suicides, AIDS, homicides, pain, and so on, we will be accomplishing one aspect of the advocated purpose of life. Of course, each of these goals has culture-specific aspects. If part of the goal is to make sure that all humans have enough exercise, this can be accomplished in many culture-specific ways, depending on the particular environment. Similarly, if a healthy diet or good interpersonal relations are the goals, they can be accomplished in a myriad of culture-specific ways.

Science tells us that our brains have not evolved much in the past 20,000 years. If we let our biology, with our selfish genes (Dawkins, 1989), control what we do we will have a dog-eat-dog culture, like the one described by Hobbes as "solitary, poor, nasty, brutish, and short." Furthermore, because our culture has developed ways to blow itself up, we are going to do just that. That will be an inglorious end of our species. The goal I set here lets our culture, rather than our biology, control what we do. We know how to organize ourselves to avoid wars—conflict resolution à la Gandhi, reduced nationalism, more democracies, more regional economic and political arrangements, such as the UN and the EU. That is the direction of desirable change. If helping as many people as possible have good health is the "new morality," we have a chance of surviving as a species. It is not going to be easy, but the alternative is terrible.

The viewpoint of this book is that all humans belong to one in-group. However, the overwhelming majority of humans use much narrower in-groups, such as family, tribe, nation, and religion. In fact, there is some evidence that humans have a need for differentiation from as well as integration with others (Brewer, 1991). This may go back to our evolutionary past when we roamed the world in small bands of no more than 50 or so people as hunters fighting other bands who intruded our territory (differentiation). We accomplished our tasks cooperatively with members of the band (integration), so both differentiation and integration were needed. In short, most humans have a need to be different from others, but they also have a need to be parts of groups. There is a point of optimal distinctiveness, where people feel most comfortable. At that point they feel sufficiently different from groups, but also sufficiently a part of groups (Brewer, 1991). Well-being requires us to be different (individualism) but also to be part of groups (collectivism). Optimal mental health requires that we use both perspectives in a balanced way (Chirkov, Ryan, Kim, & Kaplan, 2003; Diener & Suh, 1999, 2000; Triandis, 1995). But we must stress the importance of the need to belong. It is crucially linked to good physical and mental health. Also we must preserve the environment.

Another tendency for differentiation and integration is to have the urge to convince other groups that our belief system is valid and theirs is not. This tendency occurs because there is no objective criterion for supporting our point of view; the only criterion that we can use is that others agree with us. There is much research showing that social support is the only factor supporting belief systems that have no objective basis, such as religions (Festinger, 1954; Swann & Read, 1981). Festinger said, "To the extent that objective, non-social means are not available, people evaluate their opinions . . . by comparison . . . with the opinions . . . of others" (p. 117). Missionaries, for instance, want to convert people with a different religion to their own religion. If they succeed they feel that their religion must be valid because others agree with it. This is a satisfying self-deception, but it creates unnecessary conflict, and merely involves switching systems of self-deception. The world is full of missionaries, not only religious, but also political, philosophic, economic, and lifestyle proponents, all of them creating unnecessary divisions and conflicts. If we examine the factors that have been found to be associated with well-being, we will see that we should avoid such unnecessary conflicts, by tolerating differences in lifestyle and belief systems. We must use a modesty perspective: "I do not know enough to put down the views of others."

My argument then is that we are stranded on this planet and we should strive to make ourselves as cozy as possible by reducing all forms of coercion and aggression. We need to worry about the future, but the way we deal with the environment now may result in no future! Most readers may not be affected personally, but their grandchildren are likely to be alive when our global civilization collapses, unless we change course now. We should be modest about who we are, and minimize our desires, without going to a no-desire condition. The nothing in excess principle should be used.

As citizens in a democracy we can scrutinize each government policy, and each policy of the corporations we do business with, according to whether it is helpful in reducing aggression and moving us toward the goal of well-being for most humans. We need to use multiple criteria in judging the effectiveness of government policies. When making decisions, the well-being of as many humans as possible should be used in addition to economic and environmental criteria. If we do that we will find that, unfortunately, many of the actions of our governments are based on cognitively simple self-deceptions that increase aggression and take us away from the goal of helping most humans maximize their well-being. It is time to reduce the illusions associated with many government policies and many of our own behaviors and look reality squarely in the eyes.

References

Aaker, J. L., & Lee, A. Y. (2001). "I" see pleasures and "we" avoid pains. The role of self-regulatory goals information and persuasion. *Journal of Consumer Research, 27,* 33–49.

Abelson, R. P., & Levi, A. (1985). Decision and decision theory. In G. Lindzey & E. Aronson (Eds.), *Handbook of social psychology* (pp. 231–310). New York: Random House.

Abrahms, M. (2008). What terrorists really want. *International Security, 32,* 78–105.

Adams, G. (2005). The cultural grounding of personal relationships: Enemyship in North America and West African worlds. *Journal of Personality and Social Psychology, 88,* 948–968.

Adorno, T. W., Frenkel-Brunswik, E., Levinson, D. J., & Sanford, R. N. (1950). *The authoritarian personality.* New York: Harper.

Ahmed, S. (2002). *Beyond veil and holy war: Islamic teachings and Muslim practice with biblical comparisons.* Honolulu: Moving Pen Publishers.

Alcock, J. E. (2000). Alternative medicines and the psychology of belief. In W. Sampson & L. Vaughn (Eds.), *Science meets alternative medicine* (pp. 47–62). Amherst, NY: Prometheus.

Alloy, L. B., & Abramson, L. (1979). Judgment of contingency in depressed and non-depressed students: Sadder but wiser? *Journal of Experimental Psychology General, 108,* 441–485.

Allport, G. W. (1967). *The individual and his religion.* New York: Macmillan. (Original work published 1950)

Altemeyer, B. (1996). *The authoritarian specter.* Cambridge, MA: Harvard University Press.

Altemeyer, B., & Hunsberger, B. (2005). Fundamentalism and authoritarianism. In R. F. Paloutzian & C. L. Park (Eds.), *Handbook of the psychology of religion and spirituality* (pp. 378–393). New York: Guilford.

Alter, J. (2005, November 7). The price of loyalty. *Newsweek*, p. 47.

Altocchi, J., & Altocchi, L. (1995). Polyfaceted psychological acculturation in Cook islanders. *Journal of Cross-Cultural Psychology, 26*, 426–440.

Ames, R. T., & Dissanayake, W. (1996). *Self-and deception: A cross–cultural philosophical enquiry*. Albany: State University of New York Press.

Annan, K. (2004, December 4–10). Courage to fulfill our responsibilities. *The Economist*, p. 23.

Archer, M. (2003). *Structure, agency, and internal conversation*. Cambridge, UK: Cambridge University Press.

Argyle, M. (1999). Causes and correlates of happiness. In D. Kahneman, E. Diener, & N. Schwarz (Eds.), *Well-being: The foundations of hedonic psychology* (pp. 353–373). New York: Russell Sage Foundation.

Armstrong, K. (1993). *A history of God*. New York: Ballantine Books.

Armstrong, K. (2000). *The battle for God: A history of fundamentalism*. New York: Ballantine Books.

Armstrong, K. (2001). *Buddha*. London: Penguin.

Armstong, K. (2005). *A history of myth*. New York: Canongate.

Armstrong, K. (2006). *Muhammad: A prophet for our time*. New York: HarperCollins.

Aronson, E. (2004). Reducing hostility and building compassion: Lessons from the jigsaw classroom. In A. G. Miller (Ed.). *The social psychology of good and evil* (pp. 469–488). New York: Guilford.

Associated Press (2004).

Atran, S. (2002). *In Gods we trust: The evolutionary landscape of religion*. Oxford, UK: Oxford University Press.

Atran, S. (2003). Genesis of suicide terrorism. *Science, 299*, 1534–1539.

Atran, S. (2007). Religion's social and cognitive landscape: An evolutionary perspective. In S. Kitayama & D. Cohen (Eds.), *Handbook of cultural psychology* (pp. 417–453). New York: Guilford.

Atran, S., & Norenzayan, A. (2004). Religion's evolutionary landscape: Counter-intuition, commitment, compassion, communion. *Behavioral & Brain Sciences, 27*, 713–770.

Averill, J. R. (1973). Personal control over aversive stimuli and its relationship to stress. *Psychological Bulletin, 80*, 286–303.

Baker, J., A. Hamilton, L. H., & Eagleburger, L. S. (2006). *The Iraq Study Group Report*. New York: Vintage Books.

Balcetis, E., & Dunning, D. (2006). See what you want to see: Motivational influences on visual perception. *Journal of Personality and Social Psychology, 91*, 612–625.

Bandura, A. (1977). *Aggression: A social learning analysis*. Englewood Cliffs, NJ: Prentice-Hall.

Bandura, A. (1989). Perceived self-efficacy in the exercise of personal agency. *The Psychological Bulletin of the British Psychological Society, 10*, 411–424.

Bandura, A. (2004). The role of selective moral disengagement in terrorism and counterterrorism. In F. M. Moghaddam & A. J. Marsella (Eds.), *Understanding terrorism* (pp. 121–150). Washington, DC: American Psychological Association.

Barber, B. R. (1995). *Jihad vs. McWorld: Terrorism's challenge to democracy*. New York: Ballantine Books.

Bartlett, F. C. (1950). *Remembering.* Cambridge, UK: Cambridge University Press. (Original work published 1932)

Baum, A., Revenson T. A., & Singer, J. E. (Eds.). (2001). *Handbook of health psychology.* Mahwah, NJ: Erlbaum.

Baumeister, R. (1989). The optimal margin of illusion. *Journal of Social & Clinical Psychology, 8,* 176–189.

Baumeister, R. F. (1990). Suicide as escape from self. *Psychological Review, 97,* 90–113.

Baumeister, R. F. (1991). *Meanings of life.* New York: Guilford.

Baumeister, R. F. (1993). Lying to yourself: The enigma of self-deception. In M. Lewis & C. Saarni (Eds.), *Lying and deception in everyday life* (pp. 166–183). New York: Guilford.

Baumeister, R. F. (1995). *The cultural animal.* New York: Oxford University Press.

Baumeister, R. F. (1997). Identity, self-concept, and self-esteem: The self lost and found. In R. Hogan, J. Johnson, & S. Briggs (Eds.), *Handbook of personality psychology* (pp. 681–711). San Diego: Academic Press.

Baumeister, R. F. (1998). The self. In D. T. Gilbert, S. T. Fiske, & G. Lindzey (Eds.), *The handbook of social psychology* (Vol. 1, pp. 680–740). Boston: McGraw-Hill.

Baumeister, R. F., Brotslavsky, E., Finkenauer, C., & Vohs, K. D. (2001). Bad is stronger than good. *Review of General Psychology, 5,* 323–370.

Baumeister, R. F., Campbell, J. D., Krueger, J. I., & Vohs, K. D. (2003). Does self-esteem cause better performance, interpersonal success, happiness, or healthy life styles? *Psychological Science in the Public Interest, 4,* 1–44.

Baumeister, R. F., & Leary, N. R. (1995). The need to belong: Desire for interpersonal attachments as a fundamental human motivation. *Psychological Bulletin, 117,* 497–529.

Bazerman, M. H., Baron, J., & Shonk, K. (2001). *You can't enlarge the pie.* Cambridge, MA: Basic Books.

Becker, E. (1973). *The denial of death.* New York: The Free Press.

Benbow, C. P., & Stanley, J. C. (1980). Sex differences in mathematical ability: Fact or fiction? *Science, 210,* 1262–1264.

Benjamin, D., & Simon, S. (2002). *The age of sacred terror.* New York: Random House.

Berger, P. L., & Luckmann, T. (1966). *The social construction of reality: A treatise in the sociology of knowledge.* Garden City, NY: Doubleday.

Berumen, M. E. (2006). Bertrand Russell and the conquest of happiness. *Free Inquiry, 25*(6), 49–52.

Beschloss, M. (2007, May 14). A president's ultimate test. *Newsweek,* pp. 30–32.

Beveridge, W. I. B. (1950). *The art of scientific investigation.* New York: Vintage Books.

Bhikkhu, B. (1956). *Handbook for mankind.* Bangkok, Thailand: Mahachula Buddhist University Press.

Bieri, J. (1966). Cognitive complexity and personality development. In O. J. Harvey (Ed.), *Experience, structure, and adaptability* (pp. 13–37). New York: Springer.

Biswas-Diener, R. (2008). Material wealth and subjective well-being. In M. Eid & R. J. Larsen (Eds.), *The science of subjective well-being* (pp. 307–322). New York: Guilford.

Bloom, M. (2007). *Dying to kill: The allure of suicide terror.* New York: Columbia University Press.

Bloom, P. (2005). Is God an accident? *The Atlantic, 296*(5), 105–114.

Boivie, I. (2003). Buy nothing, improve everything. *The Humanist, 63*(6), 7–9.

Bond, M. H. (2004). Culture and aggression—From context to coercion. *Personality and Social Psychology Review, 8*, 62–78.

Bond, R., & Smith, P. B. (1996). Culture and conformity: A meta-analysis of studies using Asch's (1952b, 1956). Line judgment task. *Psychological Bulletin, 119*, 111–137.

Borowsky, R., Barth, F., Shweder, R. A., Rodseth, L., & Stolzenberg, N. M. (2001). A conversation about culture. *American Anthropologist, 103*, 432–446.

Bowker, J. (1997). *World religions.* New York: DK Publishing.

Bowker, J. (2000). *The Cambridge illustrated history of religions.* Cambridge, UK: Cambridge University Press.

Boyer, P. (1994). *The naturalness of religious ideals.* Berkeley: University of California Press.

Boyer, P. (2001). *Religion explained. The evolutionary origins of religious thought.* New York: Basic Books.

Brewer, M. B. (1991). The social self: On being the same and different at the same time. *Personality and Social Psychology Bulletin, 17*, 475–482.

Brewer, M. B., & Campbell, D. T. (1976). *Ethnocentrism and intergroup attitudes.* New York: Wiley.

Brewer, M. B., & Chen, Y.-R. (2007). Where (who) are collectives in collectivism? Toward a clarification of individualism and collectivism. *Psychological Review, 114*, 133–151.

Brim, O. G., Ryff, C. D., & Kessler, W. (Eds.), (2004). *How healthy are we? A national study of well-being at midlife.* Chicago: University of Chicago Press.

British Broadcasting Corporation Radio, 2005.

British Broadcasting Corporation Radio, October 7, 2007.

Brown, L. R. (2003). Rescuing a planet under stress. *The Humanist, 63*, 25–29.

Brown, R. W., & Lenneberg, E. H. (1954). A study of language and cognition. *Journal of Abnormal and Social Psychology, 49*, 454–462.

Bruner, J. (1986). *Actual minds, possible worlds.* Cambridge, MA: Harvard University Press.

Burkert, W. (1996). *Creation of the sacred: Tracks of biology in early religion.* Cambridge, MA: Harvard University Press.

Burleson, B. R., & Caplan, S. E. (1998). Cognitive complexity. In J. C. McCroskey, J. Daly, M. M. Martin, & M. J. Beatty (Eds.), *Communication and personality: Trait perspectives* (pp. 233–286). Cresskill, NJ: Hampton Press.

Buruma, I., & Margalit, A. (2004). *Occidentalism: The West in the eyes of its enemies.* New York: Penguin.

Cacciopo, J. T., Hawkley, L. Kaluil, A., Hughes, L. W., & Thisted, R. A. (2008). Happiness and the invisible thread of connection: The Chicago health, aging, and social relations study. In M. Eid & R. J. Larsen (Eds.), *The science of subjective well-being* (pp. 195–219). New York: Guilford.

Campbell, D. T., & LeVine, R. A. (1968). Ethnocentrism and intergroup relations. In R. Abelson E. Aronson, W. J. McGuire, T. M. Newcomb, M. J. Posenberg, & P. H. Tannenbaum (Eds.), *Theories of cognitive consistency: A sourcebook.* Chicago: Rand McNally.

Campbell, J. (1988). *The power of myth*. New York: Doubleday.

Camus, A. (1956). *The fall*. New York: Vintage Books.

Cantor, N., & Sanderson, C. A. (1999). Life task participation and well-being: The importance of taking part in daily life. In D. Kahneman, E. Diener, & N. Schwarz (Eds.), *Well-being: The foundations of hedonic psychology* (pp. 230–243). New York: Russell Sage Foundation.

Caracci, G. (2002). Cultural and contextual aspects of terrorism. In C. E. Stout (Ed.), *The psychology of terrorism* (Vol. 3, pp. 57–83). London: Praeger.

Carpenter, S. (2000). Effects of cultural tightness and collectivism on self-concept and causal attributions. *Cross-Cultural Research, 34*, 38–56.

Carter, J. (2007). *Palestine peace not apartheid*. New York: Simon & Schuster.

Castilla, E. J. (2004). Organizing health care—A comparative analysis of national institutions and inequity over time. *International Sociology, 19*, 403–435.

Castronova, E. (2005). *Synthetic worlds: The business and culture of online games*. Chicago: University of Chicago Press.

Center for Public Integrity (2004). *The buying of the Presidency*.

Cerf, C., & Navasky, V. S. (2008). *Mission accomplished! Or how we won the war in Iraq*. New York: Simon & Schuster.

Chang, I. (1997). *The rape of Nanking: The forgotten holocaust of World War II*. New York: Basic Books.

Charleton, W. (1926). *Epicurus' morals*. London: Peter Davies.

Chatman, J. A., & Barsade, S. G. (1995). Personality, organizational culture, and cooperation: Evidence from a business simulation. *Administrative Science Quarterly, 40*, 423–443.

Chick, G. (1997). Cultural complexity: The concept and its measurement. *Cross-Cultural Research, 31*, 275–307.

Chirkov, V., Ryan, R. M., Kim, Y., & Kaplan, U. (2003). Differentiating autonomy from individualism and independence: A self-determination theory perspective on internalization of cultural orientations and well-being. *Journal of Personality and Social Psychology, 84*, 97–110.

Chiu, C. Y., & Hong, Y. Y. (2006). *Social psychology of culture*. New York: Psychology Press.

Chu, C-N. (1991). *The Asian mind game*. New York: Rawson Associates.

Cohen, A. B., Kennick, D. T., & Li, Y. J. (2006). Ecological variability and religious beliefs. *Behavioral and Brain Sciences, 29*, 468.

Cohen, D., & Hashino-Browne, E. (2005). Insider and outsider perspectives on the self and the social world. In R. M. Sorrentino, D. Cohen, J. M. Olson, & M. P. Zanna (Eds.), *Cultural and social behavior: The Ontario Symposium* (Vol. 10, pp. 49–76). Mahwah, NJ: Erlbaum.

Cohen, D., & Nisbett, R. E. (1997). Field experiments examining the culture of honor: Explaining southern violence. *Personality and Social Psychology Bulletin, 23*, 1188–1199.

Cohen, S. (2004). Social relationships and health. *American Psychologist, 59*, 673–676.

Cohen, S. (2008). National Public System program, March 27.

Confucius. (1909). *The sayings of Confucius*. New York: A Mentor Book.

Creagan, E. T. (2001). *Mayo Clinic on healthy aging.* Rochester, MN: Mayo Clinic.

Crockett, W. H. (1965). Cognitive complexity and impression formation. In B. A. Maher (Ed.), *Progress in experimental personality research* (pp. 47–90). New York: Academic Press.

Cullison, A. (2004, September). Inside al-Quaeda's hard drive. *The Atlantic Monthly,* pp. 55–70.

Darwish, N. (2006). *Now they call me infidel: Why I renounced jihad.* New York: Sentinel, The Penguin Group.

David, H. P., Dytrych, Z., Matejcek, Z., & Schuller, V. (1988). *Born unwanted: Developmental effects of denied abortion.* Prague: Avicenum, Czechoslovak Medical Press.

Dawkins, R. (1989). *The selfish gene.* Oxford, UK: Oxford University Press.

Dawkins, R. (2003). *A devil's chaplain: Reflections on hope, lies, science and love.* Boston: Houghton Mifflin.

Dawson, J. L. M. (1974). Ecology, cultural pressures, towards conformity, and left-handedness: A bio-social psychological approach. In J. L. M. Dawson & W. J. Lonner (Eds.), *Readings in cross-cultural psychology* (pp. 124–150). Hong Kong: Hong Kong University Press.

Deaton, A. (2007, October). *Health and well-being around the world.* Lecture presented at the University of Illinois, Chicago.

DeNeve, K. M., & Cooper, H. (1998). The happy personality: A meta-analysis of 137 personality traits and subjective well-being. *Psychological Bulletin, 124,* 197–229.

Dennett, D. C. (2006). *Breaking the spell: Religion as a natural phenomenon.* London: Viking Press.

Derber, C. (2004). *Regime change begins at home: Freeing America from corporate rule.* San Francisco: Berrett-Koehler.

De Rivera, J., Kurrien, R., & Olsen, N. (2007). The emotional climate of nations and their culture of peace. *Journal of Social Issues, 63,* 255–271.

Deutsche Well, NPR Program (Sundays at 6 a.m.) in 2003.

Diamond, J. (2005). *Collapse: How societies chose to fail or survive.* London: Penguin/Allen Lane.

Diener, E. (1994). Assessing subjective well-being. Progress and opportunities. *Social Indicator Research, 31,* 103–157.

Diener, E. (2008). Myths in the science of happiness, and directions for future research. In M. Eid & R. J. Larsen (Eds.), *The science of subjective well-being* (pp. 493–514). New York: Guilford.

Diener, E., Diener, M., & Diener, C. (1995). Factors predicting the subjective well-being of nations, *Journal of Personality and Social Psychology, 69,* 851–864.

Diener, E., Lucas R. E., Oishi, S., & Suh, E. M. (2002). Looking up and looking down: Weighting good and bad information in life satisfaction judgments. *Personality and Social Psychology Bulletin, 28,* 437–445.

Diener, E., Oishi, S., & Lucas, R. (2003). Personality, culture, and subjective well-being: Emotional and cognitive evaluations of life. *Annual Review of Psychology, 54,* 403–425.

Diener, E., & Suh, E. M. (1999). National differences in subjective well-being. In D. Kahneman, E. Diener, & N. Schwarz (Eds.), *Well-being: The foundations of hedonic psychology* (pp. 434–450). New York: Russell Sage Foundation.

Diener E., & Suh E. M. (Eds.). (2000). *Culture and subjective well-being.* Cambridge, MA: MIT Press.

Dobyns, J., Doughty, P., & Lasswell, H. (1971). *Peasant, power, and applied social change: Vicos as a model.* Beverly Hills, CA: Sage.

Dogan, M. (1995). The decline of religious beliefs in Western Europe. *International Social Science Journal, 47,* 405–419.

Doob, L. (1971). *The patterning of time.* New Haven, CT: Yale University Press.

Dostoyevsky, F. (1966). *A nasty story.* London: Penguin Books.

Dulaney, S., & Fiske, A. P. (1994). Cultural rituals and obsessive-compulsive disorder: Is there a common psychological mechanism? *Ethos, 22,* 245–283.

Dunning, D. (2001). On the motives underlying social cognition. In N. Schwarz & A. Tesser (Eds.), *Blackwell handbook of social psychology. Vol. 1: Intraindividual processes* (pp. 348–374). New York: Blackwell.

Dyson, F. (2005, April 28). The bitter end. *The New York Review of Books,* pp. 56–74.

Earley, P. C., & Ang, S. (2003). *Cultural intelligence.* Palo Alto, CA: Stanford University Press.

Eckersley, R. (2004). *Well & good.* Melbourne, Australia: Text Publishing.

Eckersley, R. (2007). Culture, spirituality, religion and health: Looking at the big picture. *Medical Journal of Australia, 186*(10), 54–56.

Eckersley, R., & Dear, K. (2002). Cultural correlates of youth suicide. *Social Science and Medicine, 55,* 1893–1906.

Edgerton R. B. (1992). *Sick societies: Challenging the myth of primitive harmony.* New York: The Free Press.

Ehrlich, P. (2000). *Human natures.* Washington, DC: Inland Press.

Ehrman, B. D. (2005). *Misquoting Jesus: The story behind who changed the New Testament and why.* San Francisco: Harper.

Eid, M., & Larsen, R. J. (2008). *The science of subjective well-being.* New York: Guilford.

Eliade, M. (1967). *From primitives to zen.* New York: Harper & Row.

Eliade, M. (1978). *A history of religious ideas* (Vol. 1). Chicago: University of Chicago Press.

Eliade, M. (1982). *A history of religious ideas* (Vol. 2). Chicago: University of Chicago Press.

Eliade, M. (1985). *A history of religious ideas* (Vol. 3). Chicago: University of Chicago.

Emmons, R. A. (2008). Gratitude, subjective well-being and the brain. In M. Eid & R. J. Larsen (Eds.), *The science of subjective well-being* (pp. 469–489). New York: Guilford.

Encyclopeadia Britannica (1957).

Epicurus. (2002). *Apanta* (total work). Athens, Greece: Cactus Editions.

Erdelyi, M. H. (1974). A new look at the New Look: Perceptual defense and vigilance. *Psychological Review, 81,* 1–24.

Erdelyi, M. H. (2000). Repression. In A. E. Kazdin (Ed.), *Encyclopedia of psychology* (Vol. 7, pp. 69–71). New York: Oxford University Press.

Essock, S. M., McGuire, M. T., & Hooper, B. (1988). Self-deception in social support networks. In J. S. Lockard & D. L. Paulhus (Eds.), *Self-deception: An adaptive mechanism?* (pp. 200–211). Englewood Cliffs, NJ: Prentice-Hall.

Etzioni, A. (2004*). From empire to community*. New York: Palgrave Macmillan.

Eysenck H. (1978). *The psychological basis of ideology*. Baltimore, MD: University Park Press.

Fallows, J. (2005). Why Iraq has no army. *The Atlantic, 296*(5), 60–77.

Fanning, L. (2003, September 14). Clash of civilizations at root of war on terror. *News Gazette.*

Farazza, A. (2004). *PsychoBible: Behavior, religion, and the Holy Book*. Charlottesville, VA: Pitchstone.

Feldman, N. (2003). *After jihad: America and the struggle for Islamic democracy*. New York: Farrar, Straus, & Giroux.

Feldman, R. S., & Custrini, R. J. (1988). Learning to lie and self-deceive: Children's nonverbal communication of deception. In J. S. Lockard & D.L. Paulhus (Eds.), *Self-deception: An adaptive mechanism?* (pp. 40–53). Englewood Cliffs, NJ: Prentice-Hall.

Festinger, L. (1954). A theory of social comparison processes. *Human Relations, 7,* 117-140

Festinger, L. (1957). *A theory of cognitive dissonance*. Palo Alto, CA: Stanford University Press.

Festinger, L. (1983). *The human legacy*. New York: Columbia University Press.

Festinger, L., Riecken, H. W., & Schachter, S. (1956). *When prophesy fails: A social and psychological study of a modern group that predicted the destruction of the world.* Minneapolis: University of Minnesota Press.

Fiske, A. P., Kitayama, S., Markus, H. R., & Nisbett, R. E. (1998). The cultural matrix of social psychology. In D. T. Gilbert, S. T. Fiske, & G. Lindzey (Eds.), *The handbook of social psychology* (Vol. 2, pp. 915–980). Boston: McGraw-Hill.

Flannery, T. (2006). The weather makers: How man is changing the climate and what it means for life on earth. *Atlantic Monthly Press 298*, No. 1, pp. 56–67.

Ford, C. S., & Beach, F. A. (1951). *Patterns of sexual behavior*. New York: Harper.

Francis, L. (1992). Is psychoticism really a dimension of personality fundamental to religiosity? *Personality & Individual Differences, 13,* 645–652.

Frank, T. (2004). *What's the matter with Kansas?* New York: Metropolitan Books.

Frazer, J. G. (1960). *The golden bough*. New York: Macmillan. (Original work published 1894).

Frazer, J. G. (1968). *The new golden bough*. Garden City, NY: Anchor Books.

Frederick, D. A., & Haselton, M. G. (2007). Why is muscularity sexy? Tests of the fitness indicator hypothesis. *Personality and Social Psychology Bulletin, 33,* 1167–1183.

Fredrickson, B. L. (2008). Promoting positive affect. In M. Eid & R. J. Larsen (Eds.), *The science of subjective well-being* (pp. 449–468). New York: Guilford.

Freeney, D. J., Jr. (2002). Entrainment in Islamic fundamentalism. In C. E. Stout (Ed.), *The psychology of terrorism* (Vol. 3, pp. 191–210). London: Praeger.

Frenkel-Brunswik, E. (1939). Mechanisms of self-deception. *Journal of Social Psychology, 10,* 409–420.

Freud, S. (1964). *The future of an illusion* (Rev. Ed.). Garden City, NY: Doubleday Anchor Books.

Friedman, T. L. (2000). *The lexus and the olive tree*. New York: Farrar, Straus, & Giroux.

Friedman, T. L. (2002). *Latitudes and attitudes*. New York: Farrar, Straus, & Giroux.

Friedman, T. L. (2005, September 14). Singapore and Katrina. *New York Times*, Op-Ed page.

Funder, D. C., & Colvin, C. R. (1997). Congruence of others' and self-judgments of personality. In R. Hogan, J. Johnson, & S. Briggs (Eds.), *Handbook of personality psychology* (pp. 617–647). San Diego: Academic Press.

Galton, F. (1872). Statistical inquiries into the efficacy of prayer. *Fortnightly Review, 18,* 125–135.

Ganor, B. (2005). *The counter-terrorism puzzle: A guide for decision makers*. New Brunswick, NJ: Transaction Publishers.

Gay, P. (1999). *Mozart*. London: Penguin.

George, L. K., Ellison, C. G., & Larson, D. B. (2002). Explaining the relationship between religious involvement and health. *Psychological Inquiry, 13,* 190–200.

Geyer, A., & Baumeister, R. (2005). Religion, morality, and self-control: Values, virtues, and vice. In R. F. Paloutzian & C. L. Park (Eds.), *Handbook of the psychology of religion and spirituality* (pp. 412–432). New York: Guilford.

Gibbon, E. (1963). *The decline and fall of the Roman Empire*. New York: Dell.

Gilbert, D. T., & Cooper, J. (1985). Social psychological strategies of self-deception. In M. W. Martin (Ed.), *Self-deception and self-understanding* (pp. 75–94). Lawrence: University of Kansas Press.

Gilovich, T. (1991). *How we know what isn't so*. New York: Macmillan.

Ginges, J., Hansen, I., G. & Norenzayan, A. (In press). Religion and support for suicide attacks. *Psychological Science*.

Gladwell, M. (2002). *The tipping point: How little things can make a big difference*. New York: Little, Brown.

Gladwell, M. (2005). *Blink*. New York: Little, Brown.

Glenn, E. (1981). *Man and mankind: Conflicts and communication between cultures*. Norwood, NJ: Ablex.

Golman, D. (1985). *Vital lies, simple truths: The psychology of self-deception*. New York: Simon & Schuster.

Golman, D. (1989). What is negative about positive illusions? When benefits for the individual harm the collective. *Journal of Social and Clinical Psychology, 8,* 190–197.

Gordon, M., & Trainor, B. (2006). *Cobra II: The inside story of the invasion and occupation of Iraq*. New York: Atlantic Books.

Gore, A. (2007). *The assault on reason*. New York: Penguin Press.

Gottfredson, M. R., & Hirschi, T. (1990). *General theory of crime*. Palo Alto, CA: Stanford University Press.

Gouldner, A. W. (1960). The norm of reciprocity. A preliminary statement. *American Sociological Review, 25,* 161–178.

Grams, G. R. (1997). Self-deception in perception of personal appearance. *Dissertation Abstracts, Section B, 58,* 2709.

Gratzer, W. (2000). *The undergrowth of science: Delusion, self-deception, and human frailty*. Oxford, UK: Oxford University Press.

Green, S. (2000). Science, politics, and alternative medicine. In W. Sampson & L. Vaughn (Eds.), *Science meets alternative medicine* (pp. 33–46). Amherst, NY: Prometheus.

Greenspan, A. (2007). *The age of turbulence: Adventures in a new world*. New York: Penguin Press.

Greenwald, A. G. (1988). Self-knowledge and self-deception. In J. S. Lockard & D. L. Paulhus (Eds.), *Self-deception: An adaptive mechanism?* (pp. 113–131). Englewood Cliffs, NJ: Prentice-Hall.

Gregg, G. S. (2005). *The Middle East: A cultural psychology*. New York: Oxford University Press.

Gunaratna, R. (2002). *Inside al-Qaeda*. New York: Columbia University Press.

Gur, R. C., & Sackheim, H. A. (1979). Self-deception: A concept in search of a phenomenon. *Journal of Personality and Social Psychology, 37*, 147–169.

Hafez, M. (2004, October). *Manufacturing human bombs: Strategy, culture, and conflict in the making of Palestinian suicide terrorism*. Lecture given at the Suicide Terrorist Conference, Office of Justice Program Building, Washington, DC.

Haidt, J. (2006). *The happiness hypothesis: Finding modern truth in ancient wisdom*. New York: Basic Books.

Hall, N. R., & Crisp, R. J. (2005). Considering multiple criteria for social categorization can reduce intergroup bias. *Personality and Social Psychology Bulletin, 31*, 1345–1444.

Haney, C., Banks, W. C., & Zimbardo, P. G. (1973). Interpersonal dynamics in a simulated prison. *International Journal of Criminology and Penology, 1*, 69–97.

Hansen, I., & Norenzayan, A. (2006). Yang and ying and heaven and hell: Untangling the complex relationship between religion and intolerance. In P. McNemara (Ed.), *Where God and mind meet: How the brain and evolutionary science are revolutionizing religion and spirituality*. Westport, CT: Praeger.

Haritos-Fatourou, M. (2002). *Psychological origins of institutional torture*. New York: Routledge.

Harris, S. (2004). *The end of faith: Religion, terror, and the future of reason*. New York: Norton.

Harris, S. (2005a). Lecture on CSPAN 2, February 20.

Harris, S. (2005b, March 19). The virus of religious moderation. *The Times of London*.

Hartung, J. (1988). Deceiving down: Conjectures on the management of subordinate status. In J. S. Lockard & D. L. Paulhus (Eds.), *Self-deception: An adaptive mechanism?* (pp. 170–185). Englewood Cliffs, NJ: Prentice-Hall.

Harvey, O. J., Hunt, D. E., & Schroeder, H. M. (1961). *Conceptual systems and personality organization*. New York: Wiley.

Haselton, M. G., & Nettle, D. (2006). The paranoid optimist: An integrated evolutionary model of cognitive biases. *Personality and Social Psychology Review, 10*, 47–66.

Hatfield, E., Rapson, R. L., & Martel, L. D. (2007). Passionate love and sexual desire. In S. Kitayama & D. Cohen (Eds.), *Handbook of cultural psychology* (pp. 760–770). New York: Guilford.

Hayana, D. M. (1988). Dealing with chance: Self-deception and fantasy among gamblers. In J. S. Lockard & D. L. Paulhus (Eds.), *Self-deception: An adaptive mechanism?* (pp. 186 –199). Englewood Cliffs, NJ: Prentice-Hall.

Haybron, D. M. (2008). Philosophy and the science of subjective well-being. In M. Eid & R. J. Larsen (Eds.), *The science of subjective well-being* (pp. 17–43). New York: Guilford.

Hébert, R. (2003). In sickness or in wealth. *American Psychological Society Observer,* *16,* 30–42.

Heine, S. J., Lehman, D. R., Markus, H. R., & Kitayama, S. (1999). Is there a universal need for positive self-regard? *Psychological Review, 106,* 766–794.

Heine, S. J., Proulx, T., & Vohs, K. D. (2006). The meaning maintenance model: On the coherence of social motivation. *Personality and Social Psychology Review, 10,* 88–110.

Helson, H. (1964). *Adaptation-level theory.* New York: Harper & Row.

Henry, J. P., & Stephens, P. M. (1977). *Stress, health and social environment.* New York: Springer.

Herodotus. (1966). *The histories.* New York: Norton.

Herskovits, M. J. (1955). *Cultural anthropology.* New York: Knopf.

Higgins, E. T. (1997). Beyond pleasure and pain. *American Psychologist, 52,* 1280–1300.

Ho, D. Y-F. (1976). On the concept of face. *American Journal of Sociology 81,* 867–890.

Hobfoll, S., & Leiberman, J. (1987). Personality and social resources in immediate and continued stress resistance among women. *Journal of Personality and Social Psychology, 52,* 18–26.

Hodous, L. (1946). Confucianism. In E. J. Jurji (Ed.), *The great religions of the modern world* (pp. 1–23). Princeton, NJ: Princeton University Press.

Hofstede, G. (2001). *Culture's consequences* (2nd ed.). Thousand Oaks, CA: Sage.

Holmberg, A. R. (1969). *Nomads of the long bow.* Garden City, NY: Natural History Press. (Original work published 1950)

Holmes, D. S. (1970). Differential change in affective intensity and the forgetting of unpleasant personal experiences. *Journal of Personality and Social Psychology, 15,* 234–288.

Holtgraves, T. (1997). Styles of language use: Individual and cultural variability in conversational indirectness. *Journal of Personality and Social Psychology, 73,* 624–637.

Holton, D. C. (1946). Shintoism. In E. J. Jurji (Ed.), *The great religions of the modern world* (pp. 141–177). Princeton, NJ: Princeton University Press.

Hong, Y., Morris M. W., Chiu, C., & Benet-Martinez, V. (2000). Multiple minds: A dynamic constructivist approach to culture and cognition. *American Psychologist, 55,* 709–720.

Hood, R. W., Hill, P. C., & Williamson, W. P. (2005). *The psychology of religious fundamentalism.* New York: Guilford.

House, R. J., Hanges, P. J., Javidan, M., Dorfman, P. W., & Gupta, V. (2004). *Culture, leadership, and organizations: The GLOBE study of 62 societies.* Thousand Oaks, CA: Sage.

Houser, M. D. (2006). *Moral minds.* New York: HarperCollins.

Hu, H. C. (1944). The Chinese concept of face. *American Anthropologist, 46,* 45–64.

Hunsberger, B., & Jackson, L. M. (2005). Religion, meaning, and prejudice. *Journal of Social Issues, 61,* 807–826.

Huntington, S. P. (1996). *Clash of civilizations and the remaking of the world order.* New York: Simon & Schuster.

Huntington, S. P. (2005). *Who are we?* London: Simon & Schuster.

Hwang, Y-Y., Jung, J., & Haugtvedt, C. R. (2006). *Cultural influences on external information search and information source use.* Manuscript in preparation.

Hyman, R. (2000). The mischief making of ideomotor action. In W. Sampson & L. Vaughn (Eds.), *Science meets alternative medicine* (pp. 95–116). Amherst, NY: Prometheus.

Ibrahim, R. (2007). *The al-Qaeda reader*. New York: Broadway Books.

Ibsen, H. (1950). *Three plays: The pillars of the community, The wild duck, Hedda Gabler*. London: Penguin Books.

Inglehart, R., & Baker, W. E. (2000). Modernization, cultural change, and the persistence of traditional values. *American Sociological Review, 65*, 19–51.

Inkeles, A., & Smith, D. H. (1974). *Becoming modern*. Cambridge, MA: Harvard University Press.

International Herald Tribune, Summer 2004.

Ishay, M. R. (2004). *The history of human rights*. Berkeley: University of California Press.

Iyengar, S., & DeVoe, S. E. (2003). Rethinking the value of choice considering cultural mediators of intrinsic motivation. In V. Murphy-Berman & J. J. Berman (Eds.), *Nebraska symposium on motivation* (Vol. 49, pp. 129–174). Lincoln: University of Nebraska Press.

Iyengar, S. S., Lepper, M. R., & Ross, L. (1999). Independence from whom? Interdependence from whom? Cultural perspectives on ingroups versus outgroups. In D. A. Prentice & D. T. Miller (Eds.), *Cultural divides: Understanding and overcoming group conflict* (pp. 273–301). New York: Russell Sage Foundation.

Iwao, S. (1993). *The Japanese woman: Traditional image and changing reality*. New York: The Free Press.

Jacqard, R. (2002). *In the name of Osama Bin Laden*. Durham, NC: Duke University Press.

Jacoby, S. (2004). *Freethinkers*. New York: Metropolitan Books.

Jahoda, G. (1969). *The psychology of superstition*. London: Penguin Press.

Jahoda, M. (1958). *Current concepts of positive mental health*. New York: Basic Books.

Janis, I. L. (1982). *Groupthink: Psychological studies of policy decisions and fiascos* (2nd ed.). Boston: Houghton Mifflin.

Jannoulatos, A. (2001). *Islam*. Athens: Porefthendes. (Original work published 1975).

Janoff-Bulman, R. (1989). The benefits of illusions, the threat of disillusionment, and the limitations of accuracy. *Journal of Social & Clinical Psychology, 8*, 158–175.

Jenkins, M. (2008, April–May). A really inconvenient truth. *Miller-McCune Magazine*, pp. 38–49.

Jersild A. (1931). Memory for the pleasant as compared with the unpleasant. *Journal of Experimental Psychology, 14*, 284–288.

Johnson, D. W., & Johnson, R. T. (1993). Creative and critical thinking through academic controversy. *American Behavioral Scientist, 37*, 40–53.

Jost, J. T. (2006). The end of the end of ideology. *American Psychologist, 61*, 651–670.

Journal of the American Medical Association, 2006.

Juergensmeyer, M. (2000). *Terror in the mind of God: The global rise of religious violence*. Berkeley: University of California Press.

Kahneman, D., Diener, E., & Schwarz, N. (Eds.). (1999). *Well-being: The foundations of hedonic psychology*. New York: Russell Sage Foundation.

Kahneman, D., & Tversky, A. (1996). On the reality of cognitive illusions. *Psychological Review, 103*, 582–591.

Kant, I. (1959). *Foundations of metaphysics of morals* (L. W. Beck, Trans.). New York: Macmillan. (Original work published 1785)

Kasser, T. (2002). *The high price of materialism*. Cambridge, MA: MIT Press.

Kassin, S. M. (2007, August). Why innocents confess: Insights from the psychology research laboratory. Invited Paper presented at the 57th annual meeting of the American Psychological Association, San Francisco, CA.

Kazarian, S. S., & Evans, D. R. (2001). *Handbook of cultural health psychology*. San Diego: Academic Press.

Keeley, R. V. (2002). Trying to define terrorism. *Middle East Policy, 9*, 34.

Kepel, G. (2004). *The war for Muslim minds: Islam and the West*. Cambridge, MA: Belknap Press of Harvard University.

Khan, N. (2002). *Profiling the political violent in Pakistan: Self-construals and values*. Unpublished manuscript, University of Sussex, Sussex, UK.

Kidder, L. (1992). Requirements for being Japanese: Stories of returnees. *International Journal of Intercultural Relations, 16*, 383–394.

King, L. (2008). Interventions for enhancing subjective well-being. Can we make people happier and should we? In M. Eid & R. J. Larsen (Eds.), *The science of subjective well-being* (pp. 431–448). New York: Guilford.

Kirkpatrick, L. A. (2005). *Attachment, evolution, and the psychology of religion*. New York: Guilford.

Kitayama, S., & Cohen, D. (2007). *Handbook of cultural psychology*. New York: Guilford.

Kitayama, S., Duffy, S., & Uchida, Y. (Eds.). (2007). Self as cultural mode of being. In S. Kitayama & D. Cohen (Eds.), *Handbook of cultural psychology* (pp. 136–174). New York: Guilford.

Kitchens, G. D. (2003). Positive illusions and psychological well being in Ukraine. *Dissertation Abstracts International*, Section B: *Sciences and Engineering, 64*, 1550.

Kluckhohn, C. (1954). Culture and behavior. In G. Lindzey (Ed.), *Handbook of social psychology* (Vol. 2, pp. 921–976). Cambridge, MA: Addison-Wesley.

Koenig, H. G., McCullough, M. E., & Larson, D. B. (2001). *Handbook of religion and health*. New York: Oxford University Press.

Kolbert, E. (2006). *Field notes from a catastrophe: Man, nature and climate change*. New York: Bloomsbury Publications.

Korten, D. C. (1995). *When corporations rule the world*. San Francisco: Berrett-Kohler.

Korten, D. C. (2001). *When corporations rule the world* (2nd ed.). San Francisco: Berrett-Kohler.

Kramer, A. F., Colcombe, S. J., McAulay, E., Stalf, R., & Erickson, K. J. (2005). Fitness, aging, and neurocognitive function. *Neurobiology of Aging, 26S*, S124–S127.

Kroeber, A. L., & Kluckhohn, C. (1952). *Culture: A critical review of concepts and definitions* (Vol. 14, No. 1). Cambridge, MA: Peabody Museum.

Kruger, J., & Clement, R. W. (1994). The truly false consensus effect: An ineradicable egocentric bias in social perception. *Journal of Personality and Social Psychology, 67*, 596–610.

Kruglanski, A. W. (2004). *The psychology of close mindedness*. New York: Psychology Press.

Kruglanski, A. W., & Fishman, S. (2006). The psychology of terrorism: "Syndrome" versus "tool" perspectives. *Terrorism and Political Violence, 18,* 193–215.

Kuhn, M. H., & McPartland, T. (1954). An empirical investigation of self-attitudes. *American Sociological Review, 19,* 58–76.

Kunda, Z. (1990). The case for motivated reasoning. *Psychological Bulletin, 108,* 480–498.

Küng, H. (2005). *Why I am still a Christian*. London: Continuum. (Original work published 1987)

Kurman, J. (2003). Why is self-enhancement low in certain collectivist cultures? *Journal of Cross-Cultural Psychology, 34,* 496–510.

Kurtz, P. (1983). *In defense of secular humanism*. Amherst, NY: Prometheus.

Lambert, W. W., Triandis, L. M., & Wolf, M. (1959). Some correlates of belief in the malevolence and benevolence of supernatural beings: A cross-cultural study. *Journal of Abnormal and Social Psychology, 58,* 162–169.

Lamont, C. (1997). *The philosophy of humanism* (8th ed.). Washington, DC: Humanist Press.

Langer, E. J. (1975). The illusion of control. *Journal of Personality and Social Psychology, 32,* 311–328.

Langer, S. K. (1960). *Philosophy in a new key: A study of the symbolism of reason, rite and art* (4th ed.). Cambridge, MA: Harvard University Press.

Larsen, R. J., & Eid, M. (2008). Ed Diener and the science of subjective well-being. In M. Eid & R. J. Larsen (Eds.), *The science of subjective well-being* (pp. 1–16). New York: Guilford.

Larsen, R. J., & Prizmic, Z. (2008). Regulation of emotional well-being: Overcoming the hedonic treadmill. In M. Eid & R. J. Larsen (Eds.), *The science of subjective well-being* (pp. 258–289). New York: Guilford.

Latané, B. (1996). Dynamic social impact. The creation of culture by communication. *Journal of Communication, 46,* 13–25.

Layard, R. (2005). *Happiness: Lessons from a new science*. London: Allen Lane.

Lee, Y-T. (2003). Daoism: Humanism in ancient China: Broadening personality and counseling theories in the 21st century. *Journal of Humanistic Psychology, 43,* 64–85.

Lee, Y-T., Jussim, L. J., & McCauley, C. R. (1995). *Stereotype accuracy*. Washington, DC: American Psychological Association.

Lee, Y-T., McCauley, C., Moghaddam, F., & Worchel, S. (2004). *The psychology of ethnic and cultural conflict*. Westport, CT: Praeger.

Lee, Y-T., & Seligman, M. E. P. (1997). Are Americans more optimistic than the Chinese? *Personality & Social Psychology Bulletin, 23,* 32–40.

Leighton, A. H. (1960). *An introduction to social psychiatry*. Springfield, IL: C.C. Thomas.

Leung, K. (1997). Negotiation and reward allocations across cultures In P. C. Earley & M. Erez (Eds.), *New perspectives on international industrial and organizational psychology* (pp. 640–675). San Francisco: Lexington Press.

Levine, N. (2007). *Against the stream*. New York: Taylor & Francis.

Levine, R. V., & Bartlett, K. (1984). Pace of life, punctuality, and coronary heart disease in six countries. *Journal of Cross-Cultural Psychology, 15,* 233–255.

Levitt, S. D., & Dubner, S. J. (2005). *Freakonomics: A rogue economist explores the hidden side of everything*. London: Penguin/Allen Lane.

Lévy-Bruhl, L. (1923). *Primitive mentality*. Boston: Beacon Press.

Lévy-Bruhl, L. (1966). *How natives think*. New York: Washington Square Press. (Original work published 1910.)

Lewis, B. (1990, September). The roots of Muslim rage. *Atlantic Monthly*, pp. 47–60.

Lewis, B. (2003*). The crisis of Islam: Holy war and unholy terror*. New York: The Modern Library.

Lewis, M., & Saarni, C. (Eds.). (1993). *Lying and deception in everyday life*. New York: Guilford.

Li, S., Triandis, H. C., & Yu, Y. (2006). Cultural orientation and corruption. *Ethics & Behavior, 16*, 199–216.

Lillard, A. (1998). Ethnopsychologies: Cultural variations in theories of mind. *Psychological Bulletin, 123*, 3–32.

Lim, F., Bond, M. H., & Bond, M. K. (2005). Linking society and psychological factors to homicide rates across nations. *Journal of Cross-Cultural Psychology, 36*, 515–536.

Lin, Z. (1997). Ambiguity with a purpose. The shadow of power in communication. In P. C. Earley & M. Erez (Eds.), *New perspectives on international industrial and organizational psychology* (pp. 363–376). San Francisco: Lexington Press.

Linden, E. (2006). *The winds of change: Climate, weather and the destruction of civilizations*. New York: Simon & Schuster.

Lockard, J. S. (1988). Origins of self-deception: Is lying to oneself uniquely human? In J. S. Lockard & D. L. Paulhus (Eds.), *Self-deception: An adaptive mechanism?* (pp. 14–22). Englewood Cliffs, NJ: Prentice-Hall.

Lockard, J. S., & Mateer, C. A. (1988). Neural bases of self-deception. In J. S. Lockard & D. L. Paulhus (Eds.), *Self-deception: An adaptive mechanism?* (pp. 23–39). Englewood Cliffs, NJ: Prentice-Hall.

Lockard, J. S., & Paulhus, D. L. (Eds.). (1988). *Self-deception: An adaptive mechanism?* Englewood Cliffs, NJ: Prentice-Hall.

Luthar, S. S. (2005, February 18). Rich kid, poor kid. *Observer*, p. 11.

Lyons, A., & Kashima, Y. (2003). How are stereotypes maintained through communication? The influence of stereotype sharedness. *Journal of Personality and Social Psychology, 85*, 989–1005.

Lyubomirsky, S., Sheldon, K. M., & Schkade, D. (2005). Pursuing happiness: The architecture of sustainable change. *Review of General Psychology, 9*, 111–131.

Ma, V., & Schoeneman, T. J. (1997). Individualism versus collectivism: A comparison of Kenyan and American self-concepts. *Basic and Applied Social Psychology, 19*, 261–273.

MacAndrew, C., & Edgerton, R. B. (1969). *Drunken comportment: A social explanation*. Chicago: Aldine.

Manji, I. (2003). *The trouble with Islam*. New York: St. Martin's Press.

Malinowski, B. (1954). *Magic, science, and religion*. New York: Anchor Books.

Malinowski, B. (2004). Rational mastery by man of his surroundings. In R. Warms, J. Garber, & J. McGee (Eds.), *Sacred realms: Essays in religion, belief and society* (pp. 16–20). New York: Oxford University Press.

Mansfield, S. (2003). *The faith of George W. Bush*. New York: Penguin.

Margalit, A. (1991). Israel: The rise of the ultra-orthodox. In R. B. Silvers and B. Epstein (Eds.). *Middle East Reader* (pp. 111–124). New York: Review of Books.

Markus, H., & Kitayama, S. (1991). Culture and self: Implications for cognition, emotion, and motivation. *Psychological Review, 98,* 224–253.

Marmot, M. G., & Syme, S. L. (1976). Acculturation and coronary heart disease in Japanese Americans. *American Journal of Epidemiology, 104,* 225–247.

Marsella, A. (2004). Reflections on international terrorism: Issues, concepts, and directions. In F. M. Moghaddam & A. J. Marsella (Eds.), *Understanding terrorism* (pp. 11–48). Washington, DC: American Psychological Association.

Marsella, A. (2005). Culture and conflict. Understanding, negotiating, and reconciling conflicting constructions of reality. *International Journal of Intercultural Relations, 29,* 651–673.

Marsella, A., & Yamada, A. M. (2007). Culture and psychopathology: Foundations, issues, directions. In S. Kitayama & D. Cohen (Eds.), *Handbook of cultural psychology* (pp. 797–820). New York: Guilford.

Martin, M. W. (1986). *Self-deception and morality.* Lawrence: University Press of Kansas.

Marty, M. E., & Appleby, R. S. (1992). *The glory and the power: The fundamentalist challenge to the modern world.* Boston: Beacon Press.

Maslow, A. H. (1954). *Motivation and personality.* New York: Harper & Row.

Matlin, M. W., & Stang, D. J. (1978). *The Pollyanna principle: Selectivity in language, memory, and thought.* Cambridge, MA: Schenkman.

McBride, A. (1998). Television, individualism, and social capital. *Political Science and Politics, 31,* 542–555.

McCauley, C. (1991). *Terrorism and public policy.* London: F. Cass.

McCauley, C. (2002). Psychological issues in understanding terrorism and the response to terrorism. In C. E. Stout (Ed.), *The psychology of terrorism* (Vol. 3, pp. 3–30). London: Praeger.

McCauley, C. R. (2003). Making sense of terrorism after 9/11. In R. S. Moser & C. E. Frantz (Eds.), *Shocking violence II: Violent disaster, war and terrorism affecting our youth* (pp. 10–32). Springfield, IL: C. C. Thomas.

McMahon, D. M. (2008). The pursuit of happiness in history. In M. Eid & R. J. Larsen (Eds.), *The science of subjective well-being* (pp. 80–96). New York: Guilford.

Meaney, M. (2000). Stress. In A. E. Kazdin (Ed.), *Encyclopedia of psychology* (pp. 479–484). New York: Oxford University Press.

Meier, B. P., Hauser, D. T., Robinson, M. D., Friesen, C. C., & Schjeldahl, K. (2007). What's "up" with God? Vertical space as a representation of the divine. *Journal of Personality and Social Psychology, 93,* 699–710.

Mendoza-Denton, R., & Mischel, W. (2007). Integrating system approaches to culture and personality. The cultural cognitive-affective processing system. In S. Kitayama & D. Cohen (Eds.), *Handbook of cultural psychology* (pp. 175–195). New York: Guilford.

Milgram, S. (1974). *Obedience to authority: An experimental view.* New York: Harper & Row.

Miller, D. T., & Ross, M. (1975). Self-serving bias in the attribution of causality: Fact or fiction? *Psychological Bulletin, 82,* 213–225.

Miller, G. A. (1956). The magical number seven plus or minus two: Some limits on our capacity for processing information. *Psychological Review, 63,* 81–97.

Mills, J., & Clark, M. S. (1982). Exchange and communal relationships. In L. Wheeler (Ed.), *Review of personality and social psychology* (Vol. 3, pp. 121–144). Beverly Hills, CA: Sage.

Mneimneh, H. & Makiya, K. (2002, January 17). Manual for a "raid." *The New York Review of Books, 49,* 18–22.

Moghaddam, F. M., & Marsella, A. J. (Eds.). (2004). *Understanding terrorism.* Washington, DC: American Psychological Association.

Monts, J. K., Zurcher, L. A., & Nydegger, R. V. (1977). Interpersonal self-deception and personality correlates. *Journal of Social Psychology, 103,* 91–99.

Moomal, S., & Henzi, S. P. (2000). The evolutionary psychology of deception and self-deception. *South African Journal of Psychology, 30,* 45–51.

More, T. (1951). *Utopia and a dialogue of comfort.* New York: Dutton.

Murphy, G. (1975). *Outgrowing self-deception.* New York: Basic Books.

Myers, D. G. (1999). Close relationships and quality of life. In D. Kahneman, E. Diener, & N. Schwarz (Eds.), *Well-being: The foundations of hedonic psychology* (pp. 374–391). New York: Russell Sage Foundation.

Myers, D. G. (2008). Religioin and human flourishing. In M. Eid & R. J. Larsen (Eds.). *The science of subjective well-being* (pp. 323–343). New York: Guilford.

Myslobodsky, M. S. (1997). *The mythomanias: The nature of deception and self-deception.* Mahwah, NJ: Erlbaum.

Naroll, R. (1983). *The moral order.* Beverly Hills, CA: Sage.

National Public Radio, NOW Program, April 2004.

National Public Radio, NOW Program, May 2005.

National Public Radio, December 21, 2006.

National Public Radio, 2007.

National Public Radio, Report 2008.

National Public Television, March 27, 2008.

Nettle, D. (2005). *Happiness: The science behind the smile.* New York: Oxford University Press.

Newberg, A. B., & Newberg, S. K. (2005). The neuropsychology of religion and spiritual experience. In R. F. Paloutzian & C. L. Park (Eds.), *Handbook of the psychology of religion and spirituality* (pp. 199–215). New York: Guilford.

Nisbett, R. (2003). *The geography of thought: How Asians and Westerners think differently and why.* New York: The Free Press.

Nisbett, R. E., & Cohen, D. (1996). *Culture of honor: The psychology of violence in the South.* Boulder, CO: Westview Press.

Nisbett, R. E., & Ross, L. (1980). *Human inference: Strategies and shortcoming of social judgment.* Englewood Cliffs, NJ: Prentice-Hall.

Norenzayan, A., Choi, I., & Nisbett, R. E. (1999). Eastern and Western perceptions of causality for social behavior: Lay theories about personalities and situations. In D. A. Prentice & D. T. Miller (Eds.), *Cultural divides: Understanding and overcoming group conflict* (pp. 239–272). New York: Russell Sage Foundation.

Norenzayan, A., & Hansen, I. G. (2006). Belief in supernatural agents in the face of death. *Personality and Social Psychology Bulletin, 32,* 174–187.

Obama, B. (2006). *The audacity of hope.* New York: Crown.

Ohbuchi, K-I., Fukushima, O., & Tedeschi, J. T. (1999). Cultural values in conflict management: Goal orientation, goal attainment, and tactical decision. *Journal of Cross-Cultural Psychology, 30,* 51–71.

Oishi, S., & Koo, M. (2008). Two new questions about happiness: Is "Happiness good?" and "is happiness better?" In M. Eid & R. J. Larsen (Eds.), *The science of subjective well-being* (pp. 290–306). New York: Guilford.

Olson, K. R., Banaji, M. R., Dweck, C., & Spelke, E. S. (2006). Children's biased evaluations of lucky versus unlucky people and their social groups. *Psychological Science, 17,* 913–920.

Oman, D., & Thoresen, C. E. (2005). Do religion and spirituality influence health? In R. F. Paloutzian, & C. L. Park (Eds.), *Handbook of the psychology of religion and spirituality* (pp. 435–459). New York: Guilford.

O'Rourke, N., & Cappeliez, P. (2005). Marital satisfaction and self-deception: Reconstruction of relationship histories among older adults. *Social Behavior and Personality, 33,* 273–282.

Ortiz, D. (2007). Government-sanctioned torture and international law: A survivor's perspective. In J. D. White & A. J. Marsella (Eds.), *Fear of persecution: Global human rights, international law, and human well-being* (pp. 177–188). New York: Lexington Books.

Orwell, G. (1968). *Politics and the English language* (from *The collected essays, journalism and letters of George Orwell*). London: Secker Warburg.

Osgood, C. E., May, W., & Miron, M. (1975). *Cross-cultural universals of affective meaning.* Urbana: University of Illinois Press.

Ousmane, S. (1976). *Xala.* Westport, CT: Lawrence Hill.

Oyserman, D., & Lee, W. S. (2007). Priming "culture": Culture as situated cognition. In S. Kitayama & D. Cohen (Eds.), *Handbook of cultural psychology* (pp. 255–279). New York: Guilford.

Paloutzian, R. F., & Park, C. L. (Eds.). (2005). *Handbook of the psychology of religion and spirituality.* New York: Guilford.

Pape, W. (2005). Dying to win: *The strategic logic of suicide terrorism.* New York: Random House.

Pargament, K. I. (2002). The bitter and the sweet: An evaluation of the costs and benefits of religiousness. *Psychological Inquiry, 13,* 168–181.

Pargament, K. I., Magyar-Russell, G. M., & Murray-Swank, N. A. (2005). The sacred and the search for significance: Religion as a unique process. *Journal of Social Issues, 61,* 665–687.

Paulhus, D. L. (1985). Self-deception and impression management in test responses. In A. Angleitner & J. S. Wiggins (Eds.), *Personality assessment via questionnaire* (pp. 143–165). Berlin: Springer-Verlag.

Paulhus, D. L. (1988). Self-deception: Where do we stand? In J. S. Lockard & D. L. Paulhus (Eds.), *Self-deception: An adaptive mechanism?* (pp. 251–257). Englewood Cliffs, NJ: Prentice-Hall.

Paulhus, D. L. (1998). *Paulhus deception scales: User's manual.* North Tanawanda, NY: Multihealth Systems.

Paulhus, D. L., Friedhandler, B., & Hayes, S. (1997). Psychological defense: Contemporary theory and research. In R. Hogan, J. Johnson, & S. Briggs (Eds.), *Handbook of personality psychology,* (pp. 544–580). San Diego: Academic Press.

Paulhus, D. L., Graft, P., & Van Selst, M. (1989). Attentional load increases the positivity of self-presentation. *Social Cognition, 7,* 389–400.

Paulhus, D. L., & Suedfeld, P. (1988). A dynamic complexity model of self-deception. In J. S. Lockard & D. L. Paulhus (Eds.), *Self-deception: An adaptive mechanism?* (pp. 132–145). Englewood Cliffs, NJ: Prentice-Hall.

Pedahzur, A. (2005). *Suicide terrorism*. Cambridge, UK: Polity Press.

Peng, K., & Nisbett, R. E. (1999). Culture, dialectics, and reasoning about contradiction. *American Psychologist, 54,* 741–754.

Pennebaker, J. W. (1989). Confession, inhibition, and disease. *Advances in Experimental Social Psychology, 22,* 211–244.

Pepitone, A., & Saffiotti, L. (1997). The selectivity of nonverbal beliefs in interpreting events. *European Journal of Social Psychology, 27,* 23–35.

Pew Research Center *Bulletin,* June 23, 2006.

Pittman, T. S. (1998). Motivation. In D. T. Gilbert, S. T. Fiske, & G. Lindzey (Eds.), *The handbook of social psychology* (Vol. 1, pp. 549–590). Boston: McGraw-Hill.

Piven, J. S. (2002). On the psychosis (religion) of terrorists. In C. E. Stout (Ed.), *The psychology of terrorism* (Vol. 3, pp. 119–148). London: Praeger.

Plato. (1960). *The republic and other works*. (B. Jowett, Trans.). Garden City, NY: Dolphin Books.

Plous, S. (1993). *The psychology of judgment and decision making*. New York: McGraw-Hill.

Post, J. M., Sprinzak, E., & Denny, L. M. (2003). The terrorist in their own words: Interviews with 35 incarcerated Middle Eastern terrorists. *Terrorism and Political Violence, 15,* 171–184.

Post, S. G. (2003). *Unlimited love: Altruism, compassion and service*. Philadelphia: Templeton Foundation.

Pronin, E., Gilovich, T., & Ross, L. (2004). Objectivity in the eye of the beholder: Divergent perceptions of bias in self versus others. *Psychological Review, 111,* 781–799.

Pronin, E., Lin, D. Y., & Ross, L. (2002). The bias blind spot: Perspectives of bias in self versus others. *Personality and Social Psychology Bulletin, 28,* 361–381.

Quattrone, G. A., & Tversky, A. (1985). Self-deception and the voter's illusion. In J. Elster (Ed.), *The multiple self* (pp. 35–58). Cambridge,UK: Cambridge University Press.

Rahula, W. (1959). *What the Buddha taught*. New York: Grove Press.

Redfield, R. (1941). *The folk culture of the Yucatan*. Chicago: University of Chicago Press.

Reischauer, A. K. (1946). Buddhism. In E. J. Jurji (Ed.), *The great religions of the modern world* (pp. 90–140). Princeton, NJ: Princeton University Press.

Revel, J-F. (1991). *The flight from truth: The reign of deceit in the age of information*. New York: Random House.

Richards, F. D., Bond, C. E., & Stokes-Zoota, J. J. (2003). One hundred years of social psychology quantitatively described. *Review of General Psychology, 7,* 331–363.

Richardson, L. (2006). *What terrorists want*. New York: Random House.

Riddle, J. M., & Estes, J. W. (1992). Oral contraceptives in ancient and medieval times. *American Scientist, 80,* 226–233.

Robinson, M. P., & Riff, C. D. (1999). The role of self-deception in perception of past, present, and future happiness. *Personality and Social Psychology Bulletin, 25,* 595–606.

Roccas, S. (2005). Religion and value systems. *Journal of Social Issues, 61,* 747–759.

Rodis-Lewis, G. (1975). *Épicure et son école (Epicurus and his school)*. Paris: Gallimard.

Rohner, R. P. (1986). *The warmth dimension: Foundations of parental acceptance–rejection theor y.* Newbury Park, CA: Sage.

Rohner, R. P. (2004). The parental "acceptance–rejection syndrome": Universal correlates of perceived rejection. *American Psychologist, 59,* 827–830.

Rokeach, M. (1960). *The open and closed mind.* New York: Basic Books.

Rokeach, M. (1964). *The three Christs of Ipsilanti, a psychological study.* New York: Knopf.

Rokeach, M. (1973). *The nature of human values.* New York: The Free Press

Rosenblatt, P. C., Walsh, R. P., & Jackson, D. A. (1976). *Grief and mourning in cross-cultural perspective.* New Haven, CT: Human Relations Aria Files Press.

Rosenthal, R., & Jacobson, L. (1992). *Pygmalion in the classroom: Teacher expectations and pupils' intellectual development.* New York: Irvington.

Ross, L., & Nisbett, R. E. (1991). *The person and the situation: Perspectives of social psychology.* New York: McGraw-Hill.

Roy, O. (2004). *Globalized Islam: The search for a new Ummah.* New York: Columbia University Press.

Rozin, P., Millman, L., & Nemeroff, C. (1986). Operation of the laws of sympathetic magic in disgust and other domains. *Journal of Personality and Social Psychology, 50,* 703–712.

Rubenstein, R. E. (2002). Purification and power: The psycho-political roots of religious terrorism. In C. Kegley (Ed.), *The new global terrorism.* New York: Prentice-Hall.

Russell, B. (1940). *An inquiry into meaning and truth.* London: Allen & Unwin.

Russell, B. (1930, 1971). *The conquest of happiness.* New York: Liveright.

Ruthven, M. (2004). *Fundamentalism: The search for meaning.* New York: Oxford University Press.

Sackheim, H. A. (1983). Self-deception, self-esteem, and depression: The adaptive value of lying to oneself. In J. Maslin (Ed.), *Empirical studies of psychoanalytic theories* (pp. 101–157). Hillsdale, NJ: Erlbaum.

Sackheim, H. A. (1988). Self-deception: A synthesis. In J. S. Lockard & D. L. Paulhus (Eds.), *Self-deception: An adaptive mechanism?* (pp. 146–165). Englewood Cliffs, NJ: Prentice-Hall.

Sackheim, H. A., & Gur, R. C. (1978). Self-deception, self-confrontation and consciousness. In G. E. Schwartz & D. Shapiro (Eds.), *Consciousness and self-regulation: Advances in research and theory* (pp. 139–198). New York: Plenum.

Sackeim, H. A., & Gur, R. C. (1979). Self-deception, other deception, and self-reported psychopathology. *Journal of Consulting and Clinical Psychology, 47,* 213–215.

Sagan, C. (1980). *Cosmos.* New York: Random House.

Sageman, M. (2004, October). *The psychology of al Qaeda terrorism.* Lecture presented at the Suicide Terrorist Conference, Washington, DC.

Sampson, W., & Vaughn, L. (2000). *Science meets alternative medicine.* Amherst, NY: Prometheus.

Sarbin, T. R. (1988). Self-deception in the claims of hypnosis subjects. In J. S. Lockard & D. L. Paulhus (Eds.), *Self-deception: An adaptive mechanism?* (pp. 99–112). Englewood Cliffs, NJ: Prentice-Hall.

Saroglou, V., & Galand, P. (2004). Identities, values, and religion: A study among Muslim, other immigrants, and native Belgian young adults after the 9/11 attacks. *Identity: An International Journal of Theory and Research, 4,* 97–132.

Schneiderman, L. J. (2000). The ethics of alternative medicine. In W. Sampson, & L. Vaughn (Eds.), *Science meets alternative medicine* (pp. 203–226). Amherst, NY: Prometheus.

Schneiderman, N. (2000). Coronary heart disease. In A. E. Kazdin (Ed.), *Encyclopedia of psychology* (p. 306). New York: Oxford University Press.

Schroder, H. M., Driver, M. J., & Streufert, S. (1967). *Human information processing*. New York: Holt, Rinehart & Winston.

Schwartz, S. (1992). Universals in the content and structure of values: Theoretical advances and empirical tests in 20 countries. In M. Zanna (Ed.), *Advances in experimental social psychology* (Vol. 25, pp. 1–66). New York: Academic Press.

Schwartz, S. H. (2004). Mapping and interpreting cultural differences around the world. In H. Vinken, J. Soeters, & P. Ester (Eds.), *Comparing cultures: Dimensions of culture in comparative perspective* (pp. 43–73). Leiden, The Netherlands: Brill.

Sedikides, C., Gaertner, L., & Taguchi, Y. (2003). Pancultural self-enhancement. *Journal of Personality and Social Psychology, 84,* 60–79.

Seligman, M. E. P. (1975). *Helplessness: On depression, development, and death.* San Francisco: Freeman.

Seligman, M. E. P. (2002). *Authentic happiness.* New York: The Free Press.

Seligman, M. E. P. (2006). Positive psychotherapy. *American Psychologist, 61,* 774–790.

Sherif, C. W., Sherif, M., & Nebergall, R. E. (1965). *Attitude and attitude change.* Philadelphia: Saunders.

Sherif, M. (1936). *The psychology of social norms.* New York: Harper.

Shermer, M. (1999). *How we believe: The search for God in an age of science.* New York: W. H. Freeman.

Shteynberg, G. (2005). The cultural psychology of revenge in the United States and South Korea. Master's Thesis. University of Maryland, Department of Psychology.

Shweder, R., Minow, R., & Markus, H. R. (2002). *Engaging cultural differences: The multicultural challenge to liberal democracies.* New York: Russell Sage Foundation..

Silberman, I. (2005). Religion as a meaning system: Implications for the New Millennium. *Journal of Social Issues, 61,* 641–663.

Silberman, I., Higgins, E. T., & Dweck, C. S. (2005). Religion and world change: Violence and terrorism versus peace. *Journal of Social Issues, 61,* 761–784.

Simopoulos, A. P., & Robinson, J. (1999). *The omega diet: The lifesaving nutritional program based on the diet of the island of Crete.* New York: HarperCollins.

Sipe, A. W. R. (1995). *Sex, priests, and power: Anatomy of a crisis.* New York: Brunner/Mazel.

Sipe, A. W. R. (2003). *Celibacy in crisis.* New York: Brunner-Routledge.

Smart, N. (1998). *The world's religions.* London: Cambridge University Press.

Smith, A. (third edition in 1784, reissued in 1976). *An inquiry into the nature and causes of the wealth of nations.* Oxford, UK: Clarendon Press.

Snyder, C. R. (1985). Collaborative companions: The relationship of self-deception and excuse making. In M. W. Martin (Ed.), *Self-deception and self-understanding* (pp. 35–51). Lawrence: University Press of Kansas.

Snyder, C. R. (Ed.). (1989). Self-illusions: When are they adaptive? (Special Issue). *Journal of Social and Clinical Psychology, 8,* 1–221.

Solomon, R. C. (1993). What a tangled web: Deception and self-deceptions in philosophy. In M. Lewis & C. Saarni (Eds.), *Lying and deception in everyday life* (pp. 30-58). New York: Guilford.

Solovy, P., Rothman, A. J., & Rodin, J. (1998). Health behavior. In D. T. Gilbert, S. T. Fiske, & G. Lindzey (Eds.), *The handbook of social psychology* (Vol. 2, pp. 633–683). Boston: McGraw-Hill.

Spilka, B., Hood, R. W., & Gorsuch, R. L. (1985). *The psychology of religion: An empirical approach.* Englewood Cliffs, NJ: Prentice-Hall.

Stern, J. (2003). *Terror in the name of God.* New York: HarperCollins.

Stern, J. (2004, June 12). Holy avengers: From American anti-abortion activists to Islamic suicide bombers. *The Financial Times.*

Stevens, M. J. (2002). The unanticipated consequences of globalization: Contextualizing terrorism. In C. E. Stout (Ed.), *The psychology of terrorism* (Vol. 3, pp. 31–56). London: Praeger.

Stevenson, H. W. (1991). The development of prosocial behavior in large scale societies: China and Japan. In R. A. Hinde & J. Grobel (Eds.), *Cooperation and prosocial behaviour* (pp. 89–105). New York: Cambridge University Press.

Stewart, M. (2006). *The courtier and the heretic: Leibniz, Spinoza, and the fate of God in the modern world.* New York: Norton.

Stiglitz, J. E. (2002). *Globalization and its discontents.* New York: Norton.

Stout, C. E. (Ed.) (2002). *The psychology of terrorism* (4 vols.). Westport, CT: Praeger.

Strachman, A., & Gable, S. I. (2006). What you want (and do not want) affects what you see (and do not see). Avoidance social goals and social events. *Personality and Social Psychology Bulletin, 32,* 1446–1458.

Styers, R. (2004). *Making magic: Religion, magic, and science in the modern world.* New York: Oxford University Press.

Suedfeld, P., & Tetlock, P. E. (2001). Individual differences in information processing. In N. Schwarz & A. Tesser (Eds.), *Blackwell handbook of social psychology. Vol. 1: Intraindividual processes* (pp. 284–304). New York: Blackwell.

Suh, E., Diener, E., Oishi, S., & Triandis, H. C. (1998). The shifting basis of life satisfaction judgments across cultures: Emotions versus norms. *Journal of Personality & Social Psychology, 74,* 482–493.

Suh E. M., & Koo, J. (2008). Comparing subjective well-being across cultures and nations. In M. Eid & R. J. Larsen (Eds.), *The science of subjective well-being* (pp. 414–427). New York: Guilford.

Swann, W. G., & Read, S. J. (1981). Self-verification processes: How we sustain our self-conceptions. *Journal of Experimental Social Psychology, 17,* 351–372.

Swanson, G. E. (1960). *The birth of Gods: The origin of primitive beliefs.* Ann Arbor: University of Michigan Press.

Tahir, H. (1996). *The American campaign to suppress Islam.* London: Al-Khilafa Publications.

Tamir, M., & Robinson, M. D. (2007). The happy spotlight: Positive mood and selective attention to rewarding information. *Personality and Social Psychology Bulletin, 33,* 1124–1136.

Tavris, C., & Aronson, E. (2007). *Mistakes were made (but not by me)*. New York: Harcourt.

Taylor, S. E. (1988). Illusion and positive well-being: A social psychological perspective on mental health. *Psychological Bulletin, 103*, 193–210.

Taylor, S. E. (1989). *Positive illusions: Creative self-deception and the healthy mind*. New York: Basic Books.

Taylor, S. E. (1991). Asymmetrical effects of positive and negative events: The mobilization–minimization hypothesis. *Psychological Bulletin, 110*, 67–85.

Taylor, S. E. (1998a). Positive illusions. In H. Friedman (Ed.), *Encyclopedia of mental health* (pp. 199–208). San Diego: Academic Press.

Taylor, S. E. (1998b). The social being in social psychology. In D. T. Gilbert, S. T. Fiske, & G. Lindzey (Eds.), *The handbook of social psychology* (Vol. 1, pp. 58–98). Boston: McGraw-Hill.

Taylor, S. E. (2007). Social support. In H. S. Friedman & R. C. Silver (Eds.), *Foundations of health psychology* (pp. 145–171). New York: Oxford University Press.

Taylor S. E., & Brown, J. D. (1988). Illusion and well-being: A social psychological perspective on mental health. *Psychological Bulletin, 103*,193–210.

Taylor, S. E., Collins, R. L., Skokan, L. A., & Aspinwall, L. G. (1989). Maintaining positive illusions in the face of negative information: Getting the facts without letting them get to you. *Journal of Social & Clinical Psychology, 8,* 114–129.

Taylor, S. E., Kemeny, M. E., Reed, G. M., Bower, J. E., & Gruenewald, T. L. (2000). Psychological resources, positive illusions, and health. *American Psychologist, 55*, 99–109.

Taylor, S. E., Repetti, R. L., & Seeman, T. (1997). Health psychology: What is an unhealthy environment and how does it get under the skin? *Annual Review of Psychology, 48*, 411–447.

Tetlock, P. E. (1989). Structure and function of political belief systems. In A. R. Pratkanis, S. J. Breckler, & A. G. Greenwald (Eds.), *Attitude structure and function* (pp. 129–151). Hillsdale, NJ: Erlbaum.

Tetlock, P. E. (1998). Social psychology and world politics. In D. T. Gilbert, S. T. Fiske, & G. Lindzey (Eds.), *The handbook of social psychology* (Vol. 2, pp. 868–914). Boston: McGraw-Hill.

Thigpen, C. H., & Cleckley, H. M. (1957). *The three faces of Eve*. New York: Popular Library.

The buying of the presidency (2004). A publication of the Center for Public Integrity.

The Economist, 2003.

The Economist 2004.

The Economist, 2004, p. 75.

The Economist, 2005.

The Economist, April 8, 2005.

The Economist, 2006.

The Economist, 2007.

The Economist, July 19–25, 2008, p. 17.

The Public I, 2004.

The Public I, 2005.

Thucydides. (1934). *The complete writings of Thucydides*. New York: The Modern Library.

Time Magazine (January 17, 2005). Special issue, pp. A3–A68.

Tomaka, J., Blascovich, J., & Kelsey, R. M. (1992). Effects of self-deception, social desirability, and repressive coping on psychophysiological reactivity to stress. *Personality and Social Psychology Bulletin, 18,* 616–624.

Tov, W., & Diener, E. (2007). Culture and subjective well-being. In S. Kitayama & D. Cohen (Eds.), *Handbook of cultural psychology* (pp. 691–713). New York: Guilford.

Toyama, M., & Sakurai, S. (2001). Positive illusions in Japanese students. *Japanese Journal of Psychology, 74,* 329–335.

Trafimow, D., Triandis, H. C., & Goto, S. (1991). Some tests of the distinction between private self and collective self. *Journal of Personality and Social Psychology, 60,* 649–655.

Tredoux, C. G., Meissner, C. A., Malpass, R., & Zimmerman, L. A. (2004). Eyewitness identification. In C. Spielberger (Ed.), *Encyclopedia of applied psychology* (Vol. 1, pp. 875–888). San Diego: Academic Press.

Treisman, A. M. (1969). Strategies and models of selective attention. *Psychological Review, 76,* 282–299.

Triandis, H. C. (1971). *Attitude and attitude change.* New York: Wiley.

Triandis, H. C. (1972). *The analysis of subjective culture.* New York: Wiley.

Triandis, H. C. (1989). The self and social behavior in different cultural contexts. *Psychological Review, 96,* 506–520.

Triandis, H. C. (1990). Cross-cultural studies of individualism and collectivism. In J. Berman (Ed.), *Nebraska Symposium on Motivation, 1989* (pp. 41–133). Lincoln: University of Nebraska Press.

Triandis, H. C. (1994). *Culture and social behavior.* New York: McGraw-Hill.

Triandis, H. C. (1995). *Individualism and collectivism.* Boulder, CO: Westview Press.

Triandis, H. C., Carnevale, P. Gelfand, M., Robert, C., Wasti, A. Probst, T., et al. (2001). Culture, personality and deception: A multilevel approach. *International Journal of Cross-cultural Management, 1,* 73–90.

Triandis, H. C., Davis, E. E., & Takezawa, S. I. (1965). Some determinants of social distance among American, German and Japanese students. *Journal of Personality and Social Psychology, 2,* 540–551.

Triandis, H. C., & Gelfand, M. (1998). Converging measurements of horizontal and vertical individualism and collectivism. *Journal of Personality & Social Psychology, 74,* 118–128.

Triandis, H. C., & Singelis, T. M. (1998). Training to recognize individual differences in collectivism and individualism within culture. *International Journal of Intercultural Relations, 22,* 35–48.

Triandis, H. C., & Suh, E. M. (2002). Cultural influences on personality. *Annual Review of Psychology, 53,* 133–160.

Triandis, H. C., & Trafimow, D. (2001). Cross-national prevalence of collectivism. In C. Sedikides & M. B. Brewer (Eds.), *Individual self, relational self, collective self* (pp. 259–276). Philadelphia: Psychology Press.

Trilling, L. (1972). *Sincerity and authenticity.* London: Oxford University Press.

Trivers, R. (1988). Foreword. In J. S. Lockhard & D. L. Paulhus (Eds.), *Self-deception: An adaptive mechanism?* Englewood Cliffs, NJ: Prentice-Hall.

Trommsdorff, G., Mayer, B., & Albert, I. (2004). Dimensions of culture in intracultural comparisons. Individualism/collectivism and family related values in three generations. In H. Vinken, J. Soeters, & P. Ester (Eds.), *Comparing cultures: Dimensions of culture in comparative perspective* (pp. 157–180). Leiden, The Netherlands: Brill.

Tseng, W-S. (2001). *Handbook of cultural psychiatry.* San Diego: Academic Press.

Tuchman, B. W. (1984). *The march of folly: From Troy to Vietnam.* New York: Knopf.

Turnbull, C. M. (1972). *The mountain people.* New York: Simon & Schuster.

Uchida, Y., Kitayama, S., Mesquita, B., Reyes, J. A., & Morling, B. (2008). Is perceived emotional support beneficial? Well-being and health in independent and interdependent cultures. *Personality and Social Psychology Bulletin, 34,* 741–754.

Uchino, B. N., Cacioppo, J. T., & Kiecolt-Glaser, J. K. (1996). The relationship between social support and physiological processes: A review with emphasis on underlying mechanisms and implications. *Psychological Bulletin, 119,* 488–531.

Vandello J., & Cohen, D. (1999). Patterns of individualism and collectivism across the United States. *Journal of Personality and Social Psychology, 77,* 279–292.

Vandello, J., Cohen, D., & Ransom, S. (2008). U.S. Southern and Northern differences in perceptions of norms about aggression: Mechanisms for the perpetration of cultures of honor. *Journal of Cross-Cultural Psychology, 39,* 162–177.

Van den Bos, K., Van Ameijde, J., & Van Gorp, H. (2006). On the psychology of religion: The role of personal uncertainty in religious worldview defense. *Basic and Applied Social Psychology, 28,* 333–341.

Veenhoven, R. (2000). Well-being in the welfare state. *Journal of Comparative Policy Analysis, 2,* 91–125.

Veenhoven, R. (2008). Sociological theories of subjective well-being. In M. Eid & R. J. Larsen (Eds.), *The science of subjective well-being* (pp. 17–43). New York: Guilford.

Vico, G. (1970). *The new science.* (T. G. Bergin & M. H. Fish, Trans.). Ithaca, NY: Cornell University Press. (Original work published 1744.)

Vontess, C. E. (1991). Traditional healing in Africa: Implications for cross-cultural counseling. *Counseling & Development, 70,* 242–249.

Wagner, M. (2005, May–June). Teaching humanities in new ways—and teaching new humanities. *The Humanist,* pp. 65-73.

Wagner, R. (1954). *Religion and art.* Lincoln: University of Nebraska Press.

Walker, P. (2002). *We, the people: Developing a new democracy.* London: New Economics Foundation.

Wallace, A. F. C. (1966). *Religion: An anthropological view.* New York: Random House.

Wallis, C., (2005). The new science of happiness. *Time Magazine,* January 17, pp. A2–A9 (part of a special issue on happiness on pp. A3–A68.)

Ward, C., Bochner, S., & Furnham, A. (2001). *The psychology of culture shock* (2nd ed.). Philadelphia: Taylor & Francis.

Wasti, S. A. (2002). Affective and continuance commitment to the organization. Test of an integrated model in the Turkish context. *International Journal of Intercultural Relations, 25,* 525–550.

Wegner, D. M. (2002). *The illusion of conscious will.* Cambridge, MA: Bradford Books, the MIT Press.

Weinberg, L., & Eubank, W. (1994). Cultural differences in the behavior of terrorists. *Terrorism and Political Violence, 6,* 1–28.

Welles, J. F. (1986). Self-deception as a positive feedback mechanism. *American Psychologist, 41,* 325–326.

Welles, J. F. (1988). Societal roles in self-deception. In J. S. Lockard & D. L. Paulhus (Eds.), *Self-deception: An adaptive mechanism?* (pp. 4–70). Englewood Cliffs, NJ: Prentice-Hall.

Westen, D., Blagov, P. S. Harenski, K., Kilts, C., & Hamann, S. (2006). Neural bases of motivated reasoning: An fMRI study of emotional constraints on partisan political judgment in the 2004 U.S. presidential election. *Journal of Cognitive Neuroscience, 18,* 1947–1958.

Whiting, J. W. M. (1994). A model for psychocultural research. In E. H. Chasdi (Ed.), *Culture and human development: The selected papers of John Whiting* (pp. 89–101). New York: Cambridge University Press.

Whittaker-Bleuler, S. A. (1988). Deception and self-deception: A dominant strategy in competitive sport. In J. S. Lockard & D. L. Paulhus (Eds.), *Self-deception: An adaptive mechanism?* (pp. 212–228). Englewood Cliffs, NJ: Prentice-Hall.

Wilkinson, R. (1996). *Unhealthy societies: The afflictions of inequality.* London: Routledge.

Wilson, D. T. (1985). Self-deception without repression: Limits on access to mental states. In M. W. Martin (Ed.), *Self-deception and self-understanding* (pp. 95–116). Lawrence: University Kansas Press.

Wilson, D. T. (2002). *Strangers to ourselves.* Cambridge, MA: Harvard University Press.

Wilson, E. O. (1978). *On human nature.* Cambridge, MA: Harvard University Press.

Wilson, E. O. (2006). *The creation: An appeal to save life on earth.* New York: Norton.

Wing, R. L. (1986). *The Tao of power: A translation of the Tao Te Ching by Lao Tzu.* Garden City, NY: Dolphin/Doubleday.

Wingert, P. & Brant, M. (2005). Reading your baby's mind. *Newsweek, 146,* 33–36.

Winnicott, D. (1971). *Playing and reality.* New York: Routledge.

Wiseman, R. (1997). *Deception and self-deception.* New York: Prometheus.

World Health Organization, 1948.

Wood, W., Wong, F. Y., & Chachere, J. G. (1991). Effects of media violence on viewers' aggression in unconstrained social interaction. *Psychological Bulletin, 109,* 371–383.

Wright, R. (1985). *Sacred rage: The wrath of militant Islam.* New York: Simon & Schuster.

Yamada A., & Singelis, T. (1999). Biculturalism and self-construal. *International Journal of Intercultural Relations, 23,* 697–709.

York, R. (2004, February). Manufacturing the love of possession—The consumer trap: Big business marketing in American Life. Book Review in *Monthly Review,* pp. 79–84.

Zakaria, F. (2008). *The post-American world.* New York: Norton

Zimbardo, P. G. (2004). A situational perspective on the psychology of evil: Understanding how good people are transformed into perpetrators. In A. G. Miller (Ed.), *The social psychology of good and evil* (pp. 21–50). New York: Guilford.

Zimbardo, P. G. (2006). *The Lucifer effect: Understanding how good people turn evil.* New York: Random House.

Zipf, G. K. (1949). *Human behavior and the principle of least effort.* Cambridge, MA: Addison-Wesley.

Zuckerman, P. (2006). Is faith good for us? *Free Inquiry, 26*(5), 35–38.

Author Index

Subject Index

About the Author

HARRY C. TRIANDIS is Professor Emeritus of Psychology at the University of Illinois and a Fellow of three divisions of the American Psychological Association. His awards include APA's Distinguished International Psychologist of the Year, Distinguished Lecturer of the Year, and the award for Distinguished Contributions to International Psychology. He also earned the American Psychological Society's prestigious James M. Cattell Award. Triandis is a former Guggenheim Fellow, Ford Foundation Faculty Fellow, Fellow of the American Association for the Advancement of Science, and Fellow of the International Association of Cross-Cultural Psychology. He also served as a Distinguished Fulbright Professor and as President for the Society for the Psychological Study of Social Issues. He has authored seven books, including *Culture and Social Behavior*, and edited the six-volume *Handbook of Cross-Cultural Psychology*.